Neuroeconomics: Theory, Applications, and Perspectives

Edited by
GianMario Raggetti
Maria Gabriella Ceravolo
Lucrezia Fattobene

B
U
P

Proceedings of the
1ª Officina di Neuroeconomia

EGEA S.p.A.
Via Salasco, 5 - 20136 Milan, Italy
Phone + 39 02 5836.5751 - Fax +39 02 5836.5753
egea.edizioni@unibocconi.it - www.egeaeditore.it

First Edition: March 2018

ISBN Domestic Edition 978-88-99902-27-8
ISBN International Edition 978-88-85486-47-8
ISBN Moby pocket Edition 978-88-85486-48-5
ISBN Epub Edition 978-88-85486-49-2

Print: Digital Print Service, Segrate (Milan)

Table of contents

Part II - The Brain Functioning

Photo shoot of the event: by professional photographers of the MUSINF of Senigallia (AN)

Prelude

The "1ª Officina di Neuroeconomia", held during the 2017 Brain Awareness Week at the School of Medicine of Università Politecnica delle Marche (Ancona), has been designed to intrigue Italian students and researchers towards new visions and methods that can lead to a better understanding of economic agents' behaviour. Compared to the international academic context, Italian scholars who conduct interdisciplinary investigations to examine the neural aspects of individual decision making in the fields of economics and in finance are still few. A large number of researchers do not seem ready to overcome traditional theoretical and methodological perspectives used to explain human behaviour.

> In the Western culture, a symbol of revolutionary scientific intuition dates back to 5ᵗʰ century B.C. when Anassimandro (610 BC-546 BC), philosopher and Talete's pupil, provokes the first substantial knowledge leap, resorting to his doubt, curiosity, intuition, and observation: the basic factors of science evolution. He described how the sun, stars and sky are fixed while the Earth floats in the air and it is not circular, flat, and motionless: he went beyond the acquired version sustained by his life mentor[1].

Only recently, the innovative concept that the human brain is responsible for modulating all cognitive and motor functions, driving the decision making process, has started influencing the economics' discipline. This represented a first step of a very complex and troubled process in which the initial concept of psyche evolved to those of mind, intellect, reason and, finally, brain. This result

---

[1] See Carlo Rovelli: *Anaximander and his legacy.* Ed. Westholme Publishing. 2011. See Carlo Rovelli: *Six brief lessons on physic.* Ed: Penguins Books. 2016.

has been achieved by exploiting cultural and scientific knowledge, experiments, intuitions, confutations over a very long time. In the last decades, developments in technology and in computer science rapidly increased the efficiency of neural scientific research. Nowadays, we can observe and examine the human brain *directly, in vivo* and in a *non-invasive way*. It is possible to analyse the brain mechanisms of healthy people involved in decision making. This is a relevant innovation with respect to psychological knowledge used in behavioural economics and finance.

Neurophysiologists and neurobiologists agree that the human brain is the most complex organ largely influenced by the (inexplicable so far!) neural factor named 'emotion'. The new scientific results prove that neural functions are based on chemical-physical processes, which are automated, very fast and often unconscious. By deepening the knowledge of this wonderful organ functioning, we gather new information to understand its real (incredible) role in decision making in economics and finance. Neuroeconomics started from this opportunity. The scientific targets pursued with this new research area are not easy but it is becoming more and more necessary to reach them with tenacity, humility and new interdisciplinary visions. Surely, we need a long time before the human brain will be fully understood by… our brains.

In the meantime, among the researchers, wise ones accept the complexity of a new scientific challenge, working in multidisciplinary teams and using innovative research methods and instruments. Some other naive scholars try to take action by simply hoping to have some knowledge that is immediately convertible into an economic benefit. Finally, others, the conservative ones, consider the challenge useless and reject it. The aim of the "1ª Officina di Neuroeconomia" is to explain basic knowledge and to show recent scientific results to sustain, consolidate and satisfy the growing curiosity of the innovative group, limit the short sighted opportunism of the second group of researchers and try to seed new interest among the most conservative.

The 3-day seminar was introduced by Prof. Sauro Longhi, Rector of Università Politecnica delle Marche (UNIVPM) followed by greetings from Prof. Andrea Giovagnoni, Vice-Dean of the School of Medicine at UNIVPM. Mr. Michele Caporossi, General Manager of the Hospital "A.O.R. Ancona" welcomed all speakers, scholars and academic authorities. The "1ª Officina di

Neuroeconomia" received the patronage of the Italian Scientific Society of Neurology. A letter of congratulations had been sent by Sen. Valeria Fedeli, Ministry of Education, to the steering committee for the innovative seminar contents and the very interesting perspectives of Neuroeconomics.

The sequence of papers, in these proceedings, respects the scientific programme carried out during the 3-day seminar. The first section includes an initial synthetic description of the evolution from theoretical visions and research methods of neo-classic economics to those of behavioural economics and finance up to the introduction of the emerging theories and methods of neuroeconomics. The second paper, written by Prof. Nicola Biagio Mercuri, Dr. Rocco Cerroni and Dr. Maria Albanese, is dedicated to a basic description of the brain's anatomy structure and physiology. Dr. Girolamo Crisi, the author of the next paper, explores the use of functional Magnetic Resonance Imaging in neuroeconomics. Prof. Gabriele Polonara and Prof. Mara Fabri, in the next chapter, offer a technical description of instruments and methods used to collect, process and interpret neural correlates of decision making. The 2nd section starts with a paper by Prof. Simona Luzzi. She clarifies the way emotions influence individual decision making and highlights the pervasive role of emotions in personal preferences, choices and behaviour. The paper presented by Prof. Maria Gabriella Ceravolo and Dr. Lucrezia Fattobene offers important and new knowledge on the neural representation of perceived risk in different frameworks (risky, uncertain or ambiguous). Prof. Giuseppe Di Pellegrino and Dr. Manuela Sellitto present their recent conclusions on neural mechanisms involved in intertemporal choices. The 3rd section has been wholly dedicated to show results on neural aspects of individual decisions in economic and financial markets. Its first paper, by Prof. Frank Hartmann, describes the evolution of neuroaccounting. With the next paper, Prof. Gianpiero Lugli presents his recent interesting applications of neuroscience methods to marketing at an operational level. Neuromarketing seems a fast growing research area that some scholars try to consider this area scientifically autonomous. An impressive research in neurofinance is illustrated with the paper by Prof. Maria Gabriella Ceravolo and Dr. Lucrezia Fattobene. They present a complex research about neural correlates of traders' decision making, examined through an innovative and ecological experimental protocol. Prof.

Luca Passamonti, in his paper, illustrates a new approach to examine the link between personality and psycho-pathological behaviours driving towards individual dominance. This is an important step towards a better knowledge of the brain's role in an individual achieving leadership.

As already suggested, each presentation has encouraged a passionate debate among the participants. We have the pleasure of including three selected interesting papers. The first one, authored by Prof. Sergio Barile, Dr. Francesca Iandolo and Dr. Stefano Armenia deepens a viable social approach to social neuroscience. The second essay by Prof. Vincenzo Farina and Prof. Lucia Leonelli, with others, recommends taking advantage of neuroeconomics in finance researches and also proposes the new eye-tracking method to analyse how the brain selects information (unconsciously) through his visual system.

The third one by Mr. Riccardo Guerrini suggests different keypoints for neuroeconomists to examine new aspects of individual and collective behaviour in the insurance market.

The "1ª Officina di Neuroeconomia" ended with a panel discussion between Prof. Sauro Longhi, Rector of UNIVPM, Prof. Sergio Barile, council member of the Italian Academy of Business Economics (Accademia Italiana di Economia Aziendale - AIDEA), Prof. Leandro Provinciali, President of the Italian Scientific Society of Neurology (Società Italiana di Neurologia - SIN), Prof. Fiorenzo Conti, President of the Italian Society of Neurosciences (Società Italiana di Neuroscienze - SINS), and Prof. Roberto Grassi, incoming President of the Italian Society of Radiology (Società Italiana di Radiologia Medica-SIRM). They discussed enthusiastically about Neuroeconomics' perspectives in the domestic academic context. We considered the salient ideas emerged in the final reflections of these proceedings.

We would like to express our thanks to the Health Care Management Center of UNIVPM School of Medicine for its financial, administrative, and organisational support. We would also like to express our gratitude to everyone who has contributed in different ways to the success of this 1st Officina in Neuroeconomics: speakers, participants, students, administrative, and organisational staff.

The local academic interdisciplinary teams that are involved in neuroeconomics and neurofinance will continue to project and implement researches, seminars and events to spread Neuroeconomics in the domestic academic context. We are waiting for new ideas and collaborative proposals that should come from young forward-looking researchers.

Our hope is that the essays collected will stimulate new curiosities and interests, especially among young researchers, towards the interdisciplinary visions of neuroeconomics and neurofinance.

GianMario Raggetti
UNIVPM, Ancona

Part I
... Going inside the Black Box

1. ... and Neuroeconomics Appears and Spreads...

by GianMario Raggetti [1]

For millions of years, man has considered himself different and superior to any other living species. This conviction is based on the certainty (never proved!) that only man has some special neural skills in the animal kingdom; skill as the capacity of awareness of himself, or the possibility to reflect on what he thinks, or to perceive emotion, to have intuition, to use a complex and evolving language exchanging knowledge with his counterparts, to learn by experiences lived or heard, to memorise them, to have the perception of the inexorability of his own death, etc. Man perceives variations in the environment and he can image and implement efficient solutions to adapt himself to them. He has a curiosity, *innate* and *voluntary*, to understand how natural phenomena manifest themselves and, in particular, how the human behaviour is influenced by genetic, physiological, biological, emotional, affective, cultural, economic, and social factors.

In western culture, *Hippocrates* (400 BC) was the first natural philosopher interested in the role of the *psyche* as the source of many factors that condition human behaviour. Over time, the psyche will be named as *pneuma, breath of life, soul, mind, intellect, thought, reason*, and recently as the *whole functions* performed by the *brain. Plato* (428 BC) indicates the human brain as the location of intelligence and rationality and, therefore, of the soul. *Aristotle* (384 BC), instead, locates them in the heart. *Galen* (120 BC) detects the relationship between specific lesions in the brain of some wounded

---

[1] This work has been conducted at the Health Care Management Centre of the School of Medicine of Università Politecnica delle Marche – Ancona (I).

gladiators and the motor or cognitive deficits in their behaviour. *Vesalius* (1514) investigates the nervous system. *Descartes* (1596) proposes an interdisciplinary vision of natural science, introducing the concept of *doubt* to stimulate investigations into the cognitive functions of the human mind. John *Loke* (1690) studies the logic process of the mind involved in the learning process through the experiences.

At the beginning, *moral philosophers' reflections* facilitate the propagation of beliefs about the active presence of a metaphysical and unknown entity to explain the universe, the appearance of life, and, above all, the human species' skills to perceive these phenomena and to investigate them. Consequently, various metaphysical and religious solutions spread. For centuries, they seem to satisfy completely those basic curiosities. For a long time, the political and cultural power of religion try to limit, even in a cruel way, the development in western culture of the thought of *natural philosophers*. Many scientists have been persecuted for a long time. They have, initially, few means to investigate and their knowledge is based, above all, on their direct meticulous observations. For centuries, the knowledge of the structure and functioning of the human body and human brain is based only on post-mortem examinations. In spite of this situation, the clergy fears that scientists disseminate the doubt about dogmas and criticise their authorised interpretations of sacred texts. Despite this, their reflections evolve, slowly, to propose the *dialogue*, the *measurement* of observed natural phenomena and the *empirical verification* of knowledge. The scenario began to change.

In the age of *Enlightenment* (17th and 18th centuries), the prevalent scientific culture reinforces trust in human reason and exasperates the use of the scientific method in every activity of human thought.

The *telescope* dethroned man from his anthropocentric role in the cosmos, criticising the religious visions[2]. The *microscope* was invented and used largely by natural scientists. The *cell* is recognised as the basic element of every living organism and many infinitesimal life forms are discovered (virus and bacteria): for millennia, they have been considered divine punishments sent by God to redeem man from his sins[3]. Man is, more and more, proud of his ability to clarify the mysteries of nature using scientific

---

[2] After the astrophysical discoveries of Galileo Galilei, Johannes van Kepler, Mikolaj Kopernik and many others, man is reduced to a lone resident on a little planet rotating around a medium sized star that is his unique source of vital energy. This star is rotating inside a small and peripheral galaxy wandering in the sidereal space.

[3] John Barrow, Frank Tipler: *The antropic, cosmological principle*. Ed. Oxford Univ. Press. 1988.

methods. This liberates him from beliefs, superstitions, dogmas, and acts of faith[4]. Scientific discoveries accelerate advances in language, writing, maths, geometry, chemistry, physics, biology, technology, natural sciences, etc.[5].

New perspectives are opened continuously for scientists; they try also to satisfy many practical needs to improve the average living standards of people in Europe[6]. It is shared and usual to verify empirically any affirmation sustained. The widespread basic conceptual model adopted to explain the occurrence of natural phenomena is: "*stimulus - automatic reaction - reflex action*". The "Theory of reflex" emerges in natural sciences and in animal and human behaviour analysis.

René Descartes (1596-1650) uses it to describe the role of the brain in individual behaviour[7], distinguishing two aspects: the *simple* one and the *complex*. The first aspect considers the sensory stimuli collected; the *cause* of *automatic* processes that translate into a motor *reflex* action (*effect*). The second type is where the initial cause activates not only a motor reflex effect but also a *cognitive effect*. In this case, the cognitive effect should be attributed to the role played by the *soul* (or *mind*). The *Theory of reflex* spreads and it will be a science landmark for a long time[8]. It requires,

---

[4] A large number of scientists consider *God as a simple source of energy* (mysterious) indispensable to every movement and change in the cosmos and in the atoms that constitute every kind of matter.

[5] Isaac Newton (1643-1727), a naturalistic, mathematical, physical philosopher, discovers the role of the *Force of Gravity* that influences the evolution of matter, while not having the physical connotations of the latter; he refers to *magnetism*.

[6] James Watt (in 1764), an engineer and mathematician, designs and experiments the first *steam engine*, which profoundly innovates manufacturing, leading to the British industrial revolution. George Stephenson, an engineer, invents the *steam train* (in 1870). Samuel Morse (1863) designs and executes the *telegraph* and Alessandro Volta (in 1810), physic, invents the *electric battery*. Louis Pasteur (in 1856), chemist and biologist, discovers *vaccines* to prevent endemic pathologies. Alfred Nobel (in 1859), a chemist and engineer, invents *dynamite;* it develops the mining and transport industries (railroad, Transiberiana, Suez Canal). Thomas Alva Edison (in 1877), entrepreneur and inventor, manufactures the electric bulb. Karl Popper: *The logic of scientific discovery*. Ed. Martino Fine Books. 2014.

[7] René Descartes: *Discourse on the method and meditations on first philosophy*. Ed. Oxford University Press. 2008.

[8] There are many researches that support the dominant view of the reflex-theory on individual behavior. They start with the Marshall Hall (1790-1857) fisiologist. They continue with the studies of Ivan Pavlov (1849-1936) and Charles Sherrington (1857-1952). Marshall Hall: *Memoires on the nervous system*. Ed. Andesite Press. (2017). Daniel Todes: *Ivan Pavlov. Exploring the animal machine.*

mainly, to quantify and to interpret some changes of individual behaviour. Some initial mathematical models are devised to estimate the probable and possible reflex action expected. These visions increase the number of scientists involved in *quantitative analysis* about the life process on the planet; few of them are curious, initially, of cognitive aspects. Someone is interested in understanding the unknown interactions between *Mind-Body* considering some certain factors that are difficult to measure[9] and disapproving of the use of the *Theory of reflex* without any consideration of cognitive aspects in human behaviour.

> Then, the *evolutionist theory* drawn up in 1859 by Charles *Darwin* dethrones the man, once again: his casual and late appearance is proved relatively to the thousands of years of life on the planet[10]. This vision reinforces the relevant role of the brain in the slow, long and complicated evolution of the human species in the animal kingdom. John *Locke* (1632-1704), philosopher and doctor, and Jean Jacques *Rousseau* (1712-1778) suggested considering mental factors influencing individual behaviour[11]. Luigi *Galvani* (1737-1798) tests the role of electricity, discharged from the nervous system that excites the muscular and visceral system. He proved definitively the reflex action of muscles. In 1923, Ivan *Pavlov*, physiologist, reconsiders Descartes's conception of human behaviour and updates it investigating physiological and biological aspects in animal behaviour[12]. Despite the similarity between the mammalian and human nervous system, some doubts arise when his scientific results are automatically transferred from animals to human behaviour.

In the main stream of scientific methods, economists are obliged to consider only *quantifiable* factors of phenomena observed to interpret – at the micro-economics level - individual behaviour. In economics, the need to have a mathematical model emerges to explain the different aspects of human behaviour. It should have been based on the reflex-type mechanism, on *quantifiable causes* (*sensory stimuli*) and *quantifiable effects*.

Ed: Oxford University Press. (2000). Charles Scott Sherrington: *Man on his nature*. Ed. Cambridge Univ. Press. (reprint 2009).

[9] Karl Popper: *Knowledge and mind-body problem: In defence of interaction*. Ed. Routledge. (2000).

[10] Charles Darwin: *On the origin of species by means of natural selection*. Ed. Independently published. 2017.

[11] Jean Jacques Rousseau: *Discourse on the origin of inequality*. Ed. Hackett Publishing Comp; John Locke: *An essay concerning human understanding*. Ed. Hackett Publishing Comp. 1996.

[12] Ivan Pavlov: *Conditioned reflexes. An investigation of physiological activity of the cerebral cortex*. In: Annals of Neurosciences. Vol. 3. (Jul. 2010). (136-141).

However, the problem must be solved to consider the cognitive aspects that are often part of the final effects induced by the exogenous *stimuli*. The new target is to have a shared theoretical vision, developed mathematically, that describes the motor and cognitive aspects of human behaviour. It would eliminate the *determinism* of reflex theory opening new reflections on the *stochastic* nature of human behaviour and *free will.*

> Economists are affected diffusely by the cultural dominance of evolution in natural sciences that emerged in the *Enlightenment* century. The subsequent cultural movement, the *Romanticism,* feeds their vision introducing the distinctions between *macro* and *micro* levels in analysing economic phenomena and splitting *public interest* and *private interest.* Even in 1871, William *Javons* asserted that investigation of the role of the psyche and the human brain in people's economic behaviour is useless since the human brain would be an unintelligible *black box,* where it would have not been possible to access its functioning[13].

In reality, their analysis refers continually to the phenomena wholly influenced by cognitive factors that are not easy to be measured; many of them do not respect rigorously unchanging natural precepts and laws of nature. Personal preferences, choices, and decisions are modulated, rapidly and continuously, by emotions, mental states, affective, characterial, economic, social values, religious beliefs, cultural, elements, factors, etc. All these elements influence the cognitive aspects of observable human behaviour unpredictably and this complicates examining their role objectively.

This relevant lack of knowledge is less perceived by the spread of the metaphor of *Homo Oeconomicus.* It is a metaphor based on some naive conceptual hypotheses. The economic-financial agent is assumed, for example, *amoral, profit oriented, impermeable* to emotions, to mental states, to affections, to pleasing memories, or to regrets, etc. He is considered also *rational* in any decision assumed and *well-informed* about the *consequences* expected for any possible choice[14]. His *preferences* are hypothesised *invariables* in time and in space. The role played by emotional, affective, psychological, characterial, etc. factors in decision making are perceived as not relevant

---

[13] William S. Jevons: *The theory of political economy.* Ed. Palgrave-MacMillan. (2013) (pag.25-35).

[14] *Rationality* in economic and financial decisions (and forecasts) is called into question by the unexpected several crisis and speculative bubbles, in economic and financial markets, always imputed, *ex-post,* to the *ex-ante* individual or collective *irrationality.*

and excluded. People's behaviour is *described* and *interpreted* using a *rational-logical-consequential-quantitative* model[15].

> Despite these limits, economists and finance scholars still consider this metaphor a sort of dogma and they refer largely to it without sacrificing their vanity to adorn the outcomes of their studies with the term *"scientific"*[16]. In the meantime, somebody asks if economics and finance are to be considered as *sciences*[17].

Since the 18th century, some (few) economists perceive, with intuitive foresight, the need, for a better understanding of human economic behaviour, to consider new factors whose role in the *Mind-Body* interaction is too difficult to be quantified.

> Adam *Smith* (1723-1790), philosopher and economist, considers the role of some psychological factors to illustrate human behaviour and this vision is taken up by Alexander *Bain* (1818-1903), psychologist, and Friedrich *Von Hayek* (1889-1992), economist. In 1936, John *Watson* (1878-1958), psychologist, analyses the psychological aspects of an agent behaviour involved in *real* market negotiations (not in the lab*).* Physical knowledge pushes Burrhus Frederic *Skinner* (1904-1990), psychologist, to

---

[15] Christian Schmidt: *What neuroeconomics does really mean?* In: Revue d'économie politique. Vol. 118. N. 1. (pp.7-34). Ed. Dalloz. 2008.

[16] It is a habit that excites them, their students, and the journal editors who publish their works and it strengthens the academic approval of respective *"Scientific"* Societies. A scientist informs his reader about the level of completeness and homogeneity of data collected and processed, and about the reliability of the models used to interpret them and to forecast the possible evolution of phenomena observed. The economists rarely do it but they pretend that their traditional studies must be considered as *"scientific"* and publish their works with the editorial features of scientific papers. The result is a perfect *camouflage*. The dissemination of the *"scientific"* adjective satisfies the economist's vanity need to arouse in the reader the conviction that they offer results more reliably. For these reasons, it would be correct to continue considering Economics and Finance as *Humanities' disciplines.* Economics and Finance contexts are different from scientific disciplines, such as Physics, Chemistry, Biology, Physiology, etc., in which scientists have specific habits to face daily phenomena subject to the *immutable precepts* of Nature; a Nature divinely indifferent to the fate of the single living organism, including man. In the disciplines, named *Hard Sciences,* the researcher's discretion and subjectivity is not allowed or any consideration of the role of *emotion* and human *cognitive limits.* Usually scientists declare *all* known factors related with the evolution of phenomena observed and clarify the level of reliability of methods used to process data and information. Rarely do they interpret them with normative and predictive visions.

[17] Robert Shiller: *Is economics a science?* In: The Guardian. 06.11. 2013. Alan Wang: *No, Economics is not a science.* In: Harvard Crimson. Dec. (2013).

study the role played by *exogenous* (environmental, emotional and cultural) stimuli in human behaviour[18]. By the end of the XIX century, some scholars underline how human behaviour is associated with the individual *impulsive* search of *pleasure* avoiding pain, loss, physical separation, in particular from his currency. Francis Ysidro *Edgeworth* (1845-1927), a mathematician and economist, tries to measure the intensity of *pleasure* induced by economic decisions. John Maynard *Keynes* (1883-1946), economist and politician, expresses the need to know the role of psychological factors, resuming some insights by David *j* (1711-1776), philosopher and economist, who was attentive to the spontaneous motivations that induce people to have confidence in the future and to push to act rapidly in economics. Keynes explains the high variability of economic and financial markets, with individual psychological factors stimulated by information asymmetries [19]. He proposes the innovative concept of individual *propensity* to *consumption*, or to *saving;* a psychological suggestion that includes the role of the widespread *irrationality* in individual decisions, fuelled by emotions[20].

Other economists continue to disapprove the metaphor of *Homo Oeconomics*. They criticise its *poor scientific* hypothesis based on *partial* information. Furthermore, they disagree, particularly, with the analysis that does not consider the individual changing perception of risk level, implicit in any choice[21]. However, all the suggestions did not produce what they hoped-for.

---

[18] Adam Smith: *The theory of moral sentiments.* Ed. CreateSpace independent publishing. 2016. Friedrich Von Hayek: *The Sensory Order: An Inquiry into the Foundation of Theoretical Psychology.* Ed. University of Chicago Press. 1952. Friedrick von Hayek: *Studies on the Abuse and Decline of Reason: Text and Documents: 13.* Ed. University of Chicago. 2010. Alexander Bain: *Mind and Body. The theories of their relation.* Ed. Kessinger Publishing 2010. John Watson: *Psychology as the behaviorist views.* Ed. www.all-about-psychology.com. 2011. John Watson: *Behaviorism.* Ed. West Press. 2013. Burrhus F. Skinner: *Science and human behaviour.* Ed. Free Press. 1975.

[19] John Maynard Keynes: *The general theory of employment, interest and money. Modern macroeconomics and Keynesian revolution.* Ed. CreateSpace Independent Publishing Platform. 2015.

[20] These views are shared by John Elster (1944), sociologist and economist. John Elster: *Ulysses and sirens. Studies in rationality and irrationality.* Ed. Cambridge University Press. (1998).

[21] Some authors fear that the above-mentioned metaphor of *Homo oeconomicus* could provoke illusions, intellectual addiction or dependence on it, and excessive self-referentiality. Vilfredo Pareto: *Manual of Political Economy* Ed: Augustus M. Kelley. Publisher (reprint 1971). Alfred Marshall: *Principles of economics.* Ed. Palgrave MacMillan (reprint 2013). John M. Keynes: *A treatise on probability.* Ed. Cosimo Classics. (reprint 2007). Amos Tversky: *Judgement under uncertainty. Heuristics and biases.* Ed. Cambridge Univ. Press. 1982.

For the first time, during the 1940s, some economists initiated considering the variations in the behaviour of both counterparties involved in a negotiation. These variations emerge as a relevant element also influencing macro-economic phenomena evolution[22]. In the same period, some authors tried to produce mathematical models considering the different aspects of individual and collective behaviour of economic operators.

Paul *Samuelson* (1915-1990), economist, formulates the *Expected Utility functions* in a mathematical key[23]. Samuelson admits the limited significance of partial data used and he suggests considering, seriously, the role of psychological factors in human decision making[24]. He describes, with his foresight, how the *expressed preferences' variations* are based on the individual desire to improve personal psycho-physical well-being continuously. It is no coincidence that someone formulates the *Theory of the Games*. It refers to Keynesian concepts of *propensity*, or *aversion*, or *indifference* to *speculative* risk. This theory recalls the impulse (difficult to control) to repeat pleasant experiences, avoiding the negative ones. Mathematical models based on it could suggest the best (optimal-rational) decisions for each one of the contractors during a negotiation in the lab. However, individual preferences and strategies in effective negotiation are continuously influenced by emotion, related with memories of experiences and expectancies of gain, or loss[25].

---

[22] At the end of the 1930s, Kenneth *Arrow* (1921), economist, Gerard *Debreu* (1921-2007), economist, and Lionel Wilfred *McKenzie* (1919-2010), economist, formulated a new *Theory of general economic equilibrium*. Interactions between decisions of those who produce goods and services and the choices of those who buy them are considered relevant factors influencing prices and market evolution. Lionel McKenzie, Gerard Debreu: *Theory of value: an axiomatic analysis of economic equilibrium.* Ed: Yale University Press. 1977. Kenneth J. Arrow: *General equilibrium. Collected Papers of Kenneth Arrow.* Ed: Belknap Press of Harvard University Press. 1984. Lionel McKenzie: *Classical General Equilibrium Theory.* Ed: The MIT Press. 2002.

[23] Stanley Wong: *The Foundations of Paul Samuelson's revealed preference theory: a study by the method of rational reconstruction.* Ed. Routledge & K. Paul. 1975.

[24] Paul Samuelson, William Nordhause: *Economics.* Ed. McGraw-Hill. 2009; Hal R. Varial: *Revealed Preference.* In: Samuelsonian Economics in the 21st century. Ed. Michael Szenberg. 2006.

[25] The first theory refers to the hypothesis of a market *risky*, or *uncertain*, or *ambiguous*, in which people assume decisions. The second theory describes, mathematically, the optimal behaviour for people representing opposed interests in a negotiation. Oscar *Morgenstern* (1902-1977), economist, John *von Neumann* (1903-1957), mathematician, and John Forbes *Nash*, (1992-2015), mathematician and economist, introduce *gambling* in the *Theory of Games* as a method to analyse the psychological factor's role in non-collaborative strategies between two competitors. John von Neumann, Oskar Morgenstern: *The Theory of Games and Economic Behavior.* Ed. Princeton

Some authors study the role of *uncertainty* as a source of *irrationality* diffused in individual decision making[26]. They reflect how, on many occasions, an *irrational behaviour* is preferred; perhaps it reiterates, simply, high pleasant sensations and emotions (without any economic sense). Some psychologists start to confirm *unconscious* memories, emotions, regrets, mental status, etc. factors that support interaction between uncertainty and the (diffuse) *irrationality* in decision making[27]. Herbert *Simon* (1916-2001), psychologist, economist and computer scientist, clarifies the relevant role of the emotional, psychological and mental factors as sources of the *irrationality* of individual behaviour. In addition, he theorises that *limited rationality* be attributed also to the incomplete, unreliable information, as well as to the cognitive limits that exist in perceiving exogenous stimuli and in processing and interpreting them[28].

Applied research to produce radar during the Second World War, innovates mathematical-statistical models and technology tools to process large amounts of data

University Press. 1944; John Nash: *Games Theory: the art of thinking strategically*. Ed. 50 minute.com. 2015. John Forbes Nash: *Equilibrium points in n-person games*. In: Proceedings of the National Academy of the USA. 1950. Vol. 36. N. 1; Duncan Luce and Howard Raiffa: *Games and Decisions. Ed*: Wiley. 1957.

[26] Milton *Friedman* (1912-2006), economist, proposes new methods to investigate the role of emotional factors as source of *irrationality* in decision making. Milton Friedman, Rose Friedman: *Free to choose. A personal statement*. Ed. Marineer Bok. (1990).

[27] In the same period, Maurice *Allais* (1911-2011), a physicist and economist, with a paradox (that will have its name) reinforces substantial doubts about the reliability of certain hypotheses of *Theory of expected Utility*. Daniel *Ellsberg* (1931), an economist, in 1961 with another paradox (Ellsberg's paradox), demonstrates how people estimate the probabilities of expected events, processing partial information and assuming decisions by visceral unconscious impulses to act. Maurice Allais *"Le Comportement de l'Homme Rationnel Devant Le Risque: Critique des Postulats et Axiomes de L'Ecole Americaine"*. In: Econometrica. Vol. 21. N. 4 (pag. 503–546). (1953). Daniel Ellesberg: *Risk, ambiguity and the savage axioms*. In: Quarterly Journal of Economics. Vol. 75. N. 4. 1961. Some studies based on these theories have been furnished with an experimental collection of bio-physical responses (*Skin Conductance Response*). It is proved that bio-physical reactions derive from the (subjective) perception of exogenous (and endogenous) stimuli collected and processed in the brain *before* the neural responses reach the level of consciousness. Michael Dawson, Anne Shell: *The electrodermal System*. In: John Cacioppo, Louis Tassinary, Gary Bernston: *The handbook of psycho-physiology*. Ed. Cambridge Press. 2009.

[28] Herbert Simon: *Models of bounded rationality*. Ed. Cambridge & London MIT University Press. 1982. (Chapt. 2). Herbert Simon, Massimo Egidi, Riccardo Viale, Robin Marris: *Economics, bounded, rationality and the cognitive revolution*. Ed. Edward Elgar Publishing. 2008.

more and more quickly. The *Operational Theory* reinforces the *Theory of rational Decision*, facilitating the selection of the best (optimal in the economic sense) decisions to assume in complex, risky, uncertain or ambiguous markets. It pursues the most rational (efficient) solution (*what is the best?*) or estimates the evolution of observed phenomenon in different scenarios, changing some variables (*what if?*). Different estimations of probabilities are proposed for each scenario (*stochastic vision*). Nevertheless, the data and information used are always partial; they arise, in fact, only from quantifiable revealed preferences.

The economists try to limit the gap, arising from not considering psychological, mental, emotive factors, introducing the concepts of *ordinal utility* and *revealed preference*. This permits to build the personal *Function of expected utility;* but, it requires collecting information about the individual preference and evaluating the probabilities to satisfy each one of them. It is too much of a complicated method. The preferred and shared final solution is to equate, at a conceptual level, the preferences influenced by mental and psychological elements to *revealed preferences* (*effectively assumed and declared*). In this way, it will no longer be necessary to investigate factors arising from the brain (the so-called *black box*); however, that solution does not satisfy the scientific point of view.

During the XIXth century, modern *Psychology* strengthened and spread based on empirical analysis. In short, psychologists try to study the mind's role in a new way to solve negative effects in patients suffering from behavioural pathologies, such as compulsive craving, greed, squandering, etc.

> Wilhelm *Wundt* (1858) initiates *experimental psychology* to investigate the role of emotions and studies how they are expressed in humans and animals. William *James* (1890) introduces the *functional psychology* that connects emotional stimuli to some behavioural pathologies. John *Watson* (1913) suggests a first systemic view of *behavioural psychology* to clarify also the causes of less serious pathological behaviour. Ulrich *Neisser* (1967) introduces *cognitive psychology*, in the 1960s, especially to have a general vision of mental disorders as a source of deficit in learning processes and in the short and long-term memory. Herbert Simon (1975) investigates the psychological aspects of individual behaviour in the economy. Maurice Allais (1986) takes a next step, showing how some behavioural aspects influence the *allocation efficiency* of *resources available* in the market. Richard *Thaler* (2004) consolidates the research of *cognitive psychology* correlated with *economic and financial phenomena*, both individual and collective.

They investigate and describe the *human mind* as a *continuous information process*, activated by (exogenous and endogenous) stimuli that induce instant behavioural reactions at physical (motor) and cognitive levels. Psychologists are used to individuate the symptoms of some pathologies *externally* observing the behaviour of patient to interpret their verbal expressions with which they describe mood, emotion and mental states perceived in decision making process[29]. The psychologists try to prove how *mind outcome* modulates a large part of individual behaviour to have a better knowledge of economic behaviour in *healthy* people.

In the early 1950s, (few) economists undertook a new venture deciding to collaborate with (few) psychologists to fill the knowledge gap cited in traditional quantitative economics. Gradually, a new area of interest and study emerges and spreads: *Behavioural Economics* (and after *Behavioural Finance*). New behavioural visions permit describing and interpreting human behaviour; they are based on a mix of quantitative (traditional) economic analysis and selected methods of psychological methods. In the meantime, biologists and physiologists prove how *each living organism only makes an effort if it maximises the probability of survival of itself and, consequently, of the species*[30]. At the beginning of the XXIth century, some new mathematical models for the optimal economic choice were founded on the principle of *maximum output with minimum effort*. The *Theory of Choice* is proposed.

> The updated *Theory of Choice*, in its *normative* version, considers the role of *probability* and *uncertainty* for selecting the best (*optimal*) decision. In its *descriptive* version, it examines the *irrationality* role in individual behaviour; the experimental protocols refer to the *Game Theory*. Economists try to analyse individual behaviour considering that every negotiation occurs between two (or more) people. The best representation of it is the *Game*. Each player, safeguarding their own interests, is committed to understanding the intentions of their counterpart, to prevent his choices and decisions. Various mathematical models are built to select the *rational* (best, optimal) decision (and strategy) in a *risky*, *uncertain*, or *ambiguous* and *competitive* game context: they are named *choice-models*. All of them are based,

---

[29] Psychologists recover the *method of introspection* suggested by the philosophers of Magna Greece to clarify the role of psyche, or soul in individual behaviour. Introspection of the soul is proposed also by St. Thomas *Aquinas* (1225-1274), dominican and philosopher, to investigate if the sinner's regret was sincere, profound, or not. Barry C. Smith: *Little changes make the biggest difference*. In: John Brockman: *This will change everything*. Ed. Edge Foundation. (2010).

[30] Some biologists suggest that the intrinsic value of nature includes that a gene of any species must survive and procreate, maintaining the equilibrium in the general ecosystem. Fred Van Dyke: *Conservation biology: foundation, concepts, applications*. Ed. Springer Verlag. (2008).

obviously, on partial data (quantitative previous decisions) and include *quantitative* functions (probit) and *logarithm of probability (logit)*[31].

Some critiques highlight the weak assumptions of those models; the economic agent's daily behaviour is influenced, simultaneously, by many (different) factors and it is impossible to consider all of them in a single mathematical model for selecting the optimal (best, rational) choice. It is evident how poor the assumption is about the *theory of automatic reflex*: The cause should be only the search for an economic, or monetary, reward and the effect should be the best (optimal, rational) decision; however, this is not always plausible. The slow abandonment of this *dogma* reduces the relevance of the reflex vision to explain the variable micro-economics' decisions. To explain human behaviour, the *Probability notion* and the *Law of large numbers* are increasingly considered[32]: They offer new methods to estimate behavioural aspects, which are increasingly attractive for some economists.

   Economic Behavioural vision stimulates new interests about the intensity level of individual *emotion* and *mental states* related to the unconscious interaction between *sensation* (physical, or sensory, stimulus) and *perception* (cognitive aspect) of decision making. Behaviourists analyse this interaction hoping to translate it into mathematical functions. They consider the *mental representation* of convenience and *mental decision* as results of a specific process influenced by unconscious *sensory stimuli* and *cognitive* (emotional) *perception*. The mind seems to select its representation and decision

---

[31] With *Probit* models, the probabilities of certain evolution of the phenomena are considered, and with *Logit* models the logarithms of probabilities are considered. This second method satisfies the need to introduce the uncertainty factors. Amos Tversky, Daniel Kahneman: *Judgment under uncertainty: Heuristics and Biases*. In: Science. Vol. 185. N. 4157. (1124-1131). 1974; John Von Neuman, Oskar Morgenstern: *The theory of games and economic behavior*. Ed. Princeton Univ. Press. (1944). David Laibson: *Golden eggs and Hyperbolic discounting*. In: Quarterly Journal of Economics. Vol. 112. N. 2. (443-477). 1997.

[32] The *theory of probability* emerges, in the XVIIth century, by Blaise Pascal, Christiaan Huygene and Pierre Laplace. It offers some axioms to describe mathematically the probabilities of appearance of a certain event. This theory is based on the theorem of *Law of large numbers*. The evaluation of probabilities of the frequency of appearance of the events expected requires processing past data and information about the possible future. Gary Becker: *Irrational Behavior and Economic Theory*. In: Journal of Political Economy. Vol. 70. N. 1. (pag. 1-13). (1962). Gary King: *A solution to the ecological inference problem: reconstructing the individual behavior from agggregate data*. Ed. Princeton University Press. 1997.

without any specific relationship with the *objective identity* of the goods or services negotiated.

In fact, the mind activates a previous and complex process in which are mixed (1) the attention to select and to collect sensory information (stimuli) available (*present*), (2) the subjective visions about the expected consequences (*future*), (3) the personal memories of experiences (*past*), under the influence of (4) the context perceived (*framing effect*). The mind operates considering *present, future* and *past* factors. In a few instants, *different* mental representations appear and disappear, suddenly and unconsciously [33]. Evidently, *time* is the relevant complexity that characterises the mental process to ponder the mix of the four variables cited, *before* any evaluation regarding economic convenience or risk. The human mind often faces this complexity using the *heuristics*[34]. In this way, it simplifies the complexity and accelerates time decision.

> *Heuristics* are strategies used, automatically and unconsciously, by the mind to face immediate decisions in contexts perceived as risky, uncertain or ambiguous. They are innate or learned from experiences by trial and error. They facilitate the adaptive way[35]. Some authors found that heuristics, in the presence of limited information rather than weighting all the options, could lead to more accurate decisions and sometimes to bias. If individuals do not have the time to decide consciously, they act intuitively and emotionally.

Heuristics influence individual perception of the level of *risk, uncertainty,* or even *ambiguity* of the market continually modifying the *individual's propensity* to be *risk taker, risk averse,* or *indifferent* to the risk. Frequently, this lead to errors based on

[33] Stanislas Dehaene, Lionel Naccache: *Towards a cognitive neuroscience of consciousness. Basic evidence and workspace framework. In: Cognition.* Vol. 79. (pag. 1-379) 2001.

[34] Gerd Gigerenzer: How to make cognitive illusions disappear: beyond heuristics and biases. In: European Review of Social Psychology. Vol. 2. (pag. 83-115). 2012. Daniel Kahnemann, Amos Tversky, Paul Slovic: Judgement under uncertainty: Heuristic & biases, Ed. Cambridge University Press.1982.

[35] Gerd Gigerenzer, Wolfgang Gaissmaier: *"Heuristic Decision Making". In: Annual Review of Psychology. Ssrn.com. N. 1. (pp. 451–482). (2011). In short, the main heuristics considered are:* Anchoring and Adjustment, Representativeness, Availability, Naive Diversification, Escalation of Commitment, Familiarity, Bias-Prejudice, Obstinacy, Framing, Time, Time Coherence, Context Perception, Affect, Contagion, Gaze, Peak-end Rule, Recognition, Social Values, Social Pressure, Emotion, Mental States, etc.

cognitive bias[36]. The *behaviourists* are, more and more, intrigued about the role played by *emotion, mental states* as an important cause of *irrationality* in decision making[37]. It is a hard job for behaviourists to translate this complexity into mathematical functions and models to describe how the mind reaches a final decision. The behaviour visions inspire, in any case, pointing out the role of psychological, emotional, and mental factors and, also, the role of personality, character, cultural and social status in selecting the best decision. All of this fosters the curiosity about the role in decision making of genetic heritage, biological and physiological factors, etc.[38].

In 1979, *Prospect Theory* is developed enhancing the *speculative risk* notion and considering the *emotional sensations*[39]. *Behavioural researchers* are always referring to the notion of *speculative risk*, rarely considering the notion of *pure risk*[40]. The *Prospect Theory* also recalls the *mental representation of value*[41] and the level of *economic attraction* when we *buy* some goods or services, and the *emotional attachment* when we

---

[36] A risky context (market) means that it is possible to estimate the *probabilities* of the expected events' appearance. If this it is not allowed, the context is *uncertain,* if the data and information are contradictory, the context is *ambiguous.*

[37] Nicolas Barberis, Richard Thaler: *A survey of behavioural finance*. In: Financial markets and asset pricing. Ed. Elsevier. (Pag. 1053-1128). 2003. Richard Thaler: *Advances in behavioral finance*, Vol. 2. Ed. Princeton University Press. 2005.

[38] In 2002, Daniel *Kahneman* (1934), psychologist, and Vernon *Smith* (1927), an economist, receive the Nobel Prize for: *"Interdisciplinary Studies on Individual Behavior"*. The award was motivated by the behavioural vision adopted and the ability to quantify the effects of some factors, not just economic, in individual decisions. In 2013, the Nobel Prize is awarded to a quantitative economist, to an econometric, and to a founder of the behavioural economy, Robert *Shiller.*

[39] Daniel Kahneman, Amos Tversky: *Prospect theory: an analysis of decision under risk*. In: Econometrica. 1979. Daniel Kahneman, Amos Tversky: *Choices, values and frames*. In: American Psychologist. Vol. XXXIX. 1984.

[40] In economics and in finance, the *speculative risk* notion involves a confrontation between the probability of loss and gain (profit, reward, or an increase in the price-value of owned assets). The *basic risk* notion includes only events with the probability to cause *an economic negative result*. Technically, it is named *pure risk* and it is used generally in the insurance market.

[41] Stephen *Kosslyn* (1948), psychologist and neurologist, clarifies that mental images represent a value as an internal cognitive symbol. It facilitates the solution of complex problems. The discussion of how the brain interprets the mental representations (of value of products or services) is non-ending. Stephen Kosslyn, Wiley Miller: *Top Brain, Bottom Brain: Harnessing the power of four cognitive modes*. Ed. Simon & Schuster. (2015).

sell them. They distinguish between the buyer's behaviour and the seller's behaviour; they are different and involve different psychological mechanisms[42].

Interdisciplinary behavioural vision represents a new challenge for economists and psychologists; often, the innovative results they reach highlight the main stream of respective disciplines. It is necessary for both to learn and to master the theoretical visions, investigation methods, and technical languages of the other discipline. Particularly, psychologists must consider *normal* to investigate *healthy* people's, not patients', decision making[43]. The special attention they dedicate to the words used by the people to describe the emotional sensations and the mental states perceived when assuming decisions, justifies that the behavioural model is named the *Semantic-Model*[44].

Interdisciplinary contributions (particularly those of psychologists) make the findings more credible and the suggestions of behavioural vision more reliable. This causes a sort of irrational exuberance in marketing scholars[45]. The innovations cited induce the conviction in some of them that it would be simple to fill the gap of knowledge about individual behaviour in economics totally and easily. A belief spreads: behavioural visions can increase the effectiveness of marketing interventions in modulating *buyer's behaviour*. Many theoretical models are proposed to reinforce this professional target[46]. An increasing number of marketing advisors declare being ready to stimulate the impetus to acquire *any* potential buyers, in *any* kind of market (!). It

---

[42] Robert Dwyer, Paul Schurr, Sejo Oh: *Developing buyer-seller relationships.* In: Journal of Marketing. Vol. 51. N. 2. (pag. 11-27). 1987. Ziv Carmon, Dan Ariely: *Focusing on the forgone. How value can appear so different to buyers and sellers.* In: Journal of Consumer Research. Vol. 27. N. 3 (pag: 360-370). 2000.

[43] An *ex-ante* psychological questionnaire is used to select sample individuals: this to avoid the presence of people with serious personality pathologies (anxiety, problems with somatoform, control of impulses, dissociative connotations, etc.).

[44] The *mental state* is the spontaneous and subjective perception of a situation, fleeting, long lasting, well-being or discomfort, excitement or relaxation, optimism or pessimism, etc. Resnik Salomon, David Alcorn: *Mental space.* Ed. Karnac Books. (1994). Joel Jeffrey, Anthony Putman: *The irrationality illusion: a new paradigm for economics and behavioral economics.* In: Journal of Behavioral Finance. Vol. 14. N. 3. 2013.

[45] Luigino Bruni, Robert Sugden: *The road not taken: how psychology was removed from economics, and how it might be brought back.* In: Economic Journal. 2007. N. 117.

[46] The academic literature on *Buyer decision making* is very copious. Richard Thaler, Cass Sunstein: *Nudge: Improving decisions about health, wealth and happiness.* Ed: Penguin Books. 2009.

seems easier to satisfy the profit desire of producers, sellers and distributors of goods and services.

> Marketing scholars are drawn, more than others, by the new knowledge and suggestions arising from behavioural visions. A growing number of mangers in global industries, particularly in financial and insurance companies, invest large amounts to support behavioural research projects. Many have benefits adopting marketing behavioural suggestions in advertising, in communication, in projecting and in distribution of products or services[47].

However, it cannot be overlooked that behaviourists base their findings on *subjective* interpretation of both *external* observations of individual behaviour and analysing the *words* used by people to describe the emotional feelings experienced in decision making. Psychologists have, indeed, a lot of *discretion* selecting the research goals and experimental protocols and choosing the criteria and methods for processing and interpreting external observations and words collected. In addition, this behavioural vision contributes to spreading the dangerous habit of *humanising* institutions; it is increasingly a common to consider banks, markets, regulatory institutions, etc. as if they operate with human features.

> In academic publications, it is usual to read that: "banks *react* to market *sentiment* ..."; or: "companies *delay* investments *pending* government *decisions* ..."; or: "... markets *forecast* the *decisions* of the Central Banks", etc. These expressions induce a powerful *subliminal* effect, insidious and irreversible[48]; the authors and their readers completely forget the active role carried out by the single bank manager, central bank official, financial trader, entrepreneur, etc.

Briefly, man and his professional behaviour are not considered; his brain, mind, emotion, decision making process, etc. are transferred (and diluted) totally in the imaginary behaviour of institutions where he works. In essence, the *semantic-method* of

---

[47] Dan Ariely: *Predictably Irrational: the hidden forces that shape our decisions*. Ed: HarperCollins (2008). Richard Thaler: *Nudged: improving decisions about health, wealth and happiness*. Ed: Penguin. (2009). Phil Barden: *Decoded: the science behind why we buy*. Ed. John Wiley & Sons. (2013).

[48] Shevrin Howard, Jaak Panksepp, Linda Brakel, Michael Snodgrass: *Subliminal Affect Valence Words Change Conscious Mood Potency but Not Valence: Is This Evidence for Unconscious Valence Affect?* In: Brain Sciences. Vol. 2. N. 4 504–522. (2012).

behavioural economics has a significant weakness; it is too much *operator-dependent* and this is a serious limit to measuring, objectively, new factors of individual behaviour[49]. It is a remarkable, scientific problem. To avoid it, there is a need to have new methods to investigate behaviour in micro-economics.

After the discovery of the *microscope* in 1670, this tool significantly transformed research in biology and in physiology and it is continuously innovated accelerating the development of knowledge of infinitesimal natural phenomena[50].

> In 1893, August *Köler* (1866-1948), optical professor, innovates the microscope with *internal illumination*. In 1931, Ernst *Ruska* (1906-1988), physicist, and Max *Knoll* (1987-1969), electrical engineer, develop the prototype of the *Transmission Electron Microscope* (TEM) with a higher resolution. Max Knoll, in 1935, proposes the *Scanning Electron Microscope*. In 1981, Gerd *Binnig* (1947), physicist, and Heinrich *Rohre* (1933-2013), physicist, propose the *Electronic Probe Microscope* (EPM) and win the Nobel Prize in 1985. In 1986, the *X-ray Microscope* is used with 3D imaging, penetrating tissues. In 1995, Thomas Christoph *Cremer* introduces a *Laser Scanning Microscope* and *Spectral, Precision, Distance, Microscopy* (SPDM).

The brain is investigated at the *physiological* level and the *Black Box* is considered (*finally*) a very complex organ performing as a special CPU (*Central Processing Unit*) of the nervous system. It selects, handles, and reacts, at the same time, to a continuous flow of sensory stimuli and the more effective (and efficient) neural reactions inducing an individual, congruent behaviour (motor and cognitive) to ladapt to external changes.

> Briefly, the Human Brain[51] consists, physiologically, of 4 different structures appearing in subsequent phases of human evolution. They still interact with each other. The *Reptilian*

---

[49] Daniel Kahnemann: *Choices, values and frames*. Ed: Cambridge Univ. Press. 2000. Colin Camerer (*et al.*): *Advances in behavioral economics*. Ed. Princeton. 2003. Nassim Taleb: *Fooled by randomness. The hidden role of change in life and in the market*. Ed. Random House (2005). Nassim Taleb: *The black swan: The impact of the highly improbable*. Ed. Random House (2010 sec. ed.).

[50] Marcello Malpighi (1628-1694), biologist, discovers red blood cells and the main brain structure; Robert *Hook* (1635-1703), philosopher naturalist, proves the structure of fossil cells and proposes a first idea of biological evolution; Antoine *van Leeuwenhoke* (1632-1723), biologist, uses a microscope to analyse microorganisms, bacteria, spermatozoa, structure of cells, etc.

[51] Scientifically: *Encephalon*.

Brain is the oldest and deeper in the cranium. It is the residue of ancestral, *vertebrate,* aquatic, amphibian organisms from which the human species derives. The functions it performs are related to physical survival, to the protection of food and habitat, and to transfer genetic heritage. It has a role also in imprinting, in the selection of the leader, in imitation, in the impulse to fly into a rage, etc. During thousands of years, the reptilian brain has been physically covered, slowly, by a new neural structure: the *Limbic Brain,* or the *Mammal Brain.* This brain part accompanied man's evolution towards mammals and it manages emotions, memories, habits, decisions, protection of offspring, etc. A third structure, the *Cortex,* or *NeoCortex,* appears after thousands of years of human brain evolution. In the *Homo species,* it grows, relatively to body weight, more than in any other living organism. It physically covers completely the two ancient structures. It performs the control of all conscious decisions, higher functions, and representation and perception of the personal body, language, abstract, rational and logical thought, imagination, intuition, computation, conscience, and self-awareness. The *fourth* structure, generally less considered (the theory refers often to *Triune Brain*) is the *Cerebellum;* a very ancient neural structure that contributes to important functions, such as learning, motor control and balance, attention, concentration, etc.[52].

The *complexity* and the *specificity* of some neural functions distinguish man from the rest of the animal kingdom. Many paleontologists prove the key role played by the human brain in accompanying the very slow and long evolution from *Australipithecus* to *Homo Erectus,* and then to *Naledi's Homo,* to *Homo Faber,* to *Neanderthal Homo,* to *Homo Sapiens* and, finally, to *Homo Sapiens Sapiens,* and this evolution, surely, will continue in the future[53]! Recent development in neuroscience, genetic engineering, regenerative medicine, molecular medicine, biochemistry, artificial intelligence, and nanotechnologies allow us to glimpse a possibility of a new (and next) evolutionary phase of the human species. It would concern the appearance and spread of *Homo Cyborg.* In fact, some scientists hypothesise the diffusion of *amortal* individuals, partly human and partly machines, composed of transplanted organs and non-biological tissues, with a sensorial system and a brain enhanced and modulated with electrodes

---

[52] Paul D. MacLean: *The Triune Brain in Evolution: Role in Paleocerebral Functions.* Ed. Plenum Press. 1990. Richard Leakey: *The origin of humankind.* Ed. Basic Book, Harpers Collins Inc. 1994. John Newman, James Harris: *The scientific contributions of Paul D. MacLean (1913-2007).* In: Journal of Nervous Mental Disorders. Vol. 197. N. 1 (pag. 3-5) 2009.

[53] Charles Darwin: *The descent of man.* Ed. Penguin Classic. (repr.ed.) 2004. Christian De Duve: *Vital dust: the origin and the evolution of life on Earth.* Ed. Basic Book. 1995. Youval Noah Harry: *Sapiens: A brief history of Humankind.* Ed. Harper. 2015. Lydia Pyne: *Seven skeletons. The evolution of the world's most famous human fossils.* Ed. Viking. 2016.

and sub-skin inserted chips. Those individuals would represent an evolutionary leap influenced for the most part by scientific knowledge and, less and less, by the random intervention of nature! The next evolution phases of this new species would become ever more rapid and programmable[54].

> It is, therefore, necessary to know the evolution of the structure and functioning of the human brain to clarify its role in human behaviour. It is not easy; the Human Brain is composed of different types of two specific cells: *Neurons* and *Glia*. Their total number is estimated at about 100 billion and they do their job 24 hours a day throughout a life time, unconsciously interchanging sudden flows of *neural signals* (*spikes*), chemical and electrical, through *neural circuits* that involve many billions and billions of neural connections (*synapse concact*). The final neural outcomes modulate individual, cognitive and motor behaviour continuously[55].

Claude *Bernard* (1813-1878), physiologist, innovates medicine research definitively introducing scientific methods and the dominance of direct (empiric) observation on theoric past knowledge. He separates the concept of *induction* (from particular observation to general theory) from the concept of *deduction* (from general hypothesis to particular conclusion) and suggests considering the two concepts in any verification and disproof process. He recommends that the *cause-effect relation* (accepted in physic) should be considered in clinical research. In 1875, Richard *Caton* (1842–1926), physician, collects *neural electrical signals* in animals' brains. In 1890, Adolf *Beck* (1863-1942), physiologist, places *electrodes* on the surface of an animal brain to record the spontaneous *electrical activity* in reaction to sensory stimuli[56]. In 1929, Hans *Berger* (1873-1941), physiologist, recorded *human brain electrical activity* (ionic current

---

[54] Whoever realises these individuals, will be able to feel himself as *Homo Deus (creator)*. Yuval Noah Harari: *Sapiens. A brief History of Humankind*. Ed. Random (2015). Yuval Noah Harari: *Homo Deus. A brief history of tomorrow*. Ed. Random. (2017)

[55] Bryan Kolb, Ian Q. Wishan, G. Campbell Teskey: *An introduction to brain and behavior*. Ed. MacMillan 2016. Robin Dumbar: *Human evolution: Our brain and behavior*. Ed: Oxford University Press. 2016. Matthew F. Glasser, Timothy S. Coalson, Emma C. Robinson (*et al.*): *A multi-modal parcellation of human cerebral cortex*. In: Nature. Vol. 536. Aug. 2016.

[56] Claude Bernard, Steward Wolf: *Experimental medicine*. Ed. Routledge ed. (1999). Anton Coenen, Edward Fine, Oksana Zayachkvska: *"Adolf Beck: A Forgotten Pioneer In Electroencephalography"*. In: *Journal of the History of the Neurosciences. Vol. 23. N. 3: (pag. 276–286). 2014.*

within the cortical neurons). He uses a new, non-invasive method to investigate inside the black box using electrodes on the scalp: the *Electroencephalography* (EEG)[57].

In 1895, Wilhelm *Roentgen*, professor in Medicine, *discovers X-Rays;* the first step for rapid and amazing development of the *Radiology discipline.* In addition to recording the electrical activity of the brain, it is possible to have morphological and (lately) also functional images of the human brain. New approaches in Diagnostic Radiology emerge since the beginning of the XXth century with the support of ICT (Information, Communication, and Technology) development; new methods to light up unknown parts of the *Black Box.*

In 1986, Henry *Bequerel* (1852-1908), a physicist, points out natural *radioactivity* of some minerals (*radium*). In the same year, Thomas *Edison* (1847-1931) invents the *fluoroscope.* In 1934, Fredric and Irene *Joliot-Curie* produce *radioisotopes* processing minerals as radium and polonium. In the meantime, Nikola *Tesla* (1856-1943), among his innumerable patents in electrical and electromagnetic fields, measures the *density of magnetic flux (magnetic field).* This promotes further designs and produces new, non-invasive tools, especially for Diagnostics in Neuroradiology. In 1940, Arthur *Schuller,* neurologist, uses a contrast agent to gain better results in neuroradiology examinations. In 1950, David *Kuhl* (1929-2017) invents the *Positon Emission Tomography.* In 1963, the first *isotope brain scan* is used by Edward *Burrows.* Godfrey *Hounsfield* and Allan *Cormak,* in 1972, invent a new mathematical basis for processing *CR scanner neural signals.* In 1981, John *Mallard* uses a MRI unit and few years later he introduces the PET (Positron Emission Tomography) method.

In brief, with new tools, it becomes easier to collect *neural signals* to analyse the structure of the *nervous system[58],* the *activation* (or the *inhibition*) of single brain areas

---

[57] Barbara Swartz: *"The advantages of digital over analog recording techniques".* In: *Electroencephalography and Clinical Neurophysiology. V. 106. N. 2. (pag. 113–7). (1998).* In 1947, The American EEG Society was founded and the first International EEG congress was held.

[58] The *Nervous System* is made up of the different nerve cells in the human body. The nervous system, through the sensory stimuli collect information, processes them and reacts to them inducing emotion, action, and cognitive experience to memorise the learned results. Billions of neurons (nervous cells) are performing continuously whether we are awake or when we are asleep. Each neuron has various extensions (dendrites) and it interacts with thousands of other neurons in different parts of the system. The system is known as the *Central Nervous System* if we consider nerves in the brain (Black Box) and in the spinal cord. It is called the *Peripheral Nervous System* if we consider the other nerves in the body. The *Voluntary (somatic) nervous system* gives the sensation of control on everything we are aware of and influence. The *Vegetative* nervous system controls

of it and to measure the intensity of this phenomenon in its *electrical, physical, chemical* activities. All this information and images can be collected with *not-invasive, in vivo,* and *risk-free* procedures: the *Black Box starts to be opened.*

> The most used tools are the Transcranic Magnetic Stimulation (TMS), the Electroencephalography (EEG), the Computerised Axial Tomography (CAT), the Magnetoencephalography (MEG), the Eye-Tracking (ET), the Magnetic Resonance Imaging (MRI), the functional Magnetic Resonance Imaging (fMRI), the Diffusion Tensor Imaging (DTI), the Positron Emission Tomography (PET), and the Single Positron Emission Tomography (SPET). They are complex tools that undergo continuous innovations[59]. Only a few of them emit ionising radiation (X-ray) that, if accumulated in a big quantity, provokes damage in the genetic sequences of single brain cells. A large part of these tools emit electromagnetic waves that are not dangerous. The quality of brain imaging and the electric and physiologic neural signals collected are simply amazing.

Over the past 50 years, various *interdisciplinary* teams use a different mix of the instruments, which are more and more sophisticated, to understand what happens in a performing *"black box"*. Scientists with different skills that are involved in these teams have a shared target: the knowledge of the human *nervous system* and *brain* structure, performance, and evolution[60]. In short, some neuroscientists with their forward-looking work start to consolidate the *Neuroscience* area, including the *Cognitive sciences*[61].

> Torten Nils *Wiesel,* physiologist, receives the Nobel Prize in 1981 for his research on translation of visual stimuli in perceived images of the external environment change. David

---

unconsciously all the (chemical-physical) mechanisms inside the body. Through the nervous system, the neural reactions are quickly distributed from the brain to different parts of the body to adapt to outside changes. Robert T. Ross: *How to examine the Nervous System.* Ed: Humana Press. 2006.

[59] An exhaustive explanation of the technical aspects of each tool cited is included in the part of these proceedings written by Dr. G. Crisi and Prof. G. Polonara.

[60] Eric R. Kandel, James H. Schwartz, and Thomas M. Jessell: *Principles of Neural Science.* Ed: McGraw-Hill Education. 2012.

[61] Vernon Mountcastle: *An organizing principle for cerebral function: the unit model and the distributed system.* In: The Mindful Brain (a cura di Gerald M. Eldeman e di Vernon B. Mountcastle). Ed. MIT Press. (1978). Giovanni Berlucchi: *Revisiting the 1981 Nobel Prize to Roger Sperry, David Hubel and Torsten Wiesel on the occasion of the centennial of Prize Golgi and Cayal.* In: Journal of the History of Neurosciences. 2006. Vol. 15. Michael Gazzaniga: *Cognitive Neuroscience.* Ed: WW Northon & Co. Inc. 2016.

Hubel, neurobiologist, receives the same Nobel Prize for providing evidence of the neuron's function when a neural visual-response arises from a stimulation process. It is clarified also how interactions between visual system neurons, based on synaptic reactions and pressure reactions, are similar to the functional processes of the motor cortex cells. Vernon *Mountcastle* (1918-2015), neurophysiologist, points out the reference areas of Neurosciences: Neuroanatomy, Neurophysiology, Neurobiology, Cellular and Molecular Neurobiology, Neurochemistry, Neuropsychology, Neuroimaging, Neuropharmacology, Psychophysics, Psychiatry, Genetics, Genomics, and Computer Science. Often, the contributions of anthropologists, paleontologists, archaeologists, etc. are well accepted and considered[62].

The new sophisticated medical tools cited, used largely by neuroscientists, allow them to have perfect *resolution* and *localisation,* in the brain map, of each neural area *activated* or *inhibited,* by controlled stimuli. The knowledge the functions implemented by each neural area facilitates understanding of the brain's role in decision making in animals and in humans[63]. With these tools and having a map of functions played by each neural structure, it is easier to interpret the level of intensity of neural *activation* (or *inhibition*) to sensory stimuli. It is evident how a large part of these variations have a peculiarity; they *reveal in advance* (they are *predictive*) the final decisions assumed, anticipating the awareness of them[64].

This new information, updated continuously by neuroscientists, describes *how* the nervous system – and in particular the black-box – directly influences human (and animals'...) behaviour. The human brain carries out *three* main functions: each one can be examined at *anatomical, electrophysiological, cellular,* and *molecular* levels.

The *first* function is *sensory* function to collect, select, and process *exogenous* stimuli coming from the environment and *endogenous* stimuli coming from the organism. The *second* function is the *motor* function that organises and makes any kind of action and movement

---

[62] Vernon Mountcastle: *Daedalus.* In: *Brain science at the century's Ebb.* MIT Press. Vol. 127. (p.1-36) 1998

[63] William W. Orrison*: Atlas of brain function.* Ed. Tieme. 2008. Thomas A. Woolsey, Joseph Hanawey, Mokhtar H. Gado: *The brain atlas: A visual guide to the human central nervous system.* Ed. Wiley-Liss. 2007.

[64] Jay Gottfried, John O'Doherty, Raymond Dolan: *Encoding predictive reward value in human Amygdala, and Orbitofrontal Cortex.* In: Science. (pag. 1104-1107) Vol. 301. N. 5636. 2003. Brian Knutson, Scott Rick, Elliot Wimmer, Drazen Prelec, George Loewenstein: *Neural predictors of purchases.* In: Neuron. Vol. 53. N. 1 (pag. 146-157). 2007.

possible. The *third* one concerns the *connection* between sensory and motor functions to implement the *higher cognitive* functions.

The neuroscientists could involve the economists (and psychologists) to consider *objective* and *subjective* brain *physiology* to understand human behaviour in decision making[65]. Recent results of nuerophysiological researches (using fMRI) prove the relevance of mechanisms and processes, *automatically* and *unconsciously* activated immediately when the sensory stimuli are collected[66]. All of them emerge in the *neural substrate* of any brain functions[67]. The *plasticity of the brain* is another astonishing peculiarity of this wonderful (and in part mysterious) organ[68]. In short, the neural substrate includes all chemical and physical reactions due to the process of sensory stimuli received and influenced by emotion, arousal, and consequent mental states[69].

Furthermore, it is proved that neurons of any specific structure, *excited*, or *inhibited*, are connected with many other neurons located in other areas. These *neural connections*, estimated in billions, appear, disappear and change rapidly, automatically and unconsciously to react rapidly to all kinds of sensory stimuli collected. This phenomenon, named *Neural Plasticity*, has a genetic and physiological basis but it is modulated also by stimuli that arise from personal and professional experience, habits, education, culture, economic wealth, age, gender, characterical aspects, religion, social

---

[65] The *objective physiology* is related with chemical-physical aspects of *processes* and *mechanisms* that permit to the brain to select, elaborate and react to exogenous stimuli collected. The *subjective physiology* concerns *how* the brain *interprets* the perceptions of exogenous (and endogenous) stimuli and how it *manages* the *neural plasticity* connections caused by emotions, arousal and mental states. Robert Sussman: *The biological basis of human behavior. A critical review*. Ed. Pearson. 1998.

[66] The fMRI method detects the neural structures involved in decision making by measuring their Blood Oxygenation Level Dependent (BOLD) signal indicating the variation in arterial blood flow (or outflow) to (from) each one of them. The complexity of this method is described later.

[67] The neural substrate indicates the complex set of synaptic connections between neurons designated to perform a particular function. So there is the neural substratum of the function of language, learning, memory, intuition, prediction, calculation, expected prize, facial recognition, empathy, anxiety, fear, pleasure, etc.

[68] Michael M. Nikoletseas: *Behavioral and neural plasticity*. Ed: CreateSpace Independent Publishing platform. 2010. Moheb Costandi: *Neuroplasticity*. Ed. MIT Press. 2017.

[69] Actually, many chemical elements influence the interaction efficiency of neural connections: neurotransmitters, neuro modulators, hormones, etc.

status, social beliefs, etc.[70] Each mix of them could change the synapse connections suddenly and, consequently, the subjective perception and the interpretation of exogenous stimuli. The same external reality (context, market, risk, etc.) could be perceived in different ways and the individual behaviour unexpectedly (often unconsciously) changes.

A new scientific goal emerges; it should be necessary to have a network map of neural connections: the *Connectome*[71].

> The *Human Connectome Project* (HCP), launched in 2009, involves 16 structures of the National Institute of Health (USA) to map anatomical and functional connectivity in a healthy human brain. The tool used to observe the *neural connections* is the *Diffusion Tensor Imaging* (DTI), introduced in 1985, based on a combination between the Magnetic Resonance (MR) method and specific 3D modelling software, implemented in 1992, to have images of the *neural connections tract*. Actually, the problem is the lack of an atlas of these connections; it must be created *ex-novo* and the paucity of neuroanatomy information slows down this research project[72]. With regard to the interaction between plastic brain connections and human behaviour, the research project includes some measures of the interaction between neural functions and behaviour[73].

Economists could be amazed considering the relevant role played by *emotions* in *neural plasticity*[74] and how the brain carries out its asymptomatic role, influenced by *emotion*,

---

[70] Kevin N. Laland: *Darwin's unfinished symphony: how culture made the human mind.* Ed. Princeton University Press. 2017.

[71] Sebastian Seung: *Connectome: How the Brain's wiring makes us who we are.* Ed. Houghton Mifflin Harcourt. (2012). Olaf Sporn: *Discovering the human connectome.* Ed. MIT Press. (2012).

[72] This project would permit also individuating some solutions to brain disorder induced by Alzheimer's, Parkinson's, Schizophrenia, Autism, pathologies, etc. It receives funds from Washington University in St. Louis, University of Minnesota, Oxford University, Harvard University, Massachusetts General Hospital, and University of California in Los Angeles.

[73] The National Institute of HealthCare (USA) toolbox of measures of human behaviour includes Item Response Theory (IRT) and Computer Adaptive Test (CAT). Other areas are considered specifically (Visual processing, Personality and adaptive function, Delay discounting (neuroeconomic decision making), Fluid intelligence, and Behavioural measures of emotion processing).

[74] Joseph Le Doux: *Emotional Brain.* Ed. Simon & Schuster. 1996; Jaak Panksepp: *Affective neuro science: the foundation of human and animal emotion.* Ed. Oxford University Press. (1998); Edmund T. Rolls: *The brain and emotion.* ED. Oxford University Press. (1999); Joseph Le Doux: *Emotion circuits in the brain.* In: Annual Reviews of Neuroscience. Vol. 23. (pag. 155-184). 2000. Lisa

in perfect *compliance* with the inexorable *natural mandate*, imprinted in the genoma of any cell. This mandate obliges any cell, simply, to *nourish* itself, to *survive* and to *transmit its genetic heritage*: nothing more[75]. Consequently: *If behaviour is determined in a large part by neural automatic events and unconscious processes, it's difficult to sustain free will[76].*"

Despite such knowledge, many economists seem worried to admit that emotion, mental states, arousal and neural plasticity influence individual decision making *automatically* and *unconsciously*. They like to respect their comforting and easing traditional quantitative vision strictly, not considering that this habit turns down the level of scientific reliability of their studies. Therefore, economists need to invest time to exchange views with neuroscientists, physiologists, biologists, neurologists, neuroradiologists, etc. using innovative technological tools to examine *neural correlates* of human behaviour in economic decisions. It is the only way to discover gradually the incredible, large and continuous role played by *brain* in coordinating and modulating the interactions between the three nervous system main functions, influencing deeply individual behaviour through mechanisms and processes (chemical and physical) very fast, automatically and unconsciously[77].

It is not easy to put economists on the useful path to exchange views with experts of other scientific disciplines who are interested in human decision making. The goal is to move from self-referential to interdisciplinary study. This new target preludes an innovative rendezvous between some (few) economists (and few psychologists), curious and driven to have an interdisciplinary scientific culture. In

---

Feldman Barrett: *How emotions are made: A secret life of the brain.* Ed. Houghton Mifflin Harcourt (2017). Kin Ynn Mak: *Neural bases of emotion regulations.* Ed: Open Dissertation Press. 2017.

[75] *Biological diversity* on the planet is distilled information *over 4 billion years* of biological evolution; similarly, *the cultural diversity* of the Homo species results from the contribution of tens of thousands of years of cultural evolution. Murray Gell-Mann: *The Quark and the Jaguar.* Ed. W.H. Freeman & Co. 1994 (*preface*).

[76] Christian De Duve: *Vital Dust: The origin and evolution of life on Earth.* Ed. Basic Book. Revised Ed. 1995. Michael Platt: *Neural correlates of decisions*: In: Current Opinion in Neurobiology. Vol. 12. N. 2. (pag. 141-148). 2002. Michael Gazzaniga: *Who is in charge? Free will and science of the brain.* Ed. Ecco, Reprint edition. 2011.

[77] Joseph Le Doux: *How our brains become who we are.* Ed. Penguin Book. 2003. Daniel Kahneman: *Thinking fast and slow.* Ed. Farrar Straus & Giroux. Rep. Ed. 2013.

brief, it means moving from *simplicity* to *complexity* if they wish to examine brain role in individual behaviour in depth[78].

David M. *Green*, psychologist, and John *Swets*, psychologist, announce the need to formulate a new, shared, general theory considering the various tools to collect *neural signals* to gain a better knowledge of the brain's role in individual behaviour in economics[79]. In essence, a new vision that involves teams from which economists and neuroscientists (and other scientists) emerge. In the last decade of the XXth century, a new scientific area spreads rapidly: it is *Neuroeconomics*[80].

Neuroeconomics is rapidly raising the curiosity of a growing group in the international academic context; it permits going beyond the limits of the quantitative economy and the excessive discretion of behavioural economics. It offers a *holistic* gaze to neural factors to have a better understanding the complexity of the brain in economic decision making[81]. It involves the analysis of *neural correlates* and of the *neural substrates* of each brain function, considering the role of emotions, arousal and mental states in individual preferences, choices and decisions[82]. This depends on the new tools used to detect inside the *black box*. Neuroeconomists use the *neural-connection model* to examine brain role in economic, or financial, individual behaviour. New food for their thought emerges profusely; some new visions innovate *gradually*, and some others *radically*, the traditional economics and the behavioural economics conceptual schemes.

In 1987, Jean-Pierre *Changeux*, a neuroscientist, proposes a first conceptual basic scheme to describe the relationship of neural aspects of an individual behaviour; a new vision of the role played by the brain in *reaction-response* to exogenous, physical

---

[78] Murray Gell-Mann: *The Quark and the Jaguar: Adventures in the simple and in the complex*. Ed. W.H. Freeman & Co. 1994.

[79] See: David M. Green, John A. Swets: *Signal Detection Theory and Psychophysics*. Ed. Wiley. 1966.

[80] Michael Platt: *Neural correlates of decisions*: In: Current Opinion in Neurobiology. Vol. 12. N. 2. (pag. 141-148) 2002. Aldo Rustichini: *Neuroeconomics: what have we found, and what should we search for?* In: Current opinion in Neurobiology. Vol. 19. Pag. (672-677). 2009. Paul W. Glimcher: *Neuroeconomics: decision making and the brain*. Ed. Academic Press. 2013.

[81] Eric Kandel, Jeffrey Schwartz, Thomas Jessel: *Principles of neural sciences*. Ed. McGraw-Hill Education. 2012. See: Michael Gazzaniga: *Tales from both sides of the brain: a life in neurosciences*. Ed. Ecco (reprint 2015).

[82] In 1960, the scientific *International Brain Research Organization* was founded. In 1969, both the *European Brain and Behaviour Society*, and *Society for Neurosciences* were inaugurated. Kin Ynn Mak: *Neural bases of emotion regulations*. Ed: Open Dissertation Press. 2017.

and cognitive (emotive) stimuli[83]. Paul *Glimcher*, Colin *Camerer*, Ernst *Fehr*, and a growing number of young neuroeconomists, researching in interdisciplinary teams of Neuroeconomics, showed the scientific fertility of neurobiological investigations in economics and finance individual behaviour[84].

Neuroeconomists respect the *cause-effect relationship;* controlled exogenous stimuli are considered to be the *cause*, and the activation (or inhibition) of brain structures and the decisions taken are the *effect*. The use of fMRI, and some other tools, to collect *neural signals* related with, sensory and cognitive, stimuli, controlled by the operator, allows the thorough *locationing* of neural areas (*neural correlates*), even of very small dimensions[85] that are *activated* (or *inhibited*) during different phases of the experiments[86]. The intensity level of the *activation* (or the *inhibition*) is measured and interpreted to understand the function performed. Actually, it is possible to know exactly the basic genetically assigned function for each part of the human brain[87]. It is easy, therefore, to deduce the role that it plays in decision making; what has been very difficult, until now, is to explain the role of the *connections* (partially observed) among neurons of different structures. Nevertheless, during this complex phase of analysis, it is observed how some activations (or inhibitions) of neural structures have a *predictive* significance; they (often) *indicate in advance* (less than 1-2 sec.) the decision taken consciously by the brain[88].

---

[83] Jean-Pierre Changeaux: *Neuronal Man.* Ed. Pantheon. 1987. Colin Camerer: *The potential of Neuroeconomics.* In Economics and Philosophy. Vol. 24. Special Issue 03. (pag. 369-379). 2008.

[84] Paul W. Glimcher: *Foundations of neuroeconomic analysis.* Ed. Oxford University Press. 2010. Jean-Pierre Changeaux: *The Good, the True and the Beautiful.* Ed. Yale, University Press. 2012. Paul Glimcher: *Neuroeconomics: decision making and the brain.* Ed. Academic Press. 2013.

[85] Generally, a minimal dimension is 1 *voxel*. This is a conventional cube of neural material, displayed with a powerful scanner, in neuroradiology. The minimum side of it does not exceed usually 3-4 millimetres. In this small volume, there are hundreds of thousands of neurons and a greater number of synapse connections. It is possible to know its coordinates and to define exactly the position of the structure observed. By introducing electrodes inside the brain, the activity of individual neurons is recorded and examined. Itzhak Fried, Ueli Rutishauser, Moran Cerf, Gabriel Kreimand: *Single Neuron Studies of the Human Brain.* Ed: MIT Press. 2014.

[86] In another part of the proceedings, the reader will see an explanation about how neuroscientists can collect, observe, measure, and interpret neural signals.

[87] The *Allen Brain Atlas* is the most updated structural and functional human brain atlas in a very sophisticated 3D edition actually available.

[88] By anticipating 1-2 seconds, the definitive choice is a long time over the milliseconds of neural mechanisms and processes. Brian Knutson, Samuel Greer: *Anticipatory affect: neural correlates and*

Neuroeconomists are very curious to understand the role of the *neural substrate* of each brain function; it includes all the *automatic* and *unconscious* (*chemical-physical*) mechanisms and processes necessary to implement the specific function of the structure. The flow of emotion, the arousal, the mental states in reaction to exogenous sensory stimuli collected by the brain emerge from the neural substrates. The same factors could modify also the mental representations of economic value when we buy something, or when we sell it[89]. In this way, the perception of risk, uncertainty or ambiguity could change rapidly in the same people in different decision making.

Neuroeconomists investigate, in particular, *micro-economic* phenomena; the continuous interaction between neural correlates and motor and cognitive individual behaviour. The old vision Mind-body can be updated. The new available tools to investigate the *black box* and its role in decision making provide a high quality and quantity of brain information and functional imaging: an incomparable result with those of a few years ago. At least 40% of the functional complexity of the human brain is clarified. Therefore, prudence is necessary before conclusively defining the knowledge obtained with neurobiological investigations to understand the brain's role in individual preferences and decisions. However, they open interesting new horizons about the research of the role of the brain in decision making.

Recently, some neuroeconomists wish to understand how the brain foresees the appearance of an imminent financial market bubble[90], others analyse the irrationality level in economic behaviour induced by the *disposition* effect[91], whilst a few are interested in clarifying *how sub-cortical structures* play an important role in a large part

---

consequences for choices. In: Philosophical Transaction ORSoS: Biological Sciences. Vol. 363. N. 12. (Pag. 3771-3786). (2008). Kant Berridge: *From prediction error to incentive salience: mesolimbic computation of reward motivation.* In: European Journal of Neuroscience. Vol. 35. N. 7. (pag. 1124–1143). 2012.

[89] Camelia Kuhnen, Brian Knutson: *The neural basis of financial risk taking.* In: Neuron. Vol. 47. (pag. 763-770). 2005.

[90] Bruno De Martino, John O'Doherty, Ray Debajyoty, Peter Bossaert, Colin Camerer: *In the mind of the market: Theory of mind biases value computation during financial bubbles.* In: Neuron. Vol. 79. N. 6. (pag. 1222-1231). 2013.

[91] Martin Weber, Colin Camerer: *The disposition effect in security trading: an experimental analysis.* In: Journal of Economic Behavior and Organization. V. 33. N. 2. (Pag. 163-184). (1998). Cary Frydman, Nicholas Barberis, Colin Camerer, Peter Bossaerts, Antonio Rangel: *Using neural data to test a theory of investor behavior: an application to realization utility.* In: The Journal of Finance. Vol. 69. N. 2. (pag. 907-946). (2014).

of decision making when the time to decide is very short[92]. Some Neuroeconomics research shows the preference of the human brain to make decisions with a little discretion implying short, or shorter, waiting times to learn the outcomes achieved. This particularly affects propensity, aversion, or indifference to perceived speculative risk[93]. The important role of activations of sub-cortical structures challenges the traditional vision of economists about the rational and conscious behaviour of the agent. Often, *intuition* and *heuristics* are, *automatically* and *unconsciously,* dominant in the economic decision making[94].

Neuroeconomists consider that only the *interactions* between sub-cortical pulses (arising from the *limbic* or *reptilian* brain) and *cortical areas* make it possible for higher functions to be controlled and managed by the Cortex Frontal Lobes. They select and produce the more efficient reactions (motor and cognitive) to exogenous stimuli modulating neural *outcome* to increase the level of efficiency in the individual's ability to adapt to external changes perceived[95]. The brain is very careful to identify and understand every external stimulus that can represent, if not recognise and translate into effective response-responses, a source of imbalance in its state of physiological and biological *homeostasis*. Such monitoring and automatic prevention activities have uncontrollable genetic and physiological bases.

In the meantime, Neurophysiologists identify the structure and the role of the so-named *Reward Circuit* in decision making and the role of the *Dopamine*

---

[92] This is the typical case of decisions made by financial *scalper* traders using *Direct Access Trading*. Furthermore, a negative correlation has been found between *VentroLateral Prefrontal Cortex* and traders' professional experience. A positive correlation has been found between *DorsoLateral Prefrontal Cortex* and transaction (absolute) value; a positive correlation is shown between the *Lateral Prefrontal Cortex* and decision intervals. GianMario Raggetti, Maria Gabriella Ceravolo, Lucrezia Fattobene, Cinzia Di Dio: *Neural correlates of Direct Access Trading in a real stock market: an fMRI investigation.* In: Frontiers in Neuroscience. 29 Sept. 2017.

[93] Anthony Damasio: *Descartes' error: emotion, reason and the human brain.* Ed: Penguin Books. 2005; Joseph Le Doux: *The emotional brain: The mysterious underpinnings of emotional life.* Ed: Simons & Shuster. 1998; Jaak Pankseep: *Affective Neuroscience.* Ed. Oxford University Press. 2004; Jaak Panksepp, Lucy Biven: *The Archaeology of mind: Neuroevolutionary origin of human emotions.* Ed. W.W. Norton & Company. 2012.

[94] Daniel Kahneman, Amos Tversky, Paul Slovic: *Judgement under uncertainty: heuristics and biases.* Cambridge Univ. Press. 1982; Daniel Ariely: *Predictably irrational: the ridde forces that shape our decisions.* Ed: Harper Torch. 2011; Gerd Gigerenzer: *Risk savvy: How to make good decisions.* Ed. Penguin. 2015.

[95] Daniel Kahneman: *Thinking fast and slow.* Ed. Farrar, Straus & Giroud Inc. 2011.

neurotransmitter that reinforces or deprives the activation of this circuit[96]. This is very interesting knowledge in understanding new aspects of decision making. In 1993, *Robinson* and *Berridge's incentive-sensitises theory* includes two different psychological aspects in the same process: *wanting* (incentive) and *liking* (pleasure); it proves how the same pleasure sensation can have different neural substrates[97]. The reward system includes many *pleasure* (or *hedonic*) *centres*[98], influenced by *Dopamine*, located particularly in the *cortical-basal ganglia* and in *thalamo-cortical loop*, in the *Ventral Tegmental area*, in the *Ventral Striatum*. The different mix of activations of those centres induce different levels of motivation, desire, or craving, to receive a premium, a profit, a reward or, simply, to have an increased value of owned goods or services. The neuroscientists distinguish between *intrinsic* and *extrinsic* reward to having a pleasure sensation; pleasure is not related only to an economic, or monetary, premium, profit, or result, etc. It is proved how, at a neural level, reward may consist in positive (*not negative*) emotions and in some pleasant (or *not unpleasant*) sensations, without any economic or monetary consideration.

In the general sense, reward is the base of the *appetitive* individual behaviour; it induces pulses to satisfy, principally, basic needs of nourishment to assure *physiological homeostasis* and of sexual activity and parental care, in compliance with the *reproductive*

---

[96] Dopamine is an important neurotransmitter used by the brain to reinforce the transmission of signals among neurons. In the brain, there are different dopamine pathways to modulate the reward-motivated behaviour. Dopamine interacts with other neuromodulatories to influence the neurons' activity related with motor control, executive function, and with emotion, motivation, arousal, pleasure, and sexual gratification, etc. Roy Wise: *Additive drugs and brain stimulation reward.* In: Annual Review of Neuroscience. Vol. 19. (pag. 319-340). 1996; Oscar Arrias Carron, Ernst Poppel: *Dopamine, learning and reward-seeking behavior.* In: ActaNeurobiologiae Experimentalis. Vol. 67. N. 4. (pag. 481-488). 2007; Kent Berridge, Morten Kingelbach: *Pleasure system in the brain.* In: Neuron. Vol. 86. N. 3. (pag. 646-664) .2015.

[97] The brain *wants* an ice cream and it has a pleasure sensation in buying it. The brain *likes* to taste the ice cream and decides to *eat* it. In these *two* different circumstances, the brain has a pleasure sensation but each one is different from the other: their sensory stimuli are different. The brain distinguishes that the pleasure is induced by stimuli collected through different neural sensory and cognitive connections. Kent Berridge, Morten Kringelbach: *Neuroscience of affect: brain mechanisms of pleasure and displeasure.* In: *Current Opinion in Neurobiology. Vol. 23. N. 3. (pag. 294–303). 2013.*

[98] The main hedonic centres are inside the *Nucleus Accumbens*, the *Ventral Pallidum*, the *Insular Cortex*, in the *Orbitofrontal cortex*, etc. The dopamine neurotransmitter modulates their *liking* or *wanting* pulses. To have a consistent sensation of euphoria, it is necessary to simultaneously activate a large part of those centres. Kent Berridge, Morten Kringelbach: *The joyful mind.* In: Scientific American. (pag. 44-54) Jan. 2017.

genetic mandate. Reward expectation (..not only economic) sustains and modulates also the motivation to reiterate the memorised experiences that trigger well-being and pleasant sensations, avoiding those related with delusion, regret, suffering, etc. The role of the brain in decision making is, therefore, relevant. In addition, it is influenced by automatic and unconscious mechanisms and processes, as well as by heuristics, memories of memorised experiences and, particularly, by emotions, arousals, mental states, etc. The combinations of these factors are numerous and hardly controllable: they also change quickly.

Neureconomists know that the human brain usually takes multiple decisions simultaneously. This implies the simultaneous activation of an incredible number (billions!) of different neural circuits. The performance of each one, which is necessary to exchange information at the synaptic level, is differently modulated by the stochastic combinations of about 200 neurotransmitters, neuromodulators and hormones. Investigating the role of each one is more complex than locating a single voxel of a certain neural structure.

The model of *neural connections* typical of neuroeconomic researches offers, in spite of this, innovative and interesting information and knowledge that reinforces the need to update or integrate, on a scientific basis, the content of the schemes used by most economists, both traditional and behavioural ones. All of this leads to reflection on how to update and integrate the traditional schemes used to interpret the complexity of decision making, without hypothesising conscious behaviours and rational choices[99]. The neuroeconomics' vision obliges *rational* consideration also of the effect of the unconscious neural pulses that satisfy the genetic mandate to maintain the physiological and biological neural homeostasis, or to reiterate memorised pleasant experiences. Neuroeconomists aim to contribute to a new shared vision to clarify what should be meant by awareness and rationality, and decision making of an economic agent.

The future development of Neuroeconomics will be based not only on the curiosity of neuroeconomists but also on the interests of different stakeholders.

---

[99] Nevertheless, new visions in economics and finance are spreading. After the Nobel Prize for the first behavioural economics studies, awarded in 2002 to Prof. Daniel Kahneman, psychologist, and Prof. Vernon Smith, economist, in 2013, the premium is assigned to Prof. Robert Shiller, a behavioural economist, Prof. Eugene Fama, economist, and Prof. Lars Peter Hans for their econometric studies in behavioural finance. In 2017, Prof. Richard Thaler wins the Nobel Prize for his Behavioural Finance studies. Sooner or later, the Nobel Prize for Neuroeconomics will be awarded to one of its pioneers (Paul Glimcher, Colin Camerer, Brian Knutson, Peter Bossaert, etc.).

Neuroeconomics attracts those who study, for example, the behavioural effects of some neural pathologies, such as compulsive or repetitive purchases (*craving, gambling, etc.*). Those who design, produce, and/or sell diagnostic tools (*fMRI, EEG, Eye-tracking, etc.*) can have new buyers; these tools are bought also by managers of neuroeconomy research centres. For some time, the management of many companies competing in global or international markets use Neuroscience's, Neuroeconomics' and Neuromarketing's teams of advisors to strengthen the effectiveness of a company's production, Research & Development (R&D) policies and marketing strategies and operations. They try to increase the effectiveness of their *marketing mix* to stimulate positive emotional sensations in the brain of buyers that could provoke their neural impulses to buy (different brand-products)[100].

In the financial sector, technology and computing have dematerialised every monetary (instrument of payment) and financial instrument (share, bond...). In this way, it is easy to transfer financial wealth in time and space, and trade them instantly in global, totally computerised (virtual) markets. Since 2009, different digital-coins (cripto-coin) have spread rapidly[101]. They are traded and used in fully unregulated and highly speculative computerized markets. In financial markets, it is possible to deal with remote computers that propose, in a very short time (milliseconds), huge amounts of purchases and sales (*High Frequency Trading* - HFT) of stocks, bonds, precious metals, currencies, digital currencies, without human control but driven by algorithms, into their software. Those who design these and HFT software programs to process a large amount of financial and economic data rapidly (Data Mining, Big Data...) are interested in Neuroeconomics and Neurofinance results[102].

Their main goal, however, is to eliminate any emotional effect from trading activities in the markets. Emotion, arousal, and mental sates are removed because of sources of irrationality. They like to produce software to select optimal and rational decisions also in contests uncertain, or ambiguous without human emotional influence. They consider the knowledge offered by Neuroeconomy and Psychology

[100] Christophe Morin: *Neuromarketing: is there a 'buy button' in the brain? Selling to the old brain for instant success.* Ed: SalesBrain Publishing. 2007. Francesco Gallucci: *Marketing emozionale e neuroscienze.* Ed. Egea. 2014.
[101] The most traded and used are Bitcoin, Ethereum, Litecoin, etc.
[102] James Anderson, Edward Rosenfeld: *Neurocomputing: foundations and research.* Ed: Bradford Book. 1989. Paul McNelis: *Neural Networks in Finance: Gaining predictive edge in the market.* Ed. Academic Press. 2005; Ondrej Martinsky: *Intelligent trading systems: applying artificial intelligence to financial markets.* Ed: Harryman House, 2010.

and by researchers that use the *Mind Theory, Chaos Theory*, and *Fractal Theory* to simulate a non-linear and time-varying memory[103]. Their medium-long term (highly probable) scenario envisages that trading in the financial and monetary markets will be managed only by *automated* processes, driven by algorithms in software that is impermeable to emotions. This seems an irreversible course towards a fascinating, but disturbing, vision; in the financial markets, any (human) trader with professional skills and any (human) intuitions, emotions and preferences will be removed[104]. Robots, software, hardware and machines are preferred over human skills and unpredictable human behaviour.

Recently, new frontiers in Neuroeconomics emerge among researchers who apply theories, models, and methods of neuroeconomic investigation to explain the role of the human brain in the preferences and choices of *groups* that adhere to ideologies or to political, cultural, and religious movements; the area of *Social Neuroscience* spreads rapidly[105].

Those who operate in the *Artificial Intelligence* (AI) sector, on the contrary, are strictly concerned with Neuroeconomics- and Neurofinance-specific information about the functioning of cognitive and emotive neural circuits. They try, in fact, to transfer them out of the human brain. They try to put them inside the software, to have their robot with a behaviour more like a human (more emotional and cognitive) and able to use intuition, to make rapid (and efficient) decisions, and to learn by

---

[103] Benoit Manderbrot: *Fractals and scaling finance: discontinuity, concentration, risks.* Ed. Springer. 1997. Bill Williams: *New trading dimensions. How to profit from chaos in stocks, bonds and commodities.* Ed. Wiley. 1998. Justin Gregory Williams: *Trading Chaos: maximize profits with proven technical techniques.* Ed. Wiley. 2004. Rishi Narang: *Inside the black box: a simple guide to quantitative and high frequency trading.* Ed. Wiley. 2013.

[104] Fortunately, this is not the place to reflect on the possible effects of a long-time exasperated automatic search for rational finance decisions and, above all, on the interaction between finance and investments in the real economy. Philip Molineux, Nidal Shamroukh: *Financial Innovation.* Ed. Wiley. 1999; Nassim Taleb: *Fooled by randomness. The hidden role of chance in life and in the markets.* Ed. Random House trade paperbacks. 2005; Danilo Drago: *Securitization, CDO and Covered Bonds.* Ed. Bancaria Editrice. 2007; Nassim Taleb: *The black swan: The impact of the highly improbable.* Ed: Random House trade paperbacks. 2010.

[105] Eddie Harmon-Jones and Piotr Winkielman: *Social Neuroscience: Integrating biological and physiological explanations of social behavior.* Ed: Guildford Press. 2008; Eddie Harmon-Jones, Jennifer Beer: *Methods in Neurosciences.* Ed. Guildford Press. 2009; John Cacioppo, Penny Wisser: *Social Neurosciences: people thinking about thinking people.* Ed: Bradford Book. 2012; Russel Schutt, Larry Seydman: *Social Neuroscience: Brain, Mind, Society.* Ed: Harvard University Press. 2015.

experience. Through this effort, they consider any developments by researchers based on the *Theory of Mind* (TOM), Neurophysiology and Physics on the non-physical properties of brain matter.

Richard *Feynman* (in 1975), physicist, unites micro-macro visions in *physics of particles;* he describes the presence of *antimatter.* Matter is made up of infinitesimal particles (atoms, protons, electrons, neutrons, and the smallest quarks). Every *sub-atomic* particle strictly respects the *Law of Gravity* in its perpetual rotation. The energy sources – *quarks* - are floating in *electromagnetic waves* in an unknown environment (space), named (*improperly*) as *vacuum.* However, the vacuum does not exist: it is full of *dark matter,* or *antimatter!* Even the human brain is made up of this matter. Biologists investigate *living* matter and Physicists investigate *how* matter evolves; they describe the role of some matter's *properties* (*not physical*) as *magnetism,* in its evolution. Some study the role of magnetism in the neural process to carry out some higher human neural functions as the thought, the reflection on thought, the awareness, the consciousness, etc. [106]

The future of Neuroeconomics will be distinguished by the scientific contributions offered by a crescent number of interdisciplinary research centres around the world. Many of them are located at universities, others at some private *global* enterprises[107]. Their scientific curiosity about the role of the brain in decision

---

[106] Gerald Edelman: *The remembered present: a biological theory of consciousness.* Ed. Basic Book. 1990; Gerald Edelman: *Bright air, brilliant fire: on the matter of the mind.* Ed. Basic Book. 1993; Gerald Edelman, Giulio Tononi: *A universe of consciousness: how matter becomes imagination.* Ed: Basic Book. 2001; Chris Frith: *Making up the mind: How the brain creates our mental word.* Ed. Wiley-Blackwell. 2007; Giulio Tononi: *PHI: a voyage from the brain to the soul.* Ed: Basic Book. 2012; Michiu Kaku: *The future of mind: The scientific quest to understand, enhance, and empower the mind.* Ed. Anchor. 2015.

[107] In recent years, university research centres *devoted* to Neuroeconomics are increasing rapidly. They are located mainly in the United States and in China. In Europe, there are a certain number of them, particularly in the UK. A limited number of them are operating in Holland, Germany, France and Switzerland. Various interdisciplinary research teams (as our team, located at the School of Medicine of Università Politecnica delle Marche) are active at different European universities. The Society for Neuroeconomics (SFN) checked that in 2000, about 1,000 papers on the brain's role in decision making are published. In 2005, the number of them is over 2,000. In 2016, over 8,000 papers are issued in Neuroeconomics. Different main global enterprise have internal, or related, neuroscience and neuroeconomic research centres are different: Apple, Google, CocaCola, McDonalds, Mercedes Benz, Amazon, Microsoft, Toyota, Samsung.

making and motivations will be sustained by the different stakeholders (in scientific, economic, financial sectors) interested to clarify the individual behaviour. They justify the growing investment in support of Neuroeconomics and Neurofinance research. The positive scientific perspectives are summarised respectively by Daniel Kahneman and by Paul Glimcher in final chapters of their recent books.[108]

---

[108] Daniel Kahneman: *Thinking fast and slow*. Ed. Penguin. 2012. Paul Glimcher: *Neuroeconomics. Decision making and the brain*. Ed: Academic Press. (2nd ed.) 2013.

References

Allais, M., (1953), «Le Comportement de l'Homme Rationnel Devant Le Risque: Critique des Postulats et Axiomes de L'Ecole Americaine», *Econometrica*, 21, 4, pp. 503-546.

Anderson, J. and Rosenfeld, E., (1989), *Neurocomputing: Foundations and Research*, Bradford Book.

Ariely, D., (2011), *Predictably Irrational: The Hidden Forces That Shape our Decisions,* Harper Torch.

Arrow, K.J., (1984), *General equilibrium. Collected Paper of Kenneth Arrow*, Belknap Press of Harvard University Press.

Bain, A., (2010), *Mind and Body. The Theories and Their Relation*, Kessinger Publishing.

Barberis, N. and Thaler, R., (2003) «A Survey of Behavioral Finance», in: *Handbook of the Economics of Finance,* Edited by G.M Constantinides, M. Harris, M. & Stulz, Elsevier North Holland.

Barden, P., (2013), *Decoded: The Science Behind Why We Buy,* John Wiley & Sons.

Barrett, L.F., (2017), *How Emotions are Made. a Secret Life Of Brain,* Houghton Mifflin Harcourt.

Barrow, J. and Tipler, F., (1988), *The Anthropic, Cosmological Principle,* New York: Oxford University Press.

Becker, G., (1962), «Irrational Behavior and Economic Theory», *Journal of Political Economy,* 70, pp. 1-13.

Berlucchi G., (2006), «Revisiting the 1981 Nobel Prize to Roger Sperry, David Hubel and Torsten Wiesel on the Occasion of the Centennial of Prize Golgi and Cayal», *Journal of the History of Neurosciences,* 15, pp. 369-375.

Bernard, C. and Wolf, S., (1999), *Experimental Medicine*, Routledge.

Berridge, K., (2012), «From Prediction Error to Incentive Salience: Mesolimbic Computation of Reward Motivation», *European Journal of Neuroscience,* 35, pp. 1124-1143.

Berridge, K. and Kingelbach, M., (2013) «Neuroscience of Affect: Brain Mechanisms of Pleasure and Displeasure», *Current Opinion in Neurobiology,* 23, pp. 294-303.

Berridge, K. and Kingelbach, M., (2015), «Pleasure System in the Brain», *Neuron,* 86, pp. 646-664.

Berridge, K. and Kingelbach, M., (2017), «The Joyful Mind», *Scientific American,* 307, pp. 40-45.

Bruni, L. and Sugden, R., (2007), «The Road Not Taken: How Psychology Was Removed From Economics, and How It Might Be Brought Back», *Economic Journal,* 117, pp. 146-173.

Cacioppo, J. and Wisser, P., (2012), *Social Neurosciences: People Thinking About Thinking People,* Bradford Books.

Camerer, C., (2008), «The potential of Neuroeconomics», *Economics and Philosophy,* 24, pp. 369-379.

Camerer, C., Loewenstein, G. and Rabin, M., (2003), *Advances in Behavioral Economics,* Princeton University Press.

Carron, O.A. and Poppel, E., (2015) «Dopamine, Learning and Reward-Seeking Behaviour», *Acta Neurobiologiae Experimentalis,* 67, pp. 481-488.

Changeaux, J.P., (1987), *Neuronal Man,* Pantheon.

Changeaux, J.P., (2012), *The Good, The True and the Beautiful,* Yale University Press.

Coenen, A., Fine, E. and Zayachkvska, O., (2014), «Adolf Beck: A Forgotten Pioneer In Electroencephalography», *Journal of the History of the Neurosciences,* 23, pp. 276-286.

Costandi, M., (2017), *Neuroplasticity.* MIT Press.

Damasio, A., (2005), *Descartes' Error: Emotion, Reason and The Human Brain,* Penguin Books.

Darwin, C., (2004), *The Descent of Man,* Penguin Classic.

Darwin, C., (2017), *On the Origin of Species by Means of Natural Selection,* Independently Published.

Dawson, M. and Shell, A., (2009), «The Electrodermal System», in: *The Handbook of Psychophysiology,* John Cacioppo, Louis Tassinary, Gary Bernston (Eds), Cambridge University Press.

De Duve, C., (1995), *Vital Dust: The Origin and the Evolution of Life on Earth,* Basic Book.

De Martino, B., O'Doherty, J., Debajyoty, R., Bossaert, P. and Camerer, C., (2013) «In the Mind of the Market: Theory if Mind Biases Value Computation During Financial Bubbles», *Neuron,* 79, pp. 1222-1231.

Dehaene, S. and Naccache, L., (2001) «Towards a Cognitive Neuroscience of Consciousness. Basic Evidence and Workspace Framework», *Cognition,* 79, pp. 1-379.

Descartes, R., (2008), *A Discourse on the Method and Meditation on First Philosophy,* Oxford University Press.

Drago, D., (2007), *Securitization, CDO and Covered Bonds,* Bancaria Editrice.

Dumbar, R., (2016), *Human Evolution: Our Brain and Behavior,* Oxford University Press.

Edelman, G., (1990), *The Remembered Present: A Biological Theory of Consciousness,* Basic Book.

Edelman, G., (1993), *Bright Air, Brilliant Fire: On The Matter Of The Mind,* Basic Book.

Edelman, G. and Tononi, G., (2001), *A Universe of Consciousness: How Matter Becomes imagination,* Basic Book.

Ellesberg, D., (1961) «Risk, Ambiguity and the Savage Axioms», *Quarterly Journal of Economics,* 75, p. 4.

Ellis, G., (2016), *How Can Physics Underlie the Mind? Top Down Causation in the Human Context,* Springer.

Elster, J., (1998), *Ulysses and Sirens. Studies in Rationality and Irrationality,* Cambridge University Press.

Fried, I., Rutishauser, U., Cerf, M. and Kreimand, G., (2014), *Single Neuron Studies of the Human Brain,* MIT Press.

Friedman, M. and Friedman, R., (1990), *Free to Choose. A Personal Statement,* Mariner Books.

Frith, C., (2007), *Making up the Mind: How the Brain Creates our Mental Word,* Wiley-Blackwell.

Frydman, C., Barberis, N., Camerer, C., Bossaerts, P. and Rangel, A., (2014), «Using Neural Data to Test a Theory of Investor Behavior: An Application to Realization Utility», *The Journal of Finance,* 69, pp. 907-946.

Gallucci, F., (2014), *Marketing emozionale e neuroscienze,* Egea.

Gazzaniga, M., (2011), *Who is in Charge? Free Will and Science of The Brain*, Ecco.

Gazzaniga, M., (2015), *Tales from Both Sides of the Brain: a Life In Neurosciences*, Ecco.

Gazzaniga, M., (2016), *Cognitive Neuroscience*, Ed: WW Northon & Co. Inc.

Gell-Mann, M., (1994), *The Quark and the Jaguar. Adventures in the Simple and in the Complex*, W.H. Freeman & Co.

Gigerenzer, G., (2012), «How to Make Cognitive Illusions Disappear: Beyond Heuristics and Biases», *European Review of Social Psychology,* 2, pp. 83-115.

Gigerenzer, G., (2015), *Risk Savvy: How To Make Good Decisions*, Penguin.

Gigerenzer, G. and Gaissmaier, W., (2011), «Heuristic Decision Making», *Annual Review of Psychology,* 1, pp. 45- 482.

Glasser, M.F., Coalson, T.S., Robinson, E.C., et al., (2016), «A Multi-Modal Parcellation of Human Cerebral Cortex», *Nature,* 536, pp. 171-178.

Glimcher, P.W., (2010), *Foundations of Neuroeconomic Analysis,* Oxford University Press.

Glimcher, P.W., (2013), *Neuroeconomics: Decision Making and the Brain*, Academic Press.

Gottfried, J., O'Doherty, J. and Dolan, R., (2003), «Encoding Predictive Reward Value in Human Amygdala, and Orbitofrontal Cortex», *Science,* 301, pp. 1104-1107.

Green, D.M. and Swets, J.A., (1966), *Signal detection theory and psychophysics*, Wiley.

Hall, M., (2017), *Memoirs on the Nervous System*, Andesite Press.

Harmon-Jones, E. and Beer, J., (2009), *Methods in Neurosciences*, Guildford Press.

Harmon-Jones, E. and Winklielman, P., (2008), *Social Neuroscience: Integrating biological and Physiological Explanations of Social Behavior*, Guildford Press.

Harry, Y.N., (2015), *Sapiens: A brief history of Humankind*, Harper.

Howard, S., Panksepp, J., Brakel, L. and Snodgrass, M., (2012), «Subliminal Affect Valence Words Change Conscious Mood Potency but Not Valence: Is This Evidence for Unconscious Valence Affect?», *Brain Sciences,* 2, pp. 504–522.

Jeffrey, J. and Putman, A., (2013), «The Irrationality Illusion: A New Paradigm for Economics and Behavioral Economics», *Journal of Behavioral Finance,* 14, pp. 161-194.

Jevons, W.S., (2013), *The Theory of Political Economy*, Palgrave-MacMillan.

Kahneman, D., (2013), *Thinking Fast and Slow*, Farrar, Straus & Giroux.

Kahneman, D. and Tversky, A., (1979), «Prospect Theory: an Analysis of Decision Under Risk», *Econometrica*, 47, pp. 263-291.

Kahneman, D. and Tversky, A., (1984), «Choices, Values and Frames», *American Psychologist*, 39, pp. 341-350.

Kahneman, D., Tversky, A. and Slovic, P., (1982), *Judgement Under Uncertainty: Heuristics & Biases*, Cambridge University Press.

Kaku, M., (2015), *The Future of Mind. The Scientific Quest to Understand, Enhance, and Empower of Mind*, Anchor.

Kandel, E., Schwartz, J. and Jessel, T., (2012), *Principles of Neural Sciences*, McGraw-Hill Education.

Keynes, J. M., (2007), *A Treatise on Probability*, Cosimo Classics.

Keynes, J.M. (2015), *The General Theory of Unemployment, Interest and Money. Modern Macroeconomics and Keynesian Revolution*, CreateSpace Independent Publishing Platform.

King, G., (1997), *A Solution to the Ecological Inference Problem: Reconstructing the Individual Behavior from Aggregate Data*, Princeton University Press.

Knutson, B. and Greer, S., (2008), «Anticipatory Affect: Neural Correlates and Consequences for Choices», *Philosophical Transaction of the Royal Society*, 363, pp. 3771-3786.

Knutson, B., Rick, S., Wimmer, E., Prelec, D. and Loewenstein, G., (2007), «Neural Predictors of Purchases», *Neuron*, 53, pp. 146-157.

Kolb, B., Wishan, I.Q. and Teskey, G.C. (2016), *An Introduction to Brain and Behavior*, Palgrave-MacMillan.

Kosslyn, S. and Miller, W., (2015), *Top Brain, Bottom Brain: Harnessing the Power of Four Cognitive Modes*, Simon & Schuster.

Kuhnen, C. and Knutson, B., (2005), «The Neural Basis of Financial Risk Taking», *Neuron*, 47, pp. 763-770.

Laibson, D., (1997), «Golden Eggs and Hyperbolic Discounting», *Quarterly Journal of Economics,* 112, pp. 443-477.

Laland, K.N., (2017), *Darwin's Unfinished Symphony: How Culture Made the Human Mind,* Princeton University Press.

Le Doux, J., (1996), *The Emotional Brain: The Mysterious Underpinnings of Emotional Life,* Simon & Schuster.

Le Doux, J., (2000), «Emotion Circuits in the Brain», *Annual Reviews of Neuroscience,* 23, pp. 155-184.

Le Doux, J., (2003), *How our Brains Become Who We Are,* Penguin Book.

Leakey, R., (1994), *The origin of Humankind,* Basic Book, Harpers Collins Inc.

Locke, J., (1996), *An Essay Concerning Human Understanding,* Hackett Publishing Comp.

Luce, D. and Raiffa, H., (1957), *Games and Decisions,* New York, Wiley.

MacLean, P.D., (1990), *The Triune Brain in Evolution, Role in Paleocerebral Functions,* Plenum Press.

Mak, K.Y., (2017), *Neural Bases of Emotion Regulations,* Open Dissertation Press.

Manderbrot, B., (1997), *Fractals and Scaling Finance: Discontinuity, Concentration, Risks,* Springer.

Marshall, A., (2013), *Principles of Economics,* Palgrave MacMillan.

Martinsky, O., (2010), *Intelligent Trading System: Applying Artificial Intelligence to Financial Markets,* Harryman House.

McKenzie, L., (2002), *Classical General Equilibrium Theory,* The MIT Press.

McKenzie, L. and Debreu, G., (1977), *Theory of value: An Axiomatic Analysis of Economic Equilibrium,* Yale University Press.

McNelis, P., (2005), *Neural Network in Finance: Gaining Predictive Edge in the Market,* Academic Press.

Molineux, P. and Shamroukh, N., (1999), *Financial Innovation,* Wiley.

Morin, C., (2007), *Neuromarketing: Is There a 'Buy Button' In the Brain? Selling to the Old Brain for Instant Success,* SalesBrain Publishing.

Mountcastle, V., (1978) «An Organizing Principle for Cerebral Function: The Unit Model And The Distributed System», in Eldeman G.M. and Mountcastle V.B., (Eds), *The Mindful Brain,* MIT Press.

Mountcastle, V., (1998), «Daedalus», in *Brain Science at the Century's Ebb,* MIT Press.

Narang, R., (2013), *Inside the Black Box: A Simple Guide to Quantitative and High Frequency Trading,* Wiley.

Nash, J., (1950), «Equilibrium Points in N-Person Games», *Proceedings of the National Academy of the United States of America,* 36, pp. 48-49.

Nash, J., (2015), *Games Theory: the Art of Thinking Strategically,* Ed. 50 minute.com.

Newman, J. and Harris, J., (2009), «The Scientific Contributions» of Paul D. MacLean (1913-2007), *Journal of Nervous Mental Disorders,* 197, pp. 3-5.

Nikoletseas, M.M., (2010), *Behavioral and Neural Plasticity,* CreateSpace Independent Publishing Platform.

Orrison, W.W., (2008), *Atlas of Brain Function,* Tieme.

Panksepp, J., (1998), *Affective Neuroscience: the foundation of Human and Animal Emotion,* Oxford University Press.

Panksepp, J., (2004), *Affective Neuroscience,* Oxford University Press.

Panksepp, J. and Biven, L., (2012), *The Archaeology of Mind: Neuroevolutionary Origin of Human Emotions,* W.W. Norton & Company.

Pareto, V., (1971), *Manual of Political Economy,* Augustus M. Kelley Publisher.

Pavlov, I., (2010), «Conditioned reflexes. An Investigation of Physiological Activity of the Cerebral Cortex», *Annals of Neurosciences,* 3, pp. 136-141.

Platt, M., (2002), «Neural Correlates of Decisions», *Current Opinion in Neurobiology,* 12, pp. 141-148.

Popper, K., «Knowledge and Mind-Body Problem», in Notturno, M.A., (2000), *Defence of interaction,* London and New York, Routledge.

Popper, K., (2014), *The Logic of Scientific Discovery,* Martino Fine book.

Pyne, L., (2016), *Seven Skeletons. The Evolution of The World's Most Famous Human Fossils,* Viking.

Raggetti, G.M., Ceravolo, M.G., Fattobene, L. and Di Dio, C., (2017), «Neural Correlates of Direct Access Trading in a Real Stock Market: An Fmri Investigation», *Frontiers in Neuroscience,* 11, p. 536.

Rolls, E.T., (1999), *The Brain and Emotion,* Oxford University Press.

Ross, R.T., (2006), *How to Examine the Nervous System,* Humana Press.

Rousseau, J.J., (2004), *Discourse on the Origin of the Inequality,* Hackett Publishing Comp.

Rustichini, A., (2009), «Neuroeconomics: What Have We Found, and What Should We Search For?», *Current Opinion in Neurobiology,* 19, pp. 672-677.

Salomon, R. and Alcorn, D., (1994), *Mental Space,* Karnac Books.

Samuelson, P. and Nordhause, W.D., (2009), *Economics,* McGraw-Hill.

Schmidt, C., (2008), «What Neuroeconomics Does Really Mean?», *Revue D'économie Politique,* 118, pp. 7-34.

Schutt, R. and Seydman, L., (2015), *Social Neuroscience: Brain, Mind, Society,* Harvard University Press.

Seung, S., (2012), *Connectome: How the Brain's Wiring Makes Us Who We Are,* Houghton Mifflin Harcourt.

Sherrington, C.S., (2009), *Man on his Nature,* Cambridge University Press.

Shiller, R., (2013), «Is Economics a Science?», *The Guardian,* 6 November.

Simon, H., (1982), *Models of Bounded Rationality,* MIT University Press.

Simon, H., Egidi, M., Viale, R. and Marris, R. (2008), *Economics, Bounded, Rationality and the Cognitive Revolution,* Edward Elgar Publishing.

Skinner, B.F., (1975), *Science and Human Behaviour,* Free Press.

Smith, A., (2016), *The Theory of Moral Sentiments,* Create space Independent Publishing Platform.

Smith, B.C., (2010) «Little Changes Make the Biggest Difference», in Brockman, J., *This Will Change Everything*, (Ed.) Edge Foundation.

Sporn, O., (2012), *Discovering the Human Connectome*, MIT Press.

Sussman, R., (1998), *The Biological Basis of Human Behavior. A Critical Review*, Pearson.

Swartz, B., (1998), «The Advantages of Digital Over Analog Recording Techniques», *Electroencephalography and Clinical Neurophysiology*, 106, pp. 113–117.

Taleb, N., (2005), *Fooled by Randomness. The Hidden Role of Change in Life and in the Market*, Random House.

Taleb, N., (2010), *The Black Swan: The Impact of the Highly Improbable*, Random House.

Thaler, R., (2005), *Advances in Behavioral Finance*, Princeton University Press.

Thaler, R. and Sunstein, C., (2009), *Nudge: Improving Decisions About Health, Wealth and Happiness*, Penguin Books.

Todes, D., (2000), *Ivan Pavlov: Exploring the Animal Machine*, Oxford University Press.

Tononi, G., (2012), *PHI: A Voyage from the Brain to the Soul*, Basic Book.

Tversky, A., (1982), *Judgement under Uncertainty: Heuristics and Biases*, Cambridge University Press.

Tversky, A. and Kahneman, D., (1974), «Judgment Under Uncertainty: Heuristics and Biases», *Science*, 185, 4157, pp. 1124-1131.

Van Dyke, F., (2008), *Conservation Biology: Foundation, Concepts, Applications*, Springer.

Varian, H.R., (2006), «Revealed Preference», in Szenberg M. (Ed.) *Samuelsonian Economics and the 21st Century*, Oxford University Press.

Von Hayek, F., (1952), *The Sensory Order: An Inquiry into the Foundation of Theoretical Psychology*, University of Chicago Press.

Von Hayek, F., (2010), *Studies on the Abuse and Decline of Reason: Text and Documents: 13*, University of Chicago.

Von Neuman, J. and Morgenstern, O., (1944), *The Theory of Games and Economic Behavior*, Princeton University Press.

Wang, A., (2013), *No, Economics is Not a Science.* The Harvard Crimson, 13.12.2013.

Watson, J., (2011), *Psychology as the Behaviorist Views It*, www.all-about-psychology.com.

Watson, J., (2013), *Behaviorism*, West Press.

Weber, M. and Camerer, C., (1998) «The Disposition Effect in Security Trading: an Experimental Analysis», *Journal of Economic Behavior and Organization*, 33, pp. 163-184.

Williams, B., (1998), *New Trading Dimensions. How to Profit From Chaos in Stocks, Bonds and Commodities*, Wiley.

Williams, J.G., (2004), *Trading Chaos: Maximize Profits with Proven Technical Techniques*, Wiley.

Wise, R., (1996), «Additive Drugs and Brain Stimulation Reward», *Annual Review of Neuroscience*, 19, pp. 319-340.

Wong, S., (1975), *The Foundations of Paul Samuelson's revealed Preference Theory: A Study By The Method Of Rational Reconstruction*, Routledge & K. Paul.

Woolsey, T.A. and Hanawey, J. and Gado, M.H., (2007), *The Brain Atlas: A Visual Guide To The Human Central Nervous System*, Wiley-Liss.

2. Reward-Economic Choices-Decision Making and Dopamine

by Rocco Cerroni, Maria Albanese, Nicola Biagio Mercuri

We are our brain but we still don't know it. For this reason, we are trying to understand ourselves.

Over the last 20 years, the formidable progress that occurred in Neuroscience has increased the techniques for studying how the human brain functions. This has created new opportunities to investigate how neural circuits work and determine human behavior.

New neuroimaging methods, such as Positron Emission Tomography (PET), Single Photon Emission Computed Tomography (SPECT), Magnetic Resonance Spectroscopy (MRS), functional Magnetic Resonance Imaging (fMRI), along with non-invasive neurophysiological techniques, such as Skin Conductance Response (SCR), Electroencephalogram (EEG), Transcranial Direct Current Stimulation (TDCS) and Transcranial Magnetic Stimulation (TMS), are now available for neuroscientists to investigate the biochemical and functional basis of mental activities either *"in vivo"* in a healthy brain or in several neurological and psychiatric disorders.

Neuro-Economics is a young and interesting discipline born in the early 1990s that has benefitted from neuroscience progress. It is an interdisciplinary research area that involves Cognitive Neuroscience, Economics, Human Behavior Economics, Neurophysiology, Psychology, Marketing, Accounting, and Neuroradiology. The principal aim of neuro-economics' research is to investigate the neural aspects of decision making both in economic and financial operators and in simple consumers, starting with traditional economic theories and exploring unexpected behavioral deviations in human beings by using a series of functional neuroimaging, neurophysiologic and neuro-psychologic researches.

Furthermore, behavioral economics attempts to account for observations that seem to deviate from the predictions of standard economic theory; like the fact that individuals sometimes systematically over or underestimate probabilities or act altruistically/egoistically by considering how cognitive, emotional, or social factors interact to bias the choices. Neuro-economics brings concepts from economic theory into the realm of everyday behavior, thus providing a formalization of what makes a prospect attractive or repulsive in terms of specific, tractable computations. These computations can then be traced to the activity of single neurons or populations of neurons in different brain regions, or revealed through specific selective deficits in pathological conditions.

Decision making can be considered as the integration of three complementary abilities: choice evaluation, response selection, and feedback processing.

2.1 Behavioral economics

Historically, economists were the first to be interested in decision making; in other words how individuals create behaviors in order to maximize, consolidate, or gain benefits obtained by interaction with goods or other subjects in everyday life. They formulated theories to explain how subjects choose between different alternatives, trying to identify the variables involved in decision making.

The *"economic approach"* created a series of general models and tools/paradigms to measure the behavior of choice, using concepts derived from the economics world, like Utility, Subjective Value, Delay Discounting, Risk, and Ambiguity.

Some examples of concepts derived from economic models are:

- *Value*: between two alternatives, the subject chooses the one that has more worth.
- *Expected Value (EV= px)*: the subject chooses the alternative with the most expected value, given by the product of the "value" of the reward and the "probability" of receiving it.
- *Expected Utility*: a variable better than the "value"; the subject chooses between two alternatives based on the usefulness of obtaining a certain gain.

Some of the previous results of this approach relate to the economic concept of Utility: through **Utility theory**, it is stated that different rewards are translated into *common currency* in order to be compared. Subjects work to maximize the expected value (the ratio between value and probability of reward), however, subjects work even more to maximize the utility; the utility - better than the absolute value - determines the subject's attitude in evaluating rewards.

Shizgal was the author of early neuro-economics research focused on the utility concept. In physiological situations, our choices are rarely completely black or white, thus, predicting how people will choose requires an accurate model of how value is assigned to outcomes. The simplest possible computation of subjective value is a product of "utility", u, and its probability of occurrence, P (let us assume that the cost associated with 1-P is null). This seems like a reasonable starting point since most decisions are probabilistic.

However, options with seemingly identical expected values may lead to different choice preferences. The prospects of winning €1 with a fixed probability of P=1 or winning €10 with a fixed probability of P=1/10 lead to similar average gains but can generate different preferences depending on an individual's attitude towards risk. Furthermore, in real world settings, probabilities are generally not fixed and fluctuate over time.

Another key issue is time. Decisions generally produce outcomes in the future and outcomes that occur later are devalued relative to identical, but immediate, ones. Again, increasing experimental data show that optimal decision making in humans is based on time discounted expected values of outcomes. More complex situations arise when multiple individuals interact with each other. In behavioral economics, game-theory approaches are used to analyze scenarios in which an outcome is contingent upon mutual decisions made by two or more individuals.

Rationality assumptions posited by economic theory generate predictions that are often verified but the literature has plenty of paradoxes and violations to what is sometimes referred to as the "standard model".

2.2 Neural correlates in decision making

Over the time, thanks to the improvement in neuroimaging and neurophysiological techniques, several studies appeared to identify a neurophysiological mechanism showing brain areas involved in decision making.

Different brain areas are currently considered to be involved in decision making, also called **Distributed System for Computation and Use Comparison.**

The most important brain regions involved in this network are: orbitofrontal cortex (OFC), ventromedial prefrontal cortex (vmPFC), posterior parietal cortex

(PPC), anterior cingulate cortex (ACC), striatum, amygdala and insula (Kable and Glimcher 2007; Kim *et al.* 2008; Louie and Glimcher 2010), that integrate with each other and with serotoninergic and dopaminergic pathways (Figure 1). This network is directly involved in decision making and encodes utility, mixing different processes in different areas related to different variables.

The **OFC** is a **hub** in decision making.

A central function of the brain is to direct behavior towards essential rewards, such as food, shelter, and mates. Behavioral control mechanisms - that can flexibly adapt to changes in the subjective value of these rewards - are operationally defined as "*goal-directed behaviours*" (Balleine and Dickinson 1998; O'Doherty *et al.* 2017).

The orbitofrontal cortex (OFC) (Figure 2) is a key neural substrate for supporting goal-directed behaviour. **Goal-directed behaviour** is directly linked to the OFC representation of the **value of the reward;** thanks to OFC activity, the same reward can have a different value in different situations or depend on the alternative with which it is compared. A recent proposal is that the OFC fulfils this function by representing a variety of state and task variables ("cognitive maps"), including a conjunction of expected reward identity and value. OFC anticipatory responses are modulated according to changes in value without the need for additional stimulus–outcome learning (Gottfried *et al.* 2003; Valentin *et al.* 2007; Gremel and Costa 2013). The main feature of any goal-directed system is that representations of goals themselves must be specific. This specificity ensures that, for example, a decrease in the value of food after a meal does not affect the value of shelter or mates. Animals with lesions to the OFC continue to respond to cues predicting devalued outcomes (Gallagher *et al.* 1999; Rhodes and Murray 2013), further demonstrating that this region is critical for goal-directed behaviour.

Identity-specific goal representations in the OFC are altered to reflect changes in the value of a goal.

Specific updates could be implemented either directly by changing reward identity representations in the OFC or by changing the assignment of value to these rewards, either within the OFC or in downstream regions, such as the vmPFC. In contrast to the OFC, activity in the vmPFC reflects decision values regardless of reward identity. Whereas identity-specific OFC signals are linked to reward expectations before a decision, identity-general signals are typically observed at the time of choice.

For example, identity-specific representations of food odor reward are updated by satiety as demonstrated by Howard and Kahnt (2017); fMRI pattern based signatures of reward identity in the lateral posterior OFC are modulated after selective devaluation, and connectivity between this region and general value coding vmPFC predicts choice behaviour. In this study, scanning was conducted first while participants were hungry and then immediately after they had eaten a meal related to one of the two odours to achieve satiety. Pattern-based fMRI analyses revealed that in the lateral posterior OFC (pOFC), satiety modulated anticipatory reward identity representations for the sated (SA) odor; whereas fMRI patterns related to the non-sated (NS) food remained intact. Moreover, satiety-related changes in functional connectivity between the lateral pOFC and general value coding vmPFC predicted individual differences in how satiety altered choice behaviour. These results suggest a mechanism by which specific reward signals in the lateral OFC are flexibly and independently updated by devaluation, and how functional connections with vmPFC support goal-directed behaviour.

These results provide evidence for a mechanism by which devaluation modulates a cognitive map of expected reward in the OFC and, thereby, alters general value signals in vmPFC to guide goal-directed behaviour; in other words identity-specific signals are directly updated in the OFC and they provide critical input to representations of decision values in vmPFC. Studies in patients with OFC injuries, whilst doing tasks involving uncertainty choices, demonstrate that the OFC role does not coincide simply with the representation of utility (Damasio *et al.* 1999).

In the **Iowa Gambling Task,** subjects choosing one card from one of four decks from time to time learn to recognize safe decks (paying little but frequently) from risky decks (paying a lot but often leading to losses). The injury to decision-making areas compromises the acquisition of a proper strategy; neurophysiological studies demonstrated, in particular, that the lack of an anticipatory response (SRC) is associated with pathological performance. Moreover, the **OFC** seems to be crucial in **acquiring strategies through experience** in order to obtain behaviour that determines a long-term advantage. The OFC is not the only area involved in decision making but is part of a larger network that includes other cerebral regions and aminergic systems.

Direct recording of Lateral Intraparietal Cortex (LIP) neurons demonstrated that LIP neuron activation is correlated with expected gain. Studies focused on decision making under risk and uncertainty showed that the subject acts to maximize the relationship between utility and probability, however, in the case of two options of the same expected value, but the first riskier and the second less risky, we can distinguish different attitudes: neutral attitude, risk attitude, and risk avoidance.

Event-Related Potentials (ERP) studies investigated neural correlates of feedback processing in decision making under risk:

P200 is more marked in the frontal regions (Polezzi 2008) and did not change in relation to positive vs negative feedback; *related to the unpredictability of the outcome rather than their variance* (Polezzi 2008).

FRN represents the early feedback appraisal on binary good versus bad classification according to subject expectations. The source is located in the *medial frontal cortex* (Ghering and Willoughby 2002).

P300 is related to a more complex feedback evaluation reflecting the allocation of motivational and attentional resources and shows the larger amplitude in the *central and parietal regions* (Cui 2013).

TMS studies showed how we can modulate brain activity and, consequently, risk attitude; disruption of the right dorso-lateral pre-frontal cortex (DLPFC) by low frequency Repetitive Transcranial stimulation induces risk-taking behaviour confirming that the right brain, by its connection with the area, plays a role in suppressing options that seem more attractive. Suppression of right DLPFC activity also reduces cautious driving behaviors and computation of food values, while suppression of left DLPFC activity reduces self-control. Oppositely, right DLPFC activation reduces the appetite for risk.

2.3 Dopamine

Dopamine (DA) is a catecholamine neurotransmitter in the brain that is synthesized by mesencephalic neurons in the substantia nigra (SN) and ventral-tegmental area (VTA). DA neurons originate in the nuclei and project to the striatum, cortex, limbic system and hypothalamus (Figure 3). Dopamine is directly involved in motor behavior, pleasure and satisfaction but also in decision making and other cognitive assessments, risk processes, novelty management, and reward. Furthermore, DA regulates emotional and motivational behavior through the mesolimbic dopaminergic pathway.

2.3.1 Dopamine reward, learning and pleasure

Reward can be defined as a neural boost to the favorable experience. Dopamine is highly linked to reward. Reward is involved in learning (positive reinforcement), approach behavior, economic choices and positive emotions. The biological cornerstone of valuation processes is the brain's reward system and one of its major components is the dopamine neuronal pathway. Midbrain dopamine neurons have been implicated in different functions but, first and foremost, in signaling the hedonic value of stimuli in the environment and are, thus, often considered as forming the brain's "reward retina". Usually, brain reward starts by stimulation or disinhibition of dopaminergic neurons in the ventral tegmentum. The terminal projections of these neurons mainly release dopamine in nucleus accumbens (NAc) and prefrontal cortex, initiating reward.

For instance, the response properties of macaque dopamine neurons have been found to compute variables essentially linked to reinforcement learning, such as the difference between expected and actual reward outcomes. In simple classical conditioning experiments, dopamine neurons respond to unexpected rewards, with a sharp increase in discharge rate, and to expected but absent rewards, with a sharp decrease in discharge rate. These signals are believed to contribute to learning by signaling both positive and negative inputs from the environment, corresponding to reward or utility prediction error postulated by models of economic decision. Dopamine neurons also encode reward expectation through tonic discharges that, interestingly, scale with reward probability and, thus, convey information about risk and uncertainty (Schultz 2016).

Three brain structures, that are major components of the basal ganglia or are closely associated with the basal ganglia, namely midbrain dopamine neurons, pedunculo-pontine nucleus, and striatum (caudate nucleus, putamen, and nucleus accumbens) constitute the core of the reward system. The response of dopamine neurons to rewards consists of an early detection component and a subsequent reward component that reflect prediction error in economic utility but are unrelated to movement. Dopamine activations to non-rewarded or aversive stimuli reflect physical impact, but not punishment. Neurons in the pedunculopontine nucleus project their axons to dopamine neurons and process sensory stimuli, movements and rewards, and reward-predicting stimuli without coding outright reward prediction errors. Neurons in the striatum, besides their pronounced movement relationships, process rewards irrespective of sensory and motor aspects, integrate reward information into movement activity, code the reward value of individual actions, change their reward-related activity during learning, and code their own reward in social situations depending on whose action produces the reward. Reward is not only dopamine.

Many brain areas are activated by the possibility and receipt of reward, without reporting the same information about reward. Through carefully controlled behavioral studies, it has been shown that reward-related activities can represent reward expectations related to future outcomes, errors in those expectations, motivation, and signals related to goal and habit driven behaviors.

Explicit reward signals are found in most midbrain dopamine neurons, as well as in subsets of neurons receiving dopaminergic projections in the OFC, in the ventral striatum, and in the amygdala. These neurons further respond to conditioned stimuli that predict future reward. Another class of cells links information about reward with sensory or action information. As mentioned above, the OFC contains a representation of primary reinforcers, such as food or sexual stimuli. The neurons in this area discriminate sensory quality within and across categories but do not merely encode the physical characteristics of stimuli. For instance, activity is elicited by a specific food item when the animal is motivated to acquire it but stops if the animal is sated. In other words, reward-coding neurons respond if the "marginal utility" of that particular food is sufficiently high, specifically, if it satisfies a current need or desire. Rewards and reward expectation also affect the activity of more dorsal and medial regions of the prefrontal cortex involved in action selection and planning. In fact, many cortical (prefrontal, cingulate, parietal, inferotemporal cortex) and subcortical (striatum, amygdala, superior colliculus) structures involved in high-level sensory and/or motor integration receive reward information. Unrewarding and aversive events are also represented most commonly in distinct neuronal subpopulations in the midbrain, cortex, and amygdala. However, cells in the posterior parietal cortex have been shown to encode both rewarding and aversive stimuli, in which case activity is interpreted as reflecting motivational salience rather than value. Together, these results suggest that reward information serving to select relevant stimuli and to guide goal-directed approach and avoidance behaviour is broadcast widely throughout the primate brain.

In the late 1990s, Schultz clearly demonstrated that activity related to decision-making processes and observed behaviour can be measured, according to electrophysiological and reward studies. These results are consistent with psychological theory of learning by reward and by prediction error. Neurobiological investigations of associative learning have shown that dopamine neurons respond phasically to rewards in a manner compatible with the coding of prediction errors, whereas slower dopamine changes are involved in a larger spectrum response (Hollerman and Shultz 1998).

Furthermore reward is also conditioned by its intrinsic value.

A reward is composed of sensory and value-related components. The sensory components have an impact on sensory receptors and neurons and drive initial sensory processing that detects and, subsequently, identifies the reward. Reward value, which specifically reflects the positively motivating function of rewards, is processed only after the object has been identified. Values do not primarily reflect physical parameters but rather the brain's subjective assessment of the usefulness of the reward for survival and reproduction. This sequential process results in decisions and actions and drives reinforcement as a result of the experienced outcome.

In reward-motivated learning, mesolimbic activation precedes memory formation (Adcock *et al.* 2006). fMRI studies have shown the contrast between reward predicting cues and neutral cues; these studies demonstrated that monetary rewards activate striatum, substantia nigra, cingulate cortex and insula. fMRI studies about brain differential response in the case of reward or punishment have shown slightly different activation maps; in the "reward map", activated areas included caudate, putamen, mesial prefrontal cortex, and left motor cortex. The "Punishment map" also revealed activations in these areas, as well as the thalamus and anterior cingulate cortex.

Dopamine is closely linked to **pleasure**, mostly by determining activation in nucleus accumbens (NAc), which is the mesolimbic DA main projection target. fMRI and PET studies have shown that NAc are activated by images that anticipate monetary, alimentary or sexual rewards. Nucleus accumbens' DA is also involved in aspects of **motivation** but theoretical approaches to understanding the functions of DA have continued to evolve based upon emerging data and novel concepts. Although it has become traditional to label DA neurons as "reward" neurons, the actual findings are more complicated because they indicate that DA neurons can respond to a variety of motivationally significant stimuli. Moreover, it is important to distinguish between aspects of motivation that are differentially affected by dopaminergic manipulations. Studies involving antagonism or depletion of DA in the nucleus accumbens indicate that accumbens' DA does not mediate primary food motivation or appetite.

Nevertheless, DA is involved in appetitive and aversive motivational processes including behavioural activation, exertion of effort, sustained task engagement, and Pavlovian-to-instrumental transfer. Interference with accumbens' DA transmission affects instrumental behaviour in a manner that interacts with the response requirements of the task and also shifts effort-related choice behaviour, biasing animals towards low-effort alternatives. Dysfunctions of mesolimbic DA may contribute to motivational symptoms seen in various psychopathologies, including depression, schizophrenia, Parkinsonism, and other disorders.

Regulation of the DA system in reward-related behaviours has received a great deal of attention because of the serious consequences of dysfunction in this circuit, such as drug addiction and food reward-linked obesity, which are both major public health issues. It is now well accepted that following repeated exposure to addictive substances, adaptive changes occur at the molecular and cellular level in the DA mesolimbic pathway, which is responsible for regulating motivational behaviour and for the organisation of emotional and contextual behaviours (Nestler and Carlezon 2006; Steketee and Kalivas 2011). These modifications in the mesolimbic pathway are thought to lead to drug dependence, which is a chronic, relapsing disorder in which compulsive drug-seeking and drug-taking behaviours persist despite serious negative consequences (Thomas *et al.* 2008).

Substantial synaptic modifications of the mesolimbic DA system are associated with not only the rewarding effects of psychostimulants and other drugs of abuse but also with the rewarding effects of natural reward, such as food; however, the mechanisms by which drugs of abuse modify synaptic strength in this circuit are still elusive. In fact, DA reward signalling seems extremely complex and is also implicated in learning and conditioning processes, as revealed by studies of a DAergic response coding for a prediction error in behavioural learning (see Wise 2004; Schultz 2007, 2012), thus suggesting a need for a fine dissection at a circuit level to properly understand these motivated reward-related behaviours.

2.3.2 Dopamine and novelty

Rewarding experiences (like a glass of cold water on a hot day) can trigger dopamine neurons and studies have also shown that dopamine neurons respond to new experiences. This suggested that **novelty** may be rewarding in itself or that novelty may signal the potential for future reward. On the other hand, it may be that different groups of dopamine neurons play different roles in responding to new or rewarding experiences.

Detection of novel stimuli is advantageous for survival because novel stimuli can signal potential rewards or potential threats. Orienting towards a novel stimulus and understanding it through exploration can allow future exploitation of potential rewards. In addition to behavioural advantages, novelty detection is fundamental for computation in our brain. 'Novelty filters' (Kohonen and Oja 1976) can reduce the amount of total information so that we can focus on unexpected perceptions as inputs to pay attention to and to learn. Novelty responses are distributed over a network of many brain areas. Single unit electrophysiological recordings have shown that dopamine neurons in the midbrain increase their firing in response to the presentation of a novel stimulus in several species and in different behavioural paradigms (Horvitz *et al.* 1997; Schultz 2015; Steinfels *et al.* 1983). As animals experience the repeated association of stimulus and reward, they learn to expect the reward when the stimulus is presented (Pavlov and Anrep 1927). Dopamine neurons are thought to be the substrate underlying this type of learning because they signal reward prediction error; the difference between actual and expected reward values. These neurons are thought to guide decision making by broadcasting this information to many regions of the forebrain and reinforcing rewarding behaviours.

Novelty responses in dopamine neurons (Horvitz *et al.* 1997; Schultz 2015) were initially puzzling because animals cannot know whether a novel stimulus will reliably predict an outcome with a positive or negative value. One hypothesis was that dopamine neurons take an optimistic approach toward novel stimuli, assuming that they will predict a valuable outcome until proven wrong (Hazy *et al.* 2010; Kakade and Dayan 2002). This 'optimistic initialisation' in dopamine neurons may have advantages. For example, the novelty responses in dopamine neurons may induce orienting behaviours towards novel stimuli, similar to dopamine responses to reward or reward-predicting cues that induce orienting behaviours. Further, dopamine novelty responses may allow computational exploration or storage of the novel stimulus in the working memory (Braver and Cohen 1999), so that individuals have a better chance to associate novel stimuli to potential rewards. However, these hypotheses do not necessarily fit with conflicting observations of animals' behavioural responses to novel stimuli. Indeed, depending on the experimental context, individuals sometimes approach and sometimes avoid novel options compared to familiar ones (Gershman and Niv 2015).

One explanation for why some dopamine neurons respond to novel stimuli could be that some subpopulations of dopamine neurons are not strictly related to reward prediction error coding. Menegas *et al.* (2017) revealed opposite dynamics for learning new cue-outcome associations in the ventral striatum (VS) dopamine and the tail of striatum (TS) dopamine in mice. They observed a large response to novel cues in TS dopamine which subsequently decreased over the course of associative learning. On the other hand, they saw no response to novel cues in VS dopamine. Instead, VS dopamine gradually developed responses to reward-predicting cues during learning. These findings revealed that dopamine novelty coding is localised to the posterior part of the striatum, while VS dopamine faithfully encodes reward prediction error. Thus, novelty responses in dopamine neurons may be separated from the reward prediction error framework.

2.3.3 Inside the human being

The study of behavioural neuro-functional, neuroanatomic and neuro-synaptic correlates in humans contributes to overcoming the limits of the classic economic approach, based on models that consider decision making totally rational. Recently, research interest focused precisely on those cases where subjects systematically make irrational decisions without maximising utility and contradicting classical models; this happens when subjects have to deal their own emotions. Emotions are first and foremost innate but, when the body sensations are very intense, the brain qualifies them as emotion. It does so using concepts and not innate responses, for example, with money, which is a human created concept; those pieces of paper or coins have no objective value but they impose a function they would not otherwise have. Emotions are not only innate but also made of concepts. The brain connects the physical and social world creating many types of minds. In many daily decisions, people show aversion to losses, and greater loss sensitivity to gains of the same size.

Emotions also influence risk attitude; for example the presentation of scary faces increases the risk aversion. Human choices are remarkably susceptible to the manner in which options are presented. This so called "**framing effect**" represents a striking violation of standard economic accounts of human rationality, although its underlying neurobiology is not understood.

De Martino and colleagues in 2006 reproduced the Framing Effect with an appropriate fMRI protocol test: at the beginning of each trial, participants were shown a message indicating the starting amount of money that they would receive (e.g., 'You receive £50'). Subjects were instructed that they would not be able to retain the whole of this initial amount but would next have to choose between a sure option and a gamble option. The sure option was presented in the Gain frame trials as an amount of money retained from the starting amount (e.g., keep £20 of the £50) and in the Loss frame trials as an amount of money lost from the starting amount (e.g., lose £30 of the £50). The gamble option was represented as a pie chart depicting the probability of winning (green) or losing (red) all of the starting money. The expected outcomes of the gamble and sure options were equivalent. Gain frame trials were intermixed pseudo-randomly with Loss frame trials. No feedback concerning trial outcomes was given during the experiment.

Subjects showed a significant increase in the percentage of trials in which the gamble option was chosen in the Loss frame with respect to the Gain frame. All participants, to varying degrees, showed an effect of the framing manipulation. Using fMRI the authors found that the framing effect was specifically associated with amygdala activity, suggesting a key role for an emotional system in mediating decision biases. Moreover, across individuals, orbital and medial prefrontal cortex activity predicted a reduced susceptibility to the framing effect. The framing effect occurs because of an affective heuristic that conducts, through an intuitive-heuristic behaviour, to a shift of preferences, thereby violating the invariance principle of analytic behaviour. Conversely, some subjects' ability to control this bias, resisting to the framing effect, is an index of rationality related to OFC/vmPFC and ACC activation. This finding highlights the importance of incorporating emotional processes within models of human choice and suggests how the brain may modulate the effect of these biasing influences to approximate rationality.

Emotions and, consequently, behaviours can be influenced by modulating the levels of neurotransmitters; computation models of behavioural choice have shown that citalopram increases aversion both for themselves and others, while levodopa reduces altruism. The **"Near Miss Effect"** also constitutes unexpected behavioural deviations in human beings from classic models. A near miss is a special kind of failure to reach a goal, one that comes close to being successful. A shot at a target is said to hit the mark, or to be a near miss, or to go wide. In a game of skill, like shooting, a near miss gives useful feedback and encourages the player by indicating that success may be within reach.

By contrast, in games of pure chance, such as lotteries and slot machine games, it gives no information that could be used by a player to increase the likelihood of future success. Of course that does not imply that the player's behaviour will be unaffected. Gamblers frequently act as if they think they can influence chance outcomes. Whispering to dice, throwing gently for a low number, choosing a lottery number carefully by using family dates of birth or consulting books of lucky numbers are common examples of ineffective actions of this kind. Near misses are widely believed to encourage future play, even in games of chance where the probability of winning remains constant from trial to trial. Some commercial gambling systems, particularly instant lotteries and slot machines, are contrived to ensure a higher frequency of near misses than would be expected by chance alone. The near miss effect could be also replicated in animals, for instance, dopamine modulating reward expectancy during performance of a device similar to a slot machine in rats enhances the Near Miss Effect.

2.4 Pathology

The aberration of the mechanisms described above explains what happens in many neurological and psychiatric pathologies, where the human choice becomes systematically wrong. fMRI studies demonstrated the presence of reduced fronto-striatal activity during unexpected reward receipt in depression and even more in schizophrenia; this accounts for **anhedonia** in depressed and schizophrenic patients.

Normal maintenance of human motivation depends on the integrity of subcortical structures that link the prefrontal cortex with the limbic system. Structural and functional disruption of different networks within these circuits alters the maintenance of spontaneous mental activity and the capacity of affected individuals to associate emotions with complex stimuli. The clinical manifestations of these changes include a continuum of abnormalities in goal-oriented behaviours, known as apathy. **Apathy** is highly prevalent in Parkinson's disease (and across many neurodegenerative disorders) and can severely impact the quality of life of both patients and caregivers. Differentiation of apathy from depression, and discrimination of its cognitive, emotional, and auto-activation components, could guide an individualised approach to the treatment of symptoms. The opportunity to manipulate dopaminergic treatment in Parkinson's disease allows researchers to study a continuous range of motivational states, from apathy to impulse control disorders. Parkinson's disease can, thus, be viewed as a model that provides insight into the neural substrates of apathy.

Reward system abnormalities are directly linked to **impulse control disorders**, which include pathological gambling, compulsive shopping, binge eating disorder, hypersexuality, and excessive hobbies.

Pathological **gambling** can be defined as a behavioural addiction characterised by a persistent bad adaptive gambling attitude and as an impulse control disorder. Pathological gambling represents a serious problem in public health; it creates psycho-social problems for the involved person, causes financial problems and can lead to anxiety disorders. In addition, this disease is often associated with high rates of suicidal ideation and attempted suicide. Pathologic gamblers have a reduced activation in VLPFC, normally related to the gratification sense.

The incidence of pathological gambling in patients with **Parkinson's Disease** is significantly greater than in the general population. A correlation has been observed between dopamine agonist medication and the development of pathological gambling. However, scientists hypothesized that the affected patients have underlying risk factors: they were younger, had scored higher on novelty-seeking tests, and were more impulsive and often associated with a personal or family history of alcohol addiction. Furthermore, some genetic variations have been associated with the susceptibility of developing pathological gambling. Studies focusing on neurofunctional discrepancies between PD patients with and without pathological gambling have found increased functional activation and dopamine release in regions associated with the mesolimbic reward system. There is also evidence of increased processing of reward and decreased activation elicited by punishment, suggesting altered learning processes.

A new category of disturbances that physicians and researchers have to deal with are **compulsive buyers**. These consumers are similar to drug addicts because they are not able to control their buying behaviour; they usually experience a "high" excitement with the purchase of goods. Only recently have researchers begun to investigate the various social, psychological and financial consequences associated with the approximately 18 million compulsive purchasers.

In a series of studies, Worbe *et al.* (2011) investigated the reinforcement learning in patients having a disease characterized by motor abnormalities (tics) and vocal jerks **the Tourette syndrome**, both on and off medication. They used a simple cued go/no-go task to expose participants to cue-reward associations (monetary gain) as well as cue-punishment associations (monetary loss). Patients showed learning profiles according to their treatment status that varied in a manner consistent with the hypothesis of dopamine hyperfunctioning in Tourette syndrome. When off medication, patients had impaired punishment learning, whereas when on medication, they had impaired reward learning. The authors interpreted this pattern of findings according to the theory of dopamine's dual action in reward and punishment learning through, respectively, positive and negative prediction error signals. In untreated patients, because baseline levels of dopamine are too high, punishments cannot pull the dopamine response low enough to generate a negative prediction error signal. By contrast, in patients treated with dopamine antagonists, baseline levels of dopamine functions are kept too low and rewards cannot push the dopamine response high enough to generate a positive prediction error. In support of this hypothesis, a similar, but mirror-reversed, dissociation in the reward and punishment learning pattern has been found in patients with Parkinson disease on (high baseline dopamine) and off (low baseline dopamine) with and without L-Dopa treatment. **Aging** is not strictly pathological, but it is an interesting para-physiologic condition.

A recent study demonstrated a link between midbrain dopamine synthesis and reward-related prefrontal activity in humans, showing that healthy aging induces functional alterations in the reward system, identifying an age-related change in the direction of the relationship (from a positive to a negative correlation) between midbrain dopamine synthesis and prefrontal activity. These results indicate an age-dependent dopaminergic tuning mechanism for cortical reward processing.

Different cognitive impairments have been also reported as a result of **long-term MDMA/ecstasy use**. Increased impulsivity and altered decision making have been shown to be associated with the development and maintenance of addictive disorders pointing towards the necessity to understand a potential impairment of decision making due to MDMA use. Several studies reported increased risky decisions.

Increased impulsivity was observed both in MDMA groups and in (poly) drug subjects' groups.

2.5 Conclusions

In conclusion, the dopaminergic system is crucial for determining the behavioural aspects that drive individuals towards satisfaction and also modulate aversion. The interplay of the effects of dopamine in different brain areas is largely responsible for the choices that control the human economical behaviour.

Figures

Figure 1.
Brain areas involved in decision making

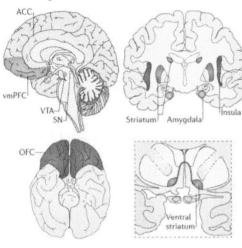

Source: Authors' elaboration.

Figure 2.
Pre-frontal areas topograpghy

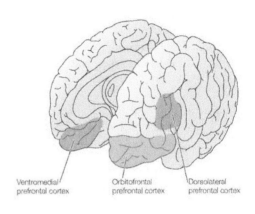

Source: Authors' elaboration.

Figure 3.
Main areas involved in dopaminergic system

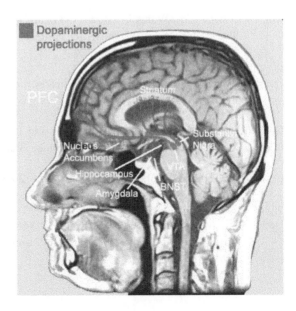

Source: Authors' elaboration.

References

Adcock, R.A., Thangavel, A., Whitfield-Gabrieli, S., Knutson, B. and Gabrieli, J.D. (2006), «Reward-Motivated Learning: Mesolimbic Activation Precedes Memory Formation», *Neuron*, 50(3), pp. 507-17.

Baik, J.H., (2013), «Dopamine Signaling in Reward-Related Behaviors», *Frontiers in Neural Circuits*, p. 7.

Balleine, B.W., Dickinson, A., (1998), «Goal-directed Instrumental Action: Contingency and Incentive Learning and Their Cortical Substrates», *Neuropharmacology*, 37(4-5), pp. 407-419.

Bissonette, G.B. and Roesch, M.R., (2016), «Neurophysiology of Reward-Guided Behavior: Correlates Related to Predictions, Value, Motivation, Errors, Attention, and Action», *Current Topics in Behavioral Neurosciences*, 27, pp. 199-230.

Braver, T.S. and Cohen, J.D., (1999), «Dopamine, Cognitive Control, and Schizophrenia: the Gating Model», *Progress in Brain Research*, 121, pp. 327-349.

Crockett, M.J., Siegel, J.Z., Kurth-Nelson, Z., Ousdal, O.T., Story, G., Frieband, C., Grosse-Rueskamp, J.M., Dayan, P., and Dolan, R.J., (2015), «Dissociable effects of Serotonin and Dopamine on the Evaluation of Harm in Moral Decision Making», *Current Biology*, 25, pp. 1852-1859.

Cui, J.F., Chen, Y.H., Wang, Y., Shum, D.H., and Chan, R.C., (2013), «Neural Correlates of Uncertain Decision Making: ERP Evidence from the Iowa Gambling Task», *Frontiers in Human Neuroscience*, 7, p. 776.

Damasio, A.R., (1999), «How the Brain Creates the Mind», *Scientific American*, 281(6), pp. 112-117.

De Martino, B., Kumaran, D., Seymour, B., and Dolan, R.J., (2006), «Frames, Biases, and Rational Decision-Making in the Human Brain», *Science*, 313(5787), pp. 684-687.

Deserno, L., Schlagenhauf, F., and Heinz, A., (2016), «Striatal Dopamine, Reward, and Decision Making in Schizophrenia», *Clinical Research*, 18(1), p. 77.

Dreher, JC, Meyer-Lindenberg, A., Kohn, P., and Berman, K.F., (2008), «Age-Related Changes in Midbrain Dopaminergic Regulation of the Human Reward System», *PNAS*, 105, pp. 15106-15111.

Gallagher, E.J., (1999), «Application of Likelihood Ratios to Clinical Decision Rules: Defining the Limits of Clinical Expertise», *Annals of Emergency Medicine*, 34(5), pp. 664-667.

Gershman, S.J. and Niv, Y., (2015), «Novelty and Inductive Generalization in Human Reinforcement Learning», *Topics in Cognitive Science*, 7(3), pp. 391-415.

Ghering, W.J., and Willoughby, A.R., (2002), «The Medial Frontal Cortex and the Rapid Processing of Monetary Gains and Losses», *Science*, 295(5563), pp. 2279-2282.

Gottfried, J.A., O'Doherty, J., and Dolan, R.J., (2003), «Encoding Predictive Reward Value in Human Amygdala and Orbitofrontal Cortex», *Science*, 301(5636), pp.1104-1107.

Gremel, C.M., and Costa, R.M., (2013), «Premotor Cortex is Critical for Goal-Directed Actions», *Frontiers in Computational Neuroscience*, 7, p.110.

Gunaydin, A., and Deisseroth, K., (2015), «Dopaminergic Dynamics Contributing to Social Behavior», *Cold Spring Harbor Symposia on Quantitative Biology*, 79, pp. 221-227.

Hazy, T.E., Frank, M.J., and O'Reilly, R.C., (2010) «Neural Mechanisms of Acquired Phasic Dopamine Responses in Learning», *Neuroscience & Biobehavioral Reviews*, 34(5), pp. 701-720.

Heiden, P., Heinz, A., and Romanczuk-Seiferth, N., (2017), «Pathological Gambling in Parkinson's Disease: What Are The Risk Factors and What is the Role of Impulsivity», *European Journal of Neuroscience*, 45, pp. 67-72.

Hollerman, J.R. and Schultz, W., (1998), «Dopamine Neurons Report an Error in the Temporal Prediction Of Reward During Learning», *Nature Neuroscience*, 1(4), pp. 304-309.

Holroyd, C.B. and Cole, M.G.H., (2002), «The Neural Basis of Human Error Processing: Reinforcement Learning, Dopamine, and the Error-Related Negativity», *Psychological Review*, 109(4), pp. 679-709.

Horvitz, J.C., Stewart, T. and Jacobs, B.L., (1997), «Burst Activity of Ventral Tegmental Dopamine Neurons is Elicited by Sensory Stimuli In The Awake Cat», *Brain Res*, 759(2), pp. 251-258.

Howard, J.D., and Kahnt, T., (2017), «Identity-Specific Reward Representations in Orbitofrontal Cortex Are Modulated by Selective Devaluation», *The Journal of Neuroscience*, 37(10), pp.2627-2638.

Kable, J.W., and Glimcher, P.W., (2007), «The Neural Correlates of Subjective Value During Intertemporal Choice», *Nature Neuroscience*, 10(12), pp. 1625-1633.

Kakade, S., and Dayan, P., (2002), «Dopamine: Generalization and Bonuses», *Neural Networks*, 15(4-6), pp. 549-559.

Kim, S., Hwang, J. and Lee, D., (2008), «Prefrontal Coding of Temporally Discounted Values during Inter-temporal Choice», *Neuron*, 59(1), pp. 161-172.

Kohonen, T. and Oja, E., (1976), «Fast Adaptive Formation of Orthogonalizing Filters and Associative Memory in Recurrent Networks of Neuron-Like Elements», *Biological Cybernetics*, 21(2), pp. 85-89.

Louie, K., and Glimcher, P.W., (2010), «Separating Value from Choice: Delay Discounting Activity in the Lateral Intraparietal Area», *J. Neurosci*, 30(16), pp. 5498-5507.

Martínez-Horta, S., Riba, J., de Bobadilla, R.F., Pagonabarraga, J., Pascual-Sedano, B., Antonijoan, R.M., Romero, S., Mañanas, M.À., García-Sanchez, C. and Kulisevsky J., (2014), *Apathy in Parkinson's Disease: Neurophysiological Evidence of Impaired Incentive Processing, The Journal of Neuroscience*, 34(17), pp. 5918-5926.

Menegas, W., Babayan, B.M., Uchida, N. and Watabe-Uchida, M., (2017), «Opposite Initialization to Novel Cues in Dopamine Signaling in Ventral and Posterior Striatum In Mice», *eLife*, e21886.

Nestler, E.J., and Carlezon, W.A., (2017), «The Mesolimbic Dopamine Reward Circuit in Depression», *Biological Psychiatry*, 59(12), pp. 1151-1159.

O'Doherty, J.P., Cockburn, J. and Pauli, W.M., (2017), «Learning, Reward, and Decision Making», *Annual Review Psychology*, 68, pp. 73-100.

Polezzi, D., Lotto, L., Daum, I., Sartori, G., Rumiati, R., (2008), «Predicting Outcomes of Decisions in the Brain», *Behavioural Brain Research*, 187(1), pp. 116-122.

Rhodes, S.E., Murray, E.A., (2013), «Differential Effects of Amygdala, Orbital Prefrontal Cortex, and Prelimbic Cortex Lesions on Goal-Directed Behavior in Rhesus Macaques», *The Journal of Neuroscience*, 33(8), pp. 3380-3389.

Shizgal, P., (1997), «Neural Basis of Utility Estimation», *Current Opinion in Neurobiology*, 7 (2), pp. 198-208.

Sirigu, A., Duhamel, J.R., (2016), «Reward and Decision Processes in The Brains Of Humans And Nonhuman Primates», *Dialogues in Clinical Neuroscience*, 18, pp. 45-53.

Schultz, W., (2016), «Dopamine Reward Prediction Error Coding», *Dialogues in Clinical Neuroscience*, 18(1), pp. 23-32.

Schultz, W., (2016), «Reward Functions of the Basal Ganglia», *Journal of Neural Transmission*, 123, pp. 679-693.

Schultz, W., (2007), «Behavioral Dopamine Signals», *Trends in Neurosciences*, 30(5), pp. 203-210.

Schultz, W., (2012), «Risky Dopamine», *Biological Psychiatry*, 71(3), pp.180-181.

Schultz, W., Carelli, R.M. and Wightman, R.M., (2015), «Phasic Dopamine Signals: From Subjective Reward Value to Formal Economic Utility», *Current Opinion in Behavioral Sciences*, 5, pp. 147-154.

Schultz, W., (2015), «Neuronal Reward and Decision Signals: From Theories to Data», *Physiological Reviews*, 95(3), pp. 853-951.

Schwartenbec, P., FitzGerald, T.H., Mathys, C., Dolan, R. and Friston, K., (2015), «The Dopaminergic Midbrain Encodes the Expected Certainty about Desired Outcomes», *Cerebral Cortex*, 25, pp. 3434-3445.

Steinfels, G.F., Heym, J., Strecker, R.E. and Jacobs, B.L., (1983), «Response of Dopaminergic Neurons in Cat to Auditory Stimuli Presented Across the Sleep-Waking Cycle», *Brain Research*, 277(1), pp. 150-154.

Steketee, J.D. and Kalivas, P.W., (2011), «Drug Wanting: Behavioral Sensitization and Relapse to Drug-Seeking Behavior», *Pharmacological Reviews*, 63(2), pp. 348-365.

Thomas, R.P., Dougherty, M.R., Sprenger, A.M. and Harbison, J.I., (2008), «Diagnostic Hypothesis Generation and Human Judgment», *Psychological Review*, 115(1), pp. 155-185.

Twome, D.M., Dougherty, M.R., Sprenger, A.M. and Harbison, J.I., (2015), «The Classic P300 Encodes A Build-To-Threshold Decision Variable», *European Journal of Neuroscience*, 42, pp. 1636-1643.

Valentin, V.V., Dickinson, A. and O'Doherty, J.P., (2007), «Determining The Neural Substrates Of Goal-Directed Learning In The Human Brain», *The Journal of Neuroscience*, 27(15), pp. 4019-4026.

Van den Bos, W., McCLure, S.M., Harris, L.T., Fiske, S.T. and Cohen, J.D., (2007), «Dissociating Affective Evaluation and Social Cognitive Processes in the Ventral

Medial Prefrontal Cortex», *Cognitive, Affective, & Behavioral Neuroscience*, 7(4), pp. 337-346.

Voon, V., Napier, T.C., Frank, M.J., Sgambato-Faure, V., Grace, A.A., Rodriguez-Oroz, M., Obeso, J., Bezard, E. and Fernagut, P.O., (2017), «Impulse Control Disorders and Levodopa-Induced Dyskinesias in Parkinson's Disease: an Update», *The Lancet Neurology*, 16, pp. 238-250.

Wise, R.A., (2004), «Dopamine, Learning and Motivation», *Nature Reviews Neuroscience*, 5(6), pp. 483-494.

Worbe, Y., Palminteri, S., Hartmann, A., Vidailhet, M., Lehéricy, S. and Pessiglione, M., (2011), «Reinforcement Learning and Gilles De La Tourette Syndrome: Dissociation of Clinical Phenotypes and Pharmacological Treatments», *Archives of General Psychiatry re Reviews Neuroscience*, 68(12), pp. 1257-1266.

3. Functional Magnetic Resonance Imaging (fMRI) in Neuroeconomics

by Girolamo Crisi

Nowadays, Economics, Psychology and Neuroscience are merging into the unified discipline of Neuroeconomics, the primary task of which is to elaborate a single, general theory regarding the decision-making process and the underlying cognitive mechanisms (Konovalov and Krajbich 2016).

In such an interdisciplinary context, Neuroeconomics, along with Psychology and Economics, seem capable of conceiving new and more efficient models for identifying the decisional processes driving our choices (Vlasceanu 2014). Through a multitude of approaches and analysis methods, Neurosciences have allowed us to explore the complexity of the anatomic and functional substratum of all kinds of brain processes: the cognitive and emotional, automatic and rational, and social and cultural ones (Vlasceanu 2014). The neurobiological mechanisms of decision making, in conditions of risk and uncertainty and trust and cooperation, represent some of the primary targets of Neuroeconomics and can be examined in real time in a non-invasive manner by means of functional Magnetic Resonance Imaging (fMRI). Despite the high costs of installation and management alongside the scarcity of available assets for research applications, this particular implementation of the MRI still represents the primary investigation procedure for exploring the cerebral functions in Neuroscience and, more recently, in Neuroeconomics. The scanner of an fMRI system is an unusual environment for Neuroeconomics' experiments; nevertheless, using specific devices for displaying stimuli and allowing people to reveal their decisions, it is possible to deliver appropriate inputs, usually with a block-design, and ask them to execute tasks while recording their neural activity to investigate a specific decision-making process. Therefore, one of the critical aspects of research in

Neuroeconomics is the opportunity of conducting experiments in realistic contexts representing plausible choices with appropriate time constraints. We have always to keep in mind the complexity of the human brain; therefore, fMRI studies aimed at investigating its functional organisation inevitably depend on the theoretical background of the experiment and the protocols of analysing the relationships between two or more variables.

As a general component of the complex physiologic phenomenon known as *neurovascular coupling*, the activation of the brain neurons implies an energy demand satisfied by an increase of oxygenated blood flow and, hence, of oxygenated haemoglobin, which induces a change in the magnetic properties of the brain tissue in the active areas that can be directly detected by the MRI device (Wells *et al.* 2015). In summary, the fMRI indirectly associates the increased flow of oxygenated haemoglobin with the increase of neural activity during the task; the so-called BOLD (*Blood Oxygen Level Dependency*) effect. Therefore, even in Neuroeconomics, the research results can be represented through anatomic maps of the active brain areas, which are shown on a colour scale, with the colour (red to yellow) being determined by the magnitude of values from the statistical parametric map (Figure 1a). While visualising such maps, we must not forget that they represent the result of a statistical analysis and the colour indicates the level of significance of the effect caused by the task, instead of a particular population of neurons. The current approach to the representation of findings of an fMRI experiment consists of the description of brain areas that activate during the execution of different tasks.

If we record the brain activities in two different conditions - "A", rest condition, and "B", during task execution (Figure 1b) - and then compare A to B, using statistical analysis, we can design a map of brain's activations (Gore 2003; Logothetis 2008). In Neuroeconomics research protocols, for example, several observations correlate the activation of specific areas/structures, like the orbitofrontal cortex, the ventromedial prefrontal cortex and the ventral striatum, to the subjective value of different options (Rushworth *et al.* 2011). It is appropriate to point out that the observation of associations between neuroanatomic substrates and psychological traits does not necessarily imply a causal relationship because such associations could result from a third (not considered) independent variable that can influence the two quoted parameters (Poldrack *et al.* 2017). In the last 20 years, from being a new method of exploring the brain activity, the fMRI has truly become a strong pillar of the cognitive neurosciences (Poldrack *et al.* 2017). The number of articles quoting the fMRI increased from just 20 in 1993 to 1800 in 2003. The use of the BOLD effect as a proxy of the brain function is not free from disadvantages; for instance, reproducibility can be far from optimal in cases where individuals or groups of subjects exhibit variable levels of physiological cerebrovascular response. A large part of the mechanisms underlying the BOLD effect has still to be understood, together with the role of specific neuron-glial networks, in determining the neurovascular coupling (Logothetis 2008). Such lack of understanding of the physiological mechanisms coupling the neural response to cerebral blood flow changes poses a few problems during the interpretation of the fMRI results. Remarkably, even though the BOLD signal is strongly related both to action potentials and local field potentials, it most likely reflects post-synaptic activities that do not depend on the former (Logothetis 2008). According to some authors, the poor fMRI sensitivity to post-synaptic events represents one of its limitations with respect to the action potentials (*spikes*), which are considered the main feature of the brain function (Logothetis 2008). Besides, it has been demonstrated that the neural inhibition is associated to a reduction of the BOLD effect (Logothetis 2008). The limitations of the fMRI-based study protocols mostly originate from their inability to take into account the functional organisation of the neural connections in its overall complexity. Therefore, the fMRI signal cannot simply differentiate between function-specific processes and chemical neuromodulation, between afferent inputs and efferent outputs, and between neuronal excitation and inhibition (Logothetis 2008). In brief, the amplitude of the fMRI signal is not a quantitative expression of functional differences, either between brain regions or between tasks in the same region. As an example, although the activation of the anterior cingulate cortex has been detected in one third of fMRI studies, a unanimous interpretation of such a result has not yet been achieved (Poldrack *et al.* 2017; Poldrack 2008; Poldrack 2017). Nonetheless, the fMRI remains the best performing and strategic technical asset for the investigation of the brain functions and the mapping of brain areas functionally involved in specific tasks.

Meta-analyses of studies involving large samples clearly point to poor reproducibility being the strongest limitation of the fMRI studies in cognitive neurosciences (David *et al.* 2013), based on a series of disadvantages, such as the high number of collected data and the low statistical power of most analyses (Button *et al 2013*), the variable analysis of input and output information (Eklund, Nichols and Knutsson 2016), and the circular analysis processes (*double dipping*) (Kriegeskorte *et al.* 2009).

In recent studies of gambling, the BOLD signal change in the nucleus *accumbens* was usually large but the effect size (Cohen's *d*) was relatively poor (Poldrack *et al.* 2017). Even so, the perspectives of MRI investigation are expanding towards the structural and functional connectivity of the neural networks, with the goal of enhancing the reproducibility and diffusion of findings (Poldrack *et al.* 2017; Poldrack and Farah, 2015). For this purpose, many innovative strategies have been developed with the aim of validating the reliability of the fMRI-based research (Poldrack 2012).

Among the most important, it is worth mentioning the computation of an adequate study sample allowing prediction of the statistical power of the study, the provision of platforms tracking the workflow of the data analysis, comparison methods based on default settings, computational virtualisation in order to boost data reproducibility and, last but not least, the realisation of a repository to enable data sharing and support for methodologists in reporting systematic reviews and meta-analyses (Poldrack 2012).

Figures

Figure 1.

Working memory: left prefrontal lateral cortex (pfclat) activation (visual *n*-back working memory task). A) 3D Volume rendering fMRI. Colour-coded statistical maps describe the functional activation of the working memory, in yellow being the most significant. Posteriorly, the occipital visual areas were activated by the processing effect of the stimuli from the projection video system. Paradigm block diagram of the task with alternating periods of stimulation and waiting (b).

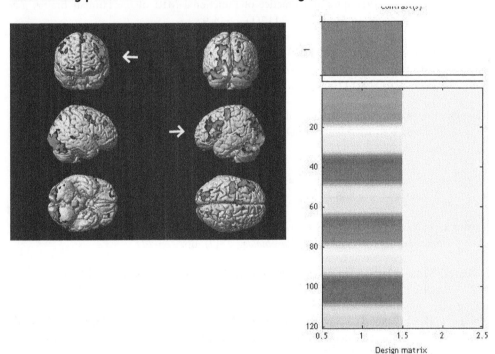

Source: Authors' elaboration.

References

Button, K.S. *et al.*, (2013), «Power Failure: Why Small Sample Size Undermines The Reliability Of Neuroscience», *Nature Review Neuroscience*, 14. pp. 365-376.

David, S.P., Ware, J.J., Chu, I.M. *et al.*, (2013), «Potential Reporting Bias in fMRI Studies of the Brain», PLoS ONE 8(7): e70104. doi:10.1371/journal.pone.0070104.

Eklund, A., Nichols T.E., Knutsson, H., (2016), «Cluster Failure: Why Fmri Inferences For Spatial Extent Have Inflated False-Positive Rates», *PNAS,* 113, pp. 7900-7905.

Gore, J.C., (2003), «Principles and Practice of Functional MRI of the Human Brain», *The Journal of Clinical Investigation*, 112(1), pp. 4-9.

Konovalov, A. and Krajbich, I., (2016), «Over a Decade of Neuroeconomics: What Have We Learned?», 1-26, *Organizational Research Methods*, DOI: 10.1177/1094428116644502.

Kriegeskorte, N., Simmons, W.K., Bellgowan, P.S., Baker C.I., (2009), «Circular Analysis in Systems Neuroscience: The Dangers Of Double Dipping», *Nature Neuroscience*, 12, pp. 535-40.

Logothetis, N.K., (2008), «What We Can Do And What We Cannot Do With FmRI», *Nature*, 453, pp. 869-878.

Poldrack, R.A., (2008), «The Role Of Fmri In Cognitive Neuroscience: Where Do We Stand?», *Current opinion in Neurobiology*, 18(2), pp. 223-227.

Poldrack, R.A., (2012), «The Future Of Fmri In Cognitive Neuroscience», *Neuroimage*, pp. 1216-1219.

Poldrack, R.A., Baker C.I., Durnez J. *et al.*, (2017), «Scanning The Horizon: Towards Transparent And Reproducible Neuroimaging Research», *Nature Review Neuroscience*, 18(2), pp. 115-126.

Poldrack, R.A., Farah, M.J., (2015), «Progress and challenges in Probing the Human Brain», *Nature*, 526, pp. 371-379.

Rushworth, M.F.S., Noonan, M.A.P., Boorman, E.D., Walton, M.E. and Behrens, T.E., (2011), «Frontal Cortex and Reward-Guided Learning and Decision Making», *Neuron*, 70, pp. 1054-1069.

Vlasceanu, S., (2014), «New Directions in Understanding the Decision-Making Process: Neuroeconomics and Neuromarketing», *Procedia - Social and Behavioral Sciences*, 127, pp. 758-762.

Wells, J.A., Christie, I.N. *et al.*, (2015), «A Critical Role for Purinergic Signalling in the Mechanisms Underlying Generation of BOLD fMRI Responses», *The Journal of Neuroscience*, 35(13), pp. 5284-5292.

4. Neuroimaging: Investigation Tools in Neuroeconomics

by Gabriele Polonara, Mara Fabri

Our brain can be considered a very efficient network that connects different cerebral areas distributed within the brain's space, each of them having its own function and role and continuously exchanging information. Our brain is, thus, a complex integrative network of functionally-linked brain regions. Multiple spatially-distributed but functionally linked brain regions continuously share information with each other, together forming interconnected resting-state communities.

For many years, all efforts have tried to understand the role of each area independently and also by means of the functional Magnetic Resonance Imaging (fMRI). By designing a functional experiment according to a sequence of activation and resting periods (block designed paradigm), it is possible to reveal the neural activity evoked by the task, which is the difference between the activation and resting state.

In recent years, an increasing amount of neuroimaging studies began to explore the functional connectivity between cerebral areas by measuring the co-activation level in the so-called "Resting-State fMRI". It has, indeed, been observed that, also during the resting state, the cerebral areas working together establish functional connections that display a high spontaneous activity level. With the use of resting-state fMRI, we can, therefore, explore the functional connections of the brain network. The study of the spontaneous oscillation of the Blood Oxygen Level Dependent (BOLD) signal during the resting state has been revealed as an interesting way to quantify the functional connectivity between cerebral areas in the whole brain.

4.1   Defining cerebral plasticity

One of the more amazing characteristics of our brain is its plasticity, i.e., the ability to modify the strength of the inter-neural relationships (synapses) to establish new connections and to eliminate some others.

This property allows the nervous system to modify its structure and function in a more or less lasting way depending on the experience. The synaptic (neural) plasticity has a role in learning and memory processes, as well as in repairing brain damage, being at the basis of the functional recovery. The processes involved in the functional cerebral recovery can be summarised as follows:

  a.   REORGANISATION of the impaired function in its original site
  b.   SHIFTING of the impaired function to a new cerebral area
  c.   TRANSFER of the impaired function

The Latin locution "repetita juvant" perfectly represents this idea.

It has been actually shown that repeating an activity many times determines a reinforcement and a consolidation of the neural circuits involved in such an activity.

4.2   Diffusion tensor imaging

One recent technique to study the structural connectivity is **Diffusion Tensor Imaging (DTI)** based on the study of water diffusion in the brain: **diffusion weighted imaging (DWI)**.

4.2.1 Isotropic and anisotropic diffusion

In pure liquid molecules freely diffuse casually, therefore, the distance covered by each molecule will be the same in any direction of the space *(Isotropic Diffusion)*. If in the diffusion medium there are parallel barriers present, the molecules will move more quickly along the barriers than perpendicularly to them; this kind of molecules motion is defined as *Anisotropic Diffusion*.

In the white matter, the diffusion is characterised by a pronounced *anisotropy*: the diffusion coefficient perpendicular to the fibres will be lower than the diffusion coefficient parallel to them.

The diffusion tensor is a mathematical model of the diffusion in a tridimensional space. It is a numerical matrix 3 x 3, arising from the measures of the diffusion in different directions, obtained by Magnetic Resonance (MR) images weighted in diffusion.

The tensor matrix can be visualised as an ellipsoid whose diameter in each direction estimates the diffusivity in that direction; the main axis is oriented according to the direction of highest diffusivity. From the mathematical point of view, at least 6 directions are needed to build the tensor (most authors use from 6 to 90 directions).

4.3   What the diffusion tensor imaging can do?

The cerebral white matter is made by axons connecting the different brain regions. Axon fibres with the same destination are assembled in larger bundles called white matter tracts. Many important tracts are present in the human brain and large enough to be observed. These tracts can be traced by DTI with an image resolution of 2-3 mm, by using the so-called tractography or fibre-tracking algorithms or monitoring algorithms. Starting with the analysis of the diffusion, the tractography is the graphic representation of the water molecules' motion. The most common fibre-tracking algorithms to sketch the white matter bundles are based on techniques of linear propagation (Deterministic Tractography), which consists of the following steps:

- Identification of a starting point for the algorithm (*seed point*),
- Propagation of the track along the estimated orientation of the fibres,
- Stop of tracking when criteria of termination are satisfied.

The main fibre tracts that can be evidenced by DTI can be classified as follows:
- PROJECTING TRACTS, which connect the cortical structures to the subcortical ones;
- COMMISSURAL TRACTS, which connect corresponding areas of the two cerebral hemispheres;
- ASSOCIATION TRACTS, which run within each hemisphere and connect distant cortical areas.

Among the PROJECTING TRACTS, the following can be recognised:

1. PIRAMIDAL TRACT (cortico-spinal and cortico-bulbar), which is the main pathway to send the motor command to the spinal cord and bulbar nuclei. It can be sketched by the Double Region Of Interest (ROI) method: an origin ROI in the posterior branch of the internal capsule, and a destination ROI at pons level.

2. MEDIAL LEMNISCUS, which is the major pathway for the ascending sensory fibres along the dorsal columns. It carries information about tactile sensitivity from the trunk and limbs. It can be sketched by placing a single ROI at the pontine level (at the mesencephalic level, the tract becomes too dispersed for discrete identification).

3. FORNIX, which connects the hippocampus to the hypothalamic nuclei. It can be sketched by a single ROI, selected at the level of the body, the columns and, if visible, the branches. In a colour map, the body appears green and the columns are blue.

COMMISSURAL TRACTS include:

CORPUS CALLOSUM: it allows the inter-hemispheric integration between cortical regions. It can be delineated by placing single ROIs at level of the genu, body and splenium; in each axial image, it can be recognised as a large red zone within the median sagittal line.

Finally, ASSOCIATION FIBRES include:

1. CINGULUM: it runs beneath the cingulate gyrus along its entire length, and connects the orbital and medial cortical areas of the frontal lobe with the hippocampus, and with posterior parietal and occipito/temporal cortical areas. Rostrally, it can be identified by single ROIs in the medial green tract, inferiorly as zones with different blue gradations, and laterally to the corpus callosum.

2. ARCUATE FASCICULUS: it is involved in the language function. It connects the Wernicke's area with the Broca's area and the inferior parietal cortex. At the corona radiata level, it can be identified by a single ROI in the half moon with medial green concavity. Inferiorly, it can be traced by single ROIs selected where the fascicle is blue.

3. UNCINATE FASCICULUS: it connects the orbital and polar frontal cortex to anterior temporal areas. It can be traced in Double ROI ways: by selecting

the origin ROI within the anterior temporal white matter, and a destination ROI in the external capsule.

4. INFERIOR LONGITUDINAL FASCICULUS: it connects the temporal with the occipital cortex. In can be delineated in Double ROI ways: by selecting the origin ROI in the occipital white matter, and a destination ROI in the anterior temporal white matter.

5. INFERIOR FRONTO-OCCIPITAL FASCICULUS: it connects the frontal cortex to the occipital cortex. It can be recognised in Double ROI ways: by selecting an origin ROI in the occipital white matter, and a destination ROI in the external capsule.

4.4 Clinical and research applications of DTI

From the beginning, it appeared clear that the great contribution of this technique is to improve the description and interpretation of many pathological conditions, for example:

- the study of patients damaged by ictus with lesions of the cortico-spinal tracts;
- the evaluation of white matter tracts travelling close to a tumor lesion or infiltrated by neoplasm;
- tractography is often used to study the brain's connectivity.

However, this marvellous technique also presents some limitations to its procedure:

1. DTI is intrinsically a technique of low resolution and with low signal to noise ratio (SNR)
2. The image quality problems are further worsened by the high sensitivity to physiological movement, such as:

- Water motions, 5 --15 micron
- Patient's motions
- Heartbeat

To avoid the heartbeat artefact, an acquisition sequence can be activated, triggered on cardiac rhythm, thus introducing a dependence of Repetition Time (TR) by cardiac frequency (scan time longer and not predictable).

The images are distorted because of effects of magnetic susceptibility and subjected to the distortion by eddy currents. The deformations are clearly visible when the colour-coded images are fused with the structural weighted T1 images. For these reasons, quality controls and strong image analysis techniques are necessary.

In addition, the reduction of the anatomical information to a tensor, i.e., to a scalar value, means that when alterations or variations of one of the scalar values is found, it is often difficult to conclude the real cause at cellular level. Actually, to retrieve more specific information about the status of the underlying neuroanatomy, information reduction needs to be avoided. For example, when fractional anisotropy (FA) is decreased, there are at least three potential cases in terms of the relative relationship among eigenvalues:

3. the longest axis of the diffusion ellipsoid (l1, parallel diffusivity) is shortened,
4. the shorter axes (l2 and l3, perpendicular diffusivity) are elongated, or
5. both of these happen simultaneously.

By contracting the 3 # 3 tensor information to a single FA value, these three cases become degenerate. Past studies have shown that myelin loss is correlated with an increase in perpendicular diffusivity, whereas axonal loss is related more to a decrease in the parallel diffusivity. However, there is the possibility that such correlations are specific to the particular disease model used and may not always hold. For instance, histological correlation studies do not support the inverse relationship (e.g., axonal loss may lead to a decrease in the parallel diffusivity but such a decrease may not necessarily mean axonal loss).

On the other hand, this limitation of the DTI technique (i.e., the systematic reduction of information) could also be an advantage considering that the following can be counted in our brain:

- more than 100 billion neurons,
- the same number of axons,
- 100 billion synapses,
- and, hundreds of billions of astrocytes (glial cells).

4.4.1 The human brain is a such a complex system that our present ability cannot provide a complete characterisation yet

The DTI is a quantitative method that, in a non-invasive way and in a short time period, through a systematic reduction of the anatomical information at a manageable dimension, is able to characterise the anatomical state and allow a comparison between different populations.

Another limitation of this attractive but simple technique is that DTI has been shown to be inadequate when studying many brain regions in which "Crossing Fibres" are present. In this case, two or more fibre tracts with different orientations coexist in the same voxel.

According to recent evaluations, fibres with different orientations can be detected in more than 90% of the white matter voxels. To solve, at least partially, this problem, a method has been developed called *spherical deconvolution*.

The noise of DTI measures introduces uncertainty in the evaluation of the fibres' orientations that, in turn, introduces errors in the traced pathways.

A small mistake in a point of the track may lead to following a different way. These mistakes could produce the identification of connections completely different from the real ones. The deterministic algorithms provide only an estimation of the white matter fibres' pathway from the seed, without any indication of the confidence interval around this value. The probabilistic algorithms try to solve this limitation by providing their results in form of a probability distribution. With this method, when the algorithm has to extend the line from a voxel to the following, to each different possible choice a probability value is assigned, which depend upon the measured value of the diffusion.

4.4.2 What, exactly, is the information produced by a tractograpy?

Starting from DTI, the **diffusion tensor tractography (DTT)** reconstructs the white matter architecture in 3D, by creating connections between adjacent voxels, which could belong to the same fibre bundle. The interpretation and validation of the results of the tractography become less certain when we look for more specific and microscopic information on the connectivity. At a more microscopic level, the connectivity is defined by the axon of a single neuron. Since an axon may display a very complex ramification pattern, even if we could entirely draw a single axon, the characterisation of its connectivity would be very demanding. *Of course the single cell connectivity has a dimension that is too microscopic to be studied by DTI!* Also, axons can join and leave the tract at any point along it. On the other hand, the advantages of the tractography are evident: **it can reconstruct white matter tracts in 3D in a non-invasive way in less than 10 minutes.**

It is very important to understand the properties and the limitations of the methods to guarantee its wise utilisation to answer to biological and/or clinical hypotheses about the brain's anatomy.

In the recent years, since sequencing of genoma, one of the most innovative research projects has been ongoing: to reconstruct the entire network of connections between cerebral areas; a map for this has been called CONNECTOMA. According to Sebastian Seung, who popularised the Connectome Theory for the human brain, "We are our CONNECTOMA". Our behaviours reflect the connectivity of the different areas of our brain, *"Nothing defines the function of a neuron better than its connections."*

4.5 Human connectome project

The Human Connectome Project (HCP) is a five-year project sponsored by the National Institutes of Health (NIH). The goal of the Human Connectome Project is to build a "network map" (connectome) that will shed light on the anatomical and functional connectivity within the healthy human brain, as well as to produce a body of data that will facilitate research into brain disorders, such as dyslexia, autism, Alzheimer's disease, and schizophrenia. In the neural activity of the brain, our memory, thinking and past experiences are stored and coded, everything make us the persons we are.

The dream of neuroscientists is to find the possibility to track this map and to study its pathways and intersections, which will lead us to accede to the biological bases of our identity.

4.6 Conclusions

DWI, and its evolutions, DTI and DTT, provide a unique way of probing tissue microstructure *in vivo* and non-invasively. It is by far the most promising tool for studying white matter and its organisation in living humans. It is, however, a difficult technique to apply correctly due to its unique imaging artefacts, the often very intricate interactions between microstructure and signal, the sophistication of the reconstruction algorithms used, and the sheer complexity of white matter itself. For these reasons, DWI and its related tensor imaging techniques are currently a very active field of research, both in terms of technical development and of its application to the study of the brain and its disorders.

As the methods evolve and mature, we expect that DWI will provide new and unforeseen insights into long-standing problems that would otherwise be impossible to study.

References

Alexander, A.L., Lee, J. E., Lazar, M. and Field, A.S., (2007), «Diffusion Tensor Imaging of the Brain», *Neurotherapeutics,* 4(3), pp. 316-329.

Bastiani, M., Shah, N.J., Goebel R. and Roebroeck, A., (2012), «Human Cortical Connectome Reconstruction from Diffusion Weighted MRI: the Effect of Tractography Algorithm», *NeuroImage,* 62(3), pp. 1732-1749.

Kolb, B., and Gibb, R., (2014), «Searching for the Principles of Brain Plasticity and Behavior», *Cortex,* 58, pp. 251-260.

Park, B., Eo, J. and Park Hae-J., (2017), «Structural Brain Connectivity Constrains within-a-Day Variability of Direct Functional Connectivity», *Frontiers in Human Neuroscience,* 11(408).

Park, Hae-J. and Friston K., (2013), «Structural and Functional Brain Networks: From Connections to Cognition», *Science,* 342(6158), 1238411.

Sebastian, S., (2013), *Connettoma. La nuova geografia della mente,* LeScienze, Codice.

Tournier, J.D., Mori, S. and Leemans, A., (2011), «Diffusion Tensor Imaging and Beyond», *Magnetic Resonance in Medicine,* 65, pp. 1532-1556.

Tournier, J.D., Yeh, C.H., Calamante, F., Cho, K.H., Connelly, A. and Lin, C.P., (2008), «Resolving Crossing Fibres Using Constrained Spherical Deconvolution: Validation Using Diffusion-Weighted Imaging Phantom Data», *Neuroimage,* 42(2), pp. 617-25.

Van den Heuvel, M.P. and Hulshoff Pol, H.E., (2010), «Exploring the Brain Network: a Review on Resting-State Fmri Functional Connectivity», *European Neuropsychopharmacology,* 20, pp, 519-534,

Van Essen, D.C., Smith, S.M, Barch, D.M., Behrens, T.E.J, Yacoub E. and Ugurbil K., (2013), «The WU-Minn Human Connectome Project: an Overview». *Neuroimage,* 80, pp.62-79.

Part II
The Brain Functioning

5. Emotions and Decision Making
by Simona Luzzi

In this mini-review, I will try to synthetise some of the current knowledge about the complex and still debated interaction between emotions and decision making.

In the first part, I will focus on emotions, and in the second part, I will try to figure out how emotions can modulate decision making.

5.1 What is an emotion?

To define emotions is quite hard work. "Emotions define who we are to ourselves as well as to others." With this sentence, Joseph LeDoux (1998) introduces the concept of emotions in one of his books, "The emotional brain", in which he posits his work on emotions.

Emotions are a fundamental experience of our life and most cognitive processes are strictly linked to emotions (Pessoa et *al.* 2008). Our episodic memory (collection of our personal life experiences) relies on emotions. Indeed, we usually remember the experiences of our life that are linked to positive or negative emotions, while the experiences which do not carry an emotional valence tend to be forgotten.

Emotions are also a way to communicate. The expression of a person's face can give us important information about his mental status ("Does he agree with me? Does he like me?"). At the same time, the emotions we show are a way to let others understand our feelings.

Emotions can be a powerful medium of communication and sometimes can "win the competition" with verbal language (e.g.: saying, "I'm going to kill you" with a fun expression on your face that leads the interlocutor to interpret this sentence in a non-literal manner, understanding that you are expressing your disappointment without be emotionally involved).

The power of emotions in communicating messages is often used in art.

Artworks arouse emotions in audiences and the more likely they are able to involve the audience from an emotional point of view, the more they are appreciated.

If we think of the enigmatic smile of the Mona Lisa, the power of the emotional message appears clear to the audience.

Some surrogates of traditional art, such as cinema, often have represented movies where the fulcrum of the story is the emotional-irrational versus the cognitive-rational dualism of the main character. "Dr. Jekyll and Mister Hyde" or the "Incredible Hulk" are examples of this dualism.

This dualism is present in most fairy tales. As an example, the well-known fairy tale, "Beauty and the Beast", is dominated by emotions and feelings: a prince who is incapable to love is transformed into a beast and his physical appearance symbolises his "heartless" state ("you will be as ugly as your heart").

5.2   The story of emotions: moving from philosophy to neurology

The relationship between reason and emotions has fascinated philosophers for centuries. In the well-known Plato's chariot allegory, a charioteer drives a chariot pulled by two winged horses. The charioteer represents cognition and reason and is the part of the soul that guides the soul to truth; one of the two horses represents the positive part of passionate nature, while the other represents the soul's irrational passions, appetites, or concupiscent nature. The charioteer has the hard task of proceeding towards enlightenment and stopping the horses from going in different directions.

After Plato, Renè Descartes is one of the philosophers that gives life to the most influential theory on the relationship between mind and emotion: the mind-body dichotomy or dualism. Descartes in his *Passions of the Soul* (1989) differentiates cognition from passion (i.e. emotions).

In 1872, Charles Darwin published "The Expression of the Emotions in Man and Animals" (2013), where he describes the facial expressions of emotions in detail. He realised there are many ways to express emotions, such as vocalisations, tears and posture.

One of the Darwin's major insights is that facial expressions of emotion have a universal meaning and that different species share mutual mechanisms responsible for producing and recognising emotion.

In 1884, William James (1884) published an influential article in "Mind", a philosophy journal: "What is an emotion?". He is likely to be the first scientist who realises that emotions are not consequent to bodily perception. "Our natural way of thinking about these standard emotions is that the mental perception of some fact excites the mental affection called the emotion, and that this latter state of mind gives rise to the bodily expression. My thesis on the contrary is that the bodily changes follow directly the perception of the exciting fact, and that our feeling of the same changes as they occur IS the emotion. Common sense says, we lose our fortune, are sorry and weep; we meet a bear, are frightened and run; we are insulted by a rival, are angry and strike. The hypothesis here to be defended says that this order of sequence is incorrect, that the one mental state is not immediately induced by the other, that the bodily manifestations must first be interposed between, and that the more rational statement is that we feel sorry because we cry, angry because we strike, afraid because we tremble, and not that we cry, strike, or tremble, because we are sorry, angry, or fearful, as the case may be. Without the bodily states following on the perception, the latter would be purely cognitive in form, pale, colourless, destitute of emotional warmth."

Edouard Claparède, a Swiss educator and psychologist, examining a lady showing severe amnesia understands that memory for emotions and episodic memory are processed by different circuits (Piccirilli, 2006). Indeed, the amnesic lady was not able to recollect facts from her personal memory but she was able to learn and remember emotional experiences.

Julian Jaynes (2000) contributes to understanding emotion processing by showing two chimeric faces to a wide number of normal subjects (Figure 1). Each subject has to say which of the two faces is happier. It is easy to understand that the two figures are specular and from a cognitive point of view they are "identical". Nevertheless, normal subjects who were asked to point to the emotional target answered in most of cases by pointing to one of the two faces. Jaynes concluded that while one hemisphere is dominant for language in most people, the opposite hemisphere is dominant for emotions.

A further step in understanding emotions and their neuroanatomical basis is performed by Paul MacLean. His well-known hypothesis of the triune brain is going to be so exhaustive that all research on emotions seem to be concluded. He postulates that from an evolutionary point of view, three different stages are identifiable, which correspond to specific brain structures. Each of these structures is "acquired" during evolution. The most ancient structures are the basal ganglia, which he names the "reptilian brain". The reptilian brain is responsible of instinctive behaviours (aggression, dominance, territoriality, etc.).

The paleomammalian brain, which is subsumed by MacLean (1990) under the name of the "limbic system", consists of the cingulate cortex, hippocampus, septum, amygdalae, and hypothalamus. MacLean believes that the limbic system processes motivation and emotion involved in feeding, reproduction, and parental behaviour. Finally, the neomammalian complex that corresponds to the neocortex is the part of the brain more recently acquired during evolution and typical of mammalian and humans in particular. It is the part of the brain responsible of cognitive functions, such as language, perception, executive planning, etc.

Even the MacLean model (1990), which influenced neuroscience for several decades, revealed many limitations. One of the most important is that, actually, the limbic system does not exist and the structures of the limbic system do not process emotions exclusively but are responsible also for some cognitive functions, such as memory.

An important step forward in understand ing how emotions work is due to the interesting work of Joseph LeDoux (1998). He focused exclusively on fear and performed several experiments to understand how fear works in our brain and which brain structures are involved in this emotion. For years, he studied mice that experienced fear and discovered that the amygdalae is the brain structure that processes fear. He described the "stress circuit" composed by several subcortical structures (for example, the thalamus) involved in the generation of body-changes that occur in dangerous situations.

Finally, a central figure in the research of emotion regulation, in particular with the main focus on the frontal lobe circuitries, is Antonio Damasio. Damasio (Damasio et al. 2000; Bechara et al. 2005, 2003, 2000, 1997; Clark et al. 2008) has studied in depth people affected by focal lesions of specific regions of the frontal lobe and formulated the somatic-marker hypothesis; a theory about how emotions and their biological underpinnings are involved in decision making. In his illuminating book (2008) "Descartes' error: emotion, reason and the human brain", he provides a scientific explanation of the linkage between feelings, the mind and the body underlying the fact that emotion plays a central role in social cognition and decision making, as expressed in the following aphorism: "We are not thinking machines that feel; rather, we are feeling machines that think."

5.3 Emotions and decision making

Decision making is a complex executive function that allows the subject to make a choice (Beauregard et *al.* 2001). To make a choice is often hard work because several possibilities are always present and the subject has to ponder all potentially positive and negative consequences of each possible choice. Decision making requires past experience, present goals, and the anticipation of an outcome. This complex mechanism relies on a wide set of brain circuits that involve both subcortical and cortical regions (Coutlee et *al.* 2012; Krain et *al.* 2006; Hsu et *al.* 2005). Within the cortical regions, a central core pertains to the frontal lobe, in particular to the orbitofrontal and dorsolateral prefrontal cortex and the anterior cingulate (Goldin et *al.* 2008).

At the same time, these crucial regions are connected with the limbic system, basal ganglia and cerebellum (Rosenbloom et *al.* 2012). Looking at the anatomofunction models of decision making, is it clear that many of the brain regions involved in decision making are the same regions involved in emotion processing. Indeed decision making is based on emotional valence. Most of our decisions are influenced by our "heart".

As a consequence, emotions have the power to mediate our ability to make a choice (Buhle et *al.* 2014; Panno et *al.* 2013; Heilman et *al.* 2010). Between the several models that have been proposed to explain the interaction between emotions, cognition, and decision making, one of the more recent and exhaustive models is "The interactive influence model of emotion and cognition" (IIEC) by Luo and Yu (2015).

This model focuses on several contexts in which emotions tend to "dominate" cognition. It is well-known that emotions play an important role in evolution; they represent a quick and powerful way by which the brain guides behavioural responses in several situations.

In their review, the authors propose two typical contexts in which emotions govern cognition: "cognition reduction" and "emotion exaggeration".

In the first context, cognition is reduced and there is a reduced control on emotions. There are several situations in which cognition is weak:

- Ambiguity: refers to situation in circumstances where the information is incomplete and the subject does not have the available information about the probabilities to make a successful choice. In these situations, the brain areas involved in modulation and integration of emotions and cognition are engaged and, in particular, the dorsomedial frontal cortex, orbital frontal cortex and amygdala. In experimental situations with ambiguity, the "intuition system" is activated generating a quick and automatic answer.

- Time constraint: these situations are characterised by a restricted time frame and the subject has to produce an answer (i.e. make a choice) within a short time range. If the subject is under pressure and has to make a choice rapidly, the intuition system is activated and preferred.
- Ego depletion: in this case, the subject cannot control him/herself adequately (loss of self-control) and then tends to use the intuitive system where the answer is usually available (Ainsworth et al. 2014; Baumeister et al. 1998; Job et al. 2010; Hagger et al. 2010; Wagner et al. 2012).

Other situations are characterised by emotion exaggeration. In this case, the emotional system is greatly enhanced and can interfere with cognitive functions and decision making.

- Proximity: there are some problems that require immediate answers. In these cases, the subject is asked to react immediately. The only rapid way the nervous system has to react quickly is to activate the emotional system. There is evidence of a different involvement of cortical vs subcortical regions in the event of proximity of threat. If there is a danger stimulus and it requires an immediate response, the subcortical structures are activated (i.e. the autonomic nervous system). In contrast, distal threat activates the prefrontal cortex. It means that in the case of a distal threat, the subject activates the structures involved in planning strategies. This schema applies both to temporal and spatial distance; if the threating stimuli are near to a spatial point of view, the subject switches to intuitive/instinctive response; if the stimuli are located far from the subject, he/she tends to use deliberative processes that allow him/her to plan a more specific strategy.
- Social distance: this implies the concept of "self" as opposed to "others". In other words, the subject reacts in different ways according to the stimuli. If the stimuli are "self-relevant" and imply reward, the subject tends to activate the emotional system in decision making. In contrast, if the stimuli are socially distant, i.e., implying changes for other persons, the subject tends to prefer a more analytic approach by using the deliberative processes. When the stimuli are self-relevant, it implies an immediate reward is activated by the same structures that are usually activated by emotional stimuli: *ventral striatum*, anterior cingulate cortex, and anterior and posterior precuneus. It is

interesting to note that, also, in the case of a delayed reward, the way in which the subject reacts does not change. This implies that making a decision about oneself in contrast with a decision about others activates two distinct systems. A more analytic system is preferred if the stimuli are not self-relevant, while an emotional activation is used when the stimuli are self-relevant.

- Social instincts: these represent a set of actions consequent to social interaction. Emotions permit giving a signal about the intentions of another person and can guide own willingness. In particular, it has demonstrated that some social stimuli, such as unfairness, activate emotion (disgust) and tend to elicit emotional responses.

If emotion can play a prominent role when cognitive capacity is reduced or when emotion is greatly strengthened, cognition can have also a regulatory role on emotions by means of attentional deployment, cognitive change, and response modulation. According to this model, there are two systems: a subcortical one (the emotional system) and a cortical one (the prefrontal cortex) that are not antagonist (as supposed in the classical dualistic models) but cooperate with a flexible answer according to the specific decision context.

Together with findings from normal subjects, there is a wide number of studies on the subject of altered functioning of the emotional system that show problems in decision making. All these findings greatly contribute to delineate the fundamental role of emotion in decision making. I will focus briefly on some psychiatric illnesses and some neurological diseases in which there is evidence of an altered emotional system and consequent impaired decision making.

5.4   Emotion and decision making in psychiatric diseases

There are a number of psychiatric disorders in which both emotion regulation and decision making are described as altered. There are a number of studies on anxiety and depression that clearly show they can alter decision making (Aldao et al. 2010; Bishop et al. 2004). One of the more intriguing chapters within the wide spectrum of psychiatric illness is autism spectrum disorder (ASD), which is a sort of umbrella term that includes several conditions all characterised by persistent deficits in social communication and interaction across multiple contexts, as well as restricted, repetitive patterns of behaviour, interests, or activities.

These deficits are present in early childhood and lead to clinically significant functional impairment. Autism usually includes deficit in language with repetitive or rigid language, poor non-verbal communication skills, including lack of eye contact, meaningful gestures and facial expressions.

Studies in autistic subjects (Shah et *al.* 2016; Schoorl et *al.* 2016) show that they are not influenced by emotional equivalents in tasks exploring decision making. For example, autistic subjects do not show the well-known "framing effect". The framing effect is noted when a subject is shown an option presented in a "gain" frame (you keep $30 of an initial $50) and is preferred to mathematically equivalent options presented in a "loss" frame (you lose $20 of an initial $50). The increase in participants choosing the option in the gain frame compared to the loss frame is known as the "framing effect". The framing effect is significantly smaller in autistic subjects than in normal subjects. Apparently, this finding should allow conclusion that the mind of an autistic person is more "rational" than that of a normal subject. If it is so, the absence of valence of emotional stimuli is the main problem these subjects show and it is the basis for their incapacity to interact with other subjects.

5.5   Emotion and decision making in degenerative brain disorders

Apathy and reduced emotion-based decision making are behavioural modifications described in Alzheimer's disease (AD) (Bayand et *al.* 2014). There is evidence that both AD and the amnestic form of mild cognitive impairment (MCI) (which is usually the prodromic form of AD) patients show decision-making impairment. The ones that fail in task exploring decision making, such as the Iowa Gambling Test (IGT), are more apathetic than the ones who show normal performance in tasks exploring decision making (Bayand et *al.* 2014).

Impaired decision-making performances have been described in many other neurodegenerative diseases, such as Parkinson's disease (Evens et *al.* 2016; Kobayakawa et *al.* 2017), Lewy Body dementia (Spotorno et *al.* 2016) frontotemporal dementia (Manes et *al.* 2011; Poletti et *al.* 2013), and Huntington's disease (Adjeroud et *al.* 2017; Gleichgerrcht et *al.* 2010). More recently, poor decision-making performances were also described in patients who are at a greater risk of developing dementia compared with healthy older adults, that is, and MCI (Zamarian et *al.* 2011). Apathy and altered emotional manifestations are very common across these neurological conditions and can play an important role in impairment of decision making with a wide range of negative consequences for the patients and the care-givers.

5.6 Conclusions

In conclusion, there is wide evidence of a prominent role of emotions in decision making. The emotional system interacts with the cortical/cognitive system to permit the subject to make a choice according to the decision context. The interplay between rational/cortical and emotional/subcortical systems is context dependent and able to allow the subject to make a flexible answer in every decisional situation.

Figures

Figure 1.
The two chimeric faces of Julian Jaynes

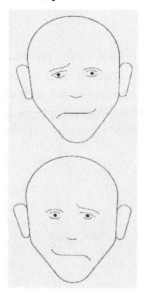

Source: Authors' elaboration.

References

Adjeroud, N., Besnard, J., Verny C, Prundean, A., Scherer, C., Gohier, B., Bonneau, D., Massioui, N.E. and Allain, P., (2017), «Dissociation Between Decision-Making Under Risk and Decision-Making Under Ambiguity in Premanifest and Manifest Huntington's Disease», *Neuropsychologia*, 103, pp. 87-95.

Ainsworth, S.E., Baumeister, R.F., Ariely, D. and Vohs, K.D., (2014), «Ego Depletion Decreases Trust in Economic Decision Making», *Journal of Experimental Social Psychology*, 54, pp. 40-49.

Albrecht, K., Volz, K.G., Sutter, M., Laibson, D.I. and VonCramon, D.Y., (2010), «What Is For Me Is Not For You: Brain Correlates of Intertemporal Choice for Self and Other», *Social Cognitive and Affective Neuroscience*, 6, pp. 218-225.

Aldao, A., Nolen-Hoeksema, S. and Schweizer, S., (2010), «Emotion-Regulation Strategies Across Psychopathology: A Meta-Analytic Review», *Clinical Psychology Review*, 30, pp. 217-237.

Bayard, S., Jacus, J.P., Raffard, S. and Gely-Nargeot, M.C., (2014), «Decision Making in AD and a MCI», *Behavioural Neurology*, 2014(231469).

Baumeister, R.F., Bratslavsky, E., Muraven, M. and Tice, D.M., (1998), «Ego Depletion: Is The Active Self a Limited Resource?», *Journal of Personality and Social Psychology*, 74, pp. 1252-1265.

Beauregard, M., Lévesque, J. and Bourgouin, P., (2001), «Neural Correlates of Conscious Self-Regulation of Emotion», *Journal of Neuroscience*, 21, RC165-RC165.

Bechara, A., Damasio, H. and Damasio, A.R., (2003), «Role of the Amygdala in Decision-Making», *Annals of the New York Academy of Sciences*, 985, pp. 356-369.

Bechara, A., Damasio, H., Tranel, D., and Damasio, A.R., (1997), «Deciding Advantageously Before Knowing the Advantageous Strategy», *Science*, 275, pp. 1293-1295.

Bechara, A., Tranel, D., and Damasio, H., (2000), «Characterization of the Decision-Making Deficit of Patients With Ventromedial Prefrontal Cortex Lesions», *Brain*, 123, pp. 2189-202.

Bechara, A., and Vand erLinden, M., (2005), «Decision-Making and Impulse Control After Frontal Lobe Injuries», *Current Opinion in Neurology*, 18, pp. 734-739.

Bishop, S., Duncan, J., Brett, M., and Lawrence, A.D., (2004), «Prefrontal Cortical Function and Anxiety: Controlling Attention to Threat-Related Stimuli», *Nature Neuroscience,* 7, pp. 184-188.

Buhle, J.T., Silvers, J.A., Wager, T.D., Lopez, R., Onyemekwu, C., Kober, H., et al., (2014), «Cognitive reappraisal Of Emotion: A Meta-Analysis of Human Neuroimaging Studies», *Cerebral Cortex,* 24, pp. 2981-2990.

Clark, L., Bechara, A., Damasio, H., Aitken, M., Sahakian, B., and Robbins, T., (2008), «Differential Effects of Insular and Ventromedial Prefrontal Cortex Lesions on Risky Decision-Making», *Brain,* 131, pp. 1311-1322.

Coutlee, C.G., Huettel S.A., (2012), «The Functional Neuroanatomy of Decision Making: Prefrontal Control of Thought and Action», *Brain Research,* 1428C, pp. 3-12.

Damasio, A., (2008), *Descartes' Error: Emotion, Reason and the Human Brain,* New York, Rand omHouse.

Damasio, A.R., Grabowski, T.J., Bechara, A., Damasio, H., Ponto, L.L., Parvizi, J., et al., (2000), «Subcortical and Cortical Brain Activity During the Feeling of Self-Generated Emotions», *Nature Neuroscience,* 3, pp. 1049-1056.

Darwin, C., (2013), *The Espresison of Emortions In Man And Animals,* BiblioLife.

Descartes, R., (1989), *The Passion of the Soul,* Hackett Publishing Company.

Evens R., Hoefler M., Biber K. and Lueken U., (2016), «The Iowa Gambling Task in Parkinson's Disease: A Meta-Analysis on Effects of Disease And Medication». *Neuropsychologia,* 91, pp. 163-172

Gleichgerrcht, E., A. Ibanez, A., Roca M., Torralva and T. Manes, F., (2010), «Decision-making Cognition in Neurodegenerative Diseases», *Nature Reviews Neurology,* 6(11), pp. 611-623.

Goldin, P.R., Mcrae, K., Ramel, W., and Gross, J.J., (2008), «The Neural Bases of Emotion Regulation: Reappraisal and Suppression of Negative Emotion», *Biological Psychiatry,* 63, pp. 577-586.

Hagger, M.S., Wood, C., Stiff, C., and Chatzisarantis, N.L., (2010), «Ego Depletion and The Strength Model of Self-Control: A Meta-Analysis», *Psychological Bulletin,* 136, pp. 495-525.

Heilman, R.M., Crisan, L.G., Houser, D., Miclea, M., and Miu, A.C., (2010), «Emotion Regulation and Decision Making Under Risk and Uncertainty», *Emotion,* 10, pp. 257-265.

Hsu, M., Bhatt, M., Adolphs, R., Tranel, D., and Camerer, C.F., (2005), «Neural Systems Responding to Degrees of Uncertainty in Human Decision-Making», *Science,* 310, pp. 1680-1683.

James, W., (1884), «What Is an Emotion?», *Mind,* os-IX(34), pp. 188-205.

Jaynes, J., (2000), *The Origin of Consciousness in the Breakdown of the Bicameral Mind,* Houghton Mifflin Harcourt.

Job, V., Dweck, C.S., and Walton, G.M., (2010), «Egodepletion-Is It All in Your Head? Implicit Theories About Willpower Affect Self-Regulation», *Psychological Science,* 21, pp. 1686-1693.

Kobayakawa M., Tsuruya N. and Kawamura M., (2017), «Decision-Making Performance in Parkinson's Disease Correlates with Lateral Orbitofrontal», *Journal of the Neurological Sciences,* volume, 372, pp. 232-238.

Krain, A.L., Wilson, A.M., Arbuckle, R., Castellanos, F.X., and Milham, M. P., (2006), «Distinct Neural Mechanisms Of Risk And Ambiguity: A Meta-Analysis Of Decision-Making», *Neuroimage,* 32, pp. 477-484.

LeDoux, J., (1998), *The Emotional Brain (The Mysterious Underpinnings of Emotional Life),* Touchstone, Simon & Schuster.

Luo, J., Yu, R., (2015), «Follow the Heart or the Head? The Interactive Influence Model of Emotion and Cognition», *Review, Frontiers in Psychology,* 6, p. 573.

MacLean, P.D., (1990), *The* Triune Brain *in Evolution: Role in Paleocerebral Functions,* Springer Science & Business Media.

Manes F., Torralva T., Ibáñez A., Roca M., Bekinschtein T. and Gleichgerrcht E., (2011), «Decision-Making in Frontotemporal Dementia: Clinical, Theoretical and Legal Implications», *Dementia and Geriatric Cognitive Disorders,* 32(1) pp. 11-17.

Panno, A., Lauriola, M., and Figner, B., (2013), «Emotion Regulation and Risk Taking: Predicting Risk Choice in Deliberative Decision Making», *Cognition & Emotion,* 27, pp. 326-334.

Pessoa, L., (2008), «On the Relationship Between Emotion and Cognition», *Nature Reviews Neuroscience*, 9, pp. 148-158.

Piccirilli, M. (2006), *Dal cervello alla mente. Appunti di neuropsicologia*, Morlacchi Editore.

Poletti, M., Baldacci, F., Cipriani G, Nuti, A. and Bonuccelli, U. (2013), «Progressive Impairment of Decision-Making in Behavioral-Variant Frontotemporal Dementia», *The Journal of Neuropsychiatry & Clinical Neurosciences*, 25(2), pp. E20-E21.

Rosenbloom, M.H., Schmahmann, J.D. and Price, B.H. (2012), «The Functional Neuroanatomy of Decision-Making», *The Journal of Neuropsychiatry and Clinical Neurosciences*, 24, pp. 266-277.

Shah, P., Catmur, C. and Bird J., (2016), «Emotional Decision-Making in Autism Spectrum Disorder: the Roles of Interoception and Alexithymia», *Molecular Autism*, 7, p. 43.

Schoorl, J., van Rijn, S., de Wied, M., van Goozen, S., Swaab, H., (2016), «Emotion Regulation Difficulties in Boys with Oppositional Defiant Disorder / Conduct Disorder and the Relation with Comorbid Autism Traits and Attention Deficit Traits». *PLoS ONE*, 11(7).

Spotorno, N., McMillan, C.T., Irwin, D.J., Clark, R., Lee, E.B., Trojanowski, J.Q., Weintraub, D. and Grossman, M., (2017), «Decision-Making Deficits Associated with Amyloidosis in Lewy. Body Disorders», *Frontiers in Human Neuroscience*, 10(693).

Wagner, D.D., and Heatherton, T.F., (2012), «Self-Regulatory Depletion Increases Emotional Reactivity in the Amygdala». *Social Cognitive and Affective Neuroscience*, 8, pp. 410-417.

Zamarian, L., Weiss, E.M., Delazer, M., (2011), «The Impact of Mild Cognitive Impairment on Decision Making in Two Gambling Tasks», *The Journals of Gerontology, series B*, 66(1), pp. 23-31.

6. Decision Making under Risk, Uncertainty and Ambiguity

by Lucrezia Fattobene, Maria Gabriella Ceravolo[1]

It is possible to distinguish two types of uncertainty: aleatory and epistemic. The former consists of the variability that is inherent in nature, is objective and irreducible (the outcome of tossing a dice), while the latter is the result of a lack of knowledge, is subjective and reducible (the percentage of sugar in a bottle of Coca-Cola). In 1921, the economist Frank Knight suggests distinguishing between risk and uncertainty; the first occurs when subjects know, with precision, the possible outcomes of different alternatives and their probability distributions, the second occurs when the probability of manifestation of the outcome is not known with mathematical precision. In the domain of uncertainty, it is then possible to separate the case when nothing is known about probabilities – uncertainty - from the case when partial information is available - ambiguity (Ellsberg 1961). Recently, Schmidt (2013) proposed extending the definition of ambiguity also to cases when information emanating from different sources is conflicting.

6.1 Traditional models of choice under risk

Over time, different models of decision making under risk have been proposed. According to the Expected Value (EV) theory, the EV of a variable is the weighted average of the possible outcome and is computed by adding up the different values

[1] We would like to thank Prof. GM. Raggetti for contributing to the numerous discussions and for the valuable advices he provided during the writing of the chapter.

obtained and multiplying the outcome and its probability of manifestation. As a formula:

$$EV(X) = \sum_{x} p(x) \cdot x$$

where X is the lottery, x the possible outcome and p(x) the likelihood of its occurrence. For instance, in the case of a lottery, a coin toss pays 100 for heads and 0 for tails, the EV=0.5(100) + 0.5(0) = 50.

This model predicts that the subject always chooses the option that maximises the EV.

The St. Petersburg paradox is an example where despite an infinite EV, subjects were found to be willing to pay no more than a few ducats; it challenged the rigour and the acceptability of the EV model to predict subjects' decision making under risk.

The main limitation of this model is that it does not take into account the decrease of utility that derives from the increase of the availability of the goods (or the service).

In this sense, two famous researchers assert that:

> "The determination of the value of an item must not be based on the price, but rather on the utility it yields [...]. There is no doubt that a gain of one thousand ducats is more significant to the pauper than to a rich man though both gain the same amount." (Bernoulli 1738, trans 1954)

and that:

> "The mathematicians estimate money in proportion to its quantity, and men of good sense in proportion to the usage that they may make of it." (Cramer 1728)

Cramer and Bernoulli solved the paradox introducing a utility function that aimed at translating the objective value into a subjective one, taking into account the decrease of pleasure associated with the saturation coming from larger doses. By way of example, consider the pleasure associated with drinking a glass of water. That value perception changes from a thirsty person to a not thirsty person, being the same person, as long as he keeps drinking water. A concave utility function that converts the objective amount into a personal utility is able to express this declining marginal satisfaction.

The Expected Utility Theory, translated into a normative decision-making model by von Neumann and Morgenstern in 1947, suggests that people tend not to maximise the objective value but rather the personal utility. As a formula:

$$EU(X) = \sum_{x} p(x)u(x)$$

where X is the lottery, EU the expected utility of the lottery, u(x) utility associated to each possible outcome and p(x) the outcome manifestation probability.

It is interesting to underline that this type of function is the same one Fechner - a physicist and an experimental psychologist - used to express the relationship between an external stimulus and a subject's perception. This episode reveals that even if psychophysics and economics are two disparate research fields, they share the common hypothesis of an existing link between the transformation of information present in the external world and the subjective internal sensations, which guide choices and behaviour.

The limitations of the Expected Utility Theory emerged through the famous Ellsberg Paradox.

In the last decades, besides these normative models that fail to capture actual individual behaviour, different descriptive models that illustrate real behaviour have been developed. Among these descriptive models, some are based on the use of heuristics (representativeness, availability, anchoring), i.e. mental short cut resulting from evolutionary processes that reduce problem complexities.

A different model is that of Kahneman and Tversky (1979) who propose the Prospect Theory (PT) that is now a milestone in behavioural economics. In particular, Kahneman and Tversky observe that subjects:

- underweight large probabilities and overweight small probabilities;
- attribute value to changes in level and not to absolute amounts (final assets)
- display risk seeking behaviour in the domain of losses (where the function is convex) and risk averse behaviour for gains (concave function);
- are more sensitive to losses than to gains.

Other types of models of decision making under risk, rather than decomposing risky choice into outcome – probability, consider first and second or even higher order moments (Glimcher and Fehr 2014). Briefly, the options are represented as outcome distributions that can be expressed through their moments, generally, the mean, the variance and the skew. According to the Markowitz framework (1959), a subject's Willingness To Pay (WTP) for a lottery is the difference between the average return and the variance of the possible outcome, and varies according to the individual's weight attributed to the trade-off between the maximisation of the return on one hand and the minimisation of the risk on the other hand. As a formula:

$$WTP(X) = V(X) - bR(X)$$

where X is the lottery, V(X) the mean return of the lottery, R(X) the variance associated to the outcome and b the subject's parameter of risk attitude.

The parameter of risk attitude is generally supposed to synthetise the curvature or the slope of the utility function, capturing the personal disposition to face risk. The word "attitude" seems to suggest that this disposition is a psychological trait that characterises individual behaviour and is constant across different situations (Bromiley and Curley 1992).[2] This unsophisticated view has been extensively challenged, since it emerges that the same person can display a different level of risk aversion in the same period of life for different domains (health, finance) or for the same domain in different periods of life (adolescence, old age). Talking about different periods of life generally recalls ample time windows; actually, neuroscience reveals that individual attitudes can change also in very short time. To understand these concepts better, it is useful to adopt a neuroeconomics' approach and explore the neurobiological concepts of reward and risk jointly.

6.2 A neuroeconomics perspective of risk

To define utility, pleasure, reward, and above all, to measure them, economists face several difficulties. Over time, the monetary value of the object, ordinal or cardinal utility, willingness to pay, etc. has been used. Most of the limitations of these measures have emerged since it is extremely complicated to translate personal internal perceptions into quantitative measures using an external or a self-reported perspective. Neuroscientists, on the contrary, know much more about reward and pleasure than economists do. Moreover, they systematically use investigation techniques that permit objectively quantifying all those aspects that economists and psychologists consider abstract and subjective, measuring the neurophysiological states associated to them.

---

[2] Until now, the identification of a risk-seeking or risk-averse phenotype has faced numerous difficulties.

From a neurobiological point of view, an object has a value only if the subject makes an effort to obtain it; on the contrary, a punishment is something to make an effort to avoid. In 1954, Olds and Milner inserted an electrode in a rat's brain, providing the rat with the possibility to stimulate the brain area by simply pressing a lever (Figure 1). The researchers observed that when the electrode stimulated a specific brain area, the rat continued to press the lever for receiving nothing more than this electrical stimulation, completely losing interest in other external and internal stimuli (hunger, thirst ...).

In this case, one way to measure the subjective value is the frequency and the rapidity with which the rat presses the lever. This experiment revealed the existence of a "reward centre", the nucleus *accumbens*, and of a reward circuitry, that have been lately confirmed by hundreds of studies. The reward system consists of the *mesolimbic dopamine pathway* (the most important one) that connects the ventral tegmental area and nucleus *accumbens*, and of the *mesocortical dopamine pathway* that connects the ventral tegmental area and prefrontal cortex. These pathways, in turn, consists of parallel and integrated circuits that include several brain areas, such as the amygdala, associated to learning, emotion[3], memory, attention and perception, hippocampus, involved in long-term and declarative memories, ventral pallidum and lateral hypothalamus.

Among the different studies on the reward system, in 2006 Schultz observed that a specific population of neurons, the dopaminergic neurons located in the nucleus *accumbens*, reacts to stimuli associated to a reward that does not react to neutral stimuli. He also observed that during the Pavlovian conditioning, at the beginning, neurons react to positive stimuli, but over time, they stop reacting to rewards and start reacting to stimuli that anticipate the rewards. This allows asserting that a specific population of neurons that codify expected values exists. Bridging these discoveries in the neuroscience field with the current economics' theoretical frameworks can definitely help to overcome some of the limitations that lead to failing normative models and imprecise descriptive ones in economics and finance. The discipline of neuroeconomics, therefore, managed to provide a quantitative and objective measure of reward, pleasure and utility that have been considered qualitative and not objectively measurable constructs for a long time. Utility can be roughly defined as the

---

[3] The word *emotion* is often used in neuroeconomics: with this expression, researchers refer to its *neurobiology,* to the *physiological* changes that occur as responses to some events. (In 1937, the neuroanatomist J. M. Papez asked "Is emotion a magic product, or is it a physiologic process which depends on an anatomic mechanism?")

average firing rate[4] of the population of neurons that codifies the subjective value of the object. As a formula:

$$U = r \text{ (firing rate)} = \sum \frac{r_n}{N}$$

Broadly, the neuronal firing (or spike per second) in a trial, defined in the unit of frequency (Hz), is the spike[5] count in an interval of duration t divided by t (Figure 2).

Risk can be considered an inversely related function of probability whose value is minimal when p is 0 or 1 and maximum when p is 0.5. When p=0.5, in fact, there is identical probability to obtain or miss the reward, while when value is lower or higher than 0.5, gains are respectively less and more probable and, thus, less risky. The following image (Figure 3) graphically reports the time interval from the stimulus to the reward; the risk response (arrow) occurs after the activation related to the stimulus (triangle).

Several studies indicate that dopaminergic neurons in the *ventral striatum* codify both the magnitude (Tobler, Fiorillo and Schultz 2005) and the probability (Fiorillo, Tobler and Schultz 2003) of reward, and their integration into the expected value (Tobler, Fiorillo and Schultz 2005). Interestingly, a part of this population of neurons has been found to be more sensitive to magnitude while another part to probability, allowing a *spatial separation* into the *ventral striatum* of the two components (Yacubian *et al.* 2006). In any case, a large part of the activations related to probabilities and to magnitude overlaps in this brain area. Preuschoff, Bossaerts and Quartz (2006) find evidence of also a *temporal separation* and they report immediate neural correlates of expected reward and delayed neural correlates of risk. Therefore, as for reward, also the risk seems to be coded by the dopamine neurons in that brain area, but with a delay with respect to reward. The reward-sensitive dopamine neurons that react to risk show a slow and sustained reaction to risk.

---

[4] The expression "roughly" is used to underline that some definitions represent merely a simplification of very complex and sophisticated constructs in neuroscience. In recent years, several methods for estimating neural firing rates have been developed from the fields of machine learning, statistics, and computational neuroscience. Specifically, firing rates are a measure of different quantities depending on different contexts (time-dependent firing rate, spike-count rate, average firing rate, etc.)

[5] A spike, or an impulse, is the action potential that occurs when neurons send information through their axons.

6.2.1 Why is it important to delve into the concept of reward when studying the risk?

From a neurobiological perspective, the relevant element in the relationship between choice and risk is the expectation associated to the reward, which motivates the subject. While for economists the uncertainty follows the choice, for neurobiologists, it is intrinsic in the act of choosing itself and, therefore, it is impossible to talk about choice and risk as separate elements. Surprisingly, in 2007, Knutson *et al.* discovered that neural correlates for purchasing decisions – where probability is not a key element – are similar to those related to financial risk (Knutson *et al.* 2003; Kuhnen and Knutson 2005). The above-mentioned Prospect Theory of Kahneman and Tversky (1979) deserves credit for highlighting that risk, before being a mathematical calculation, is a personal and subjective perception that is later processed and elaborated by our brain. Therefore, risk is not just something inherent with the complexity and the chaos of the external world but is a mental representation to which underlie neural correlates and neural processes. Neuroeconomics' research aims at filling the gap of understanding these neural processes that drive the choice.

6.3   Anticipatory affect model

According to Expected Utility theories, decision making is merely based on the integration of severity and likelihood of possible outcomes, and emotions represent an epiphenomenon. These models assume that the assessment of risky and uncertain situations is a cognitive activity where affective states play no role at all. This consequentialist approach has been improved through a perspective that integrates anticipated emotions, namely affective processes that are not actually experienced at the time of the decision but are expected to be experienced after the decision is taken. Examples of anticipated emotions are regret or disappointment. In 2001, Loewenstein *et al.* proposed distinguishing between *anticipated emotions* and *anticipatory emotions* that, in turn, consist of affective processes experienced at the time of the decision. By integrating and improving a large series of studies that during the years have considered several psychological dimensions of risk (for instance, the affect-as-information hypothesis, the affect heuristic rule, etc.), the authors proposed the *risk-as-feeling hypothesis*, according to which, emotional reactions anticipate the choice, diverging sometimes with cognitive evaluations, and dominating behaviour in this last case. In more detail, according to this theoretical framework, behaviour is the result of the interplay of two systems. A first process consists of cognitive evaluations of risk (the integration of likelihood and magnitude of the possible outcome). During these cognitive evaluations, some internal states and automatic emotional reactions play a role in influencing individual behaviour. At the same time, also the process itself of cognitively evaluating a risky situation, above all focusing on the final consequences, triggers some feelings that influence, in turn, these cognitive evaluations and the outcome. According to this perspective, these systems mutually influence each other and can conflict; the behaviour displayed is the result of the dominance of one of the two systems. Finally, the behaviour leads to outcomes that trigger other emotions that are stored in the subject's memory and influences subsequent decision-making processes.

Historically, the available techniques have not permitted clear detection if emotions anticipate and influence individual choices. As for all the feelings or the internal states, the only available measures are self-reported and retrospective and, therefore, prone to a large number of biases and inaccuracies. Imaging techniques, on the contrary, allow measuring both temporal and spatial resolution of brain activations. In 2008, Knutson and Greer proposed the Anticipatory Affect Model, according to which the anticipation of possible outcomes influences the two dimensions of affective processes: the valence, which ranges from appetitive to aversive, and the salience that varies from low to high.[6] In the Anticipatory Affect Model, cues play a significant role in initiating the anticipatory process; when cues signal potential gains, valence increases, positive arousal increases, and approach behaviour is promoted; on the contrary, when cues signal potential losses, valence decreases, negative arousal increases, and avoidance behaviour is fostered. Evidence reveals that specific neural circuits activate (or deactivate) during anticipation; nucleus *accumbens* activations increases when anticipating positive outcomes, and are generally followed by purchase decision or risky choices, while anterior insula activations correlate both with the anticipation of positive and negative outcomes but precedes the avoidance of over-priced products or the low-risky gambles. Functional Magnetic Resonance Imaging (fMRI) has, therefore, permitted temporal and spatial localisation of neural activity that predicts risk taking behaviour. Summing up, an incentive cue can trigger activations in two main brain circuits, whose most prominent brain area are nucleus *accumbens* and anterior *insula*; the dominance of these circuits, in turn, cause an approach or an avoidance behaviour towards potential gains or losses. In

---

[6] This two-dimensional scheme has been originally proposed by the experimental psychologist William Wundt in 1897 and lately translated in the affective circumplex by Watson et al. (1999).

other words, if positive arousal increases, potential gains should appear more prominent, and people would approach the risky situation; on the contrary, if negative arousal increases, potential losses appear more prominent and people avoid the risky situation.

6.4 Risk perception

The anticipatory affect model has revealed that the positive emotional state promotes approach behaviour while the negative emotional state promotes avoidance behaviour. Using this framework, Kuhnen and Knutson (2011) aim to test if change in emotional states or in the corresponding brain area activations modifies individuals' risk preferences. Besides the value that it adds to the literature, it is worth mentioning this experiment since it reveals that neuroeconomics is relevant as it allows creating new theoretical frameworks to test new hypotheses; and even without using neuroscience techniques but just building on previous findings. The methodology used by the authors in fact comes from experimental finance; what makes the study a neuroeconomics one is the conceptual framework on which the hypotheses are developed.

To test their hypothesis, the authors asked students to choose, over several rounds, between bonds that represent a safe asset, or stocks that represent a risky asset. At the beginning of each trial, a picture was presented in order to exogenously manipulate the emotional state. In particular, three types of picture have been used: highly arousing with positive valence (a), highly arousing with negative valence (b), and neutral (c) (Figure 4). Pictures of type (a) are supposed to stimulate nucleus *accumbens'* activations that foster excitement and shift to risk seeking behaviour, while picture of type (b), on the contrary, stimulates anterior *insula* activation and risk avoidance behaviour; finally, the neutral picture (c) is used as a benchmark.

Interestingly, results reveal that the percentage of trials where risky assets are chosen is lower when negative stimuli are presented to participants before investment decisions, compared with positive and neutral stimuli. In other words, after subjects have seen a negative and highly arousing picture, they are more risk averse and less prone to choose stocks, relative to trials where the other two types of stimuli are presented. Besides these external stimuli, internal ones also have been found to influence risk-taking behaviour. In fact, the analysis shows that there is an increase of 11% in the probability of switching from safe to risky securities when the previous trial pays a high dividend, which would represent a positive stimulus, compared to trials where low dividends are paid. Overall, this study highlights that emotional states matter in financial risk taking, both if exogenously or endogenously induced; therefore, institutions and policymakers might have to take into account the possibility that decisions could be shaped by external features of the market or environment in general, and by internal states that might be provoked by previous decisions. Other streams of implications of these findings are related both to the micro level of learning theories and investors' behaviour, and to the macro one of financial bubbles.

From the canonical view that considers individuals always risk averse, prospect theory represented a step forward highlighting that people are context-dependent and display opposite behaviours in the domains of losses and gains. The study conducted by Kuhnen and Knutson (2011) has demonstrated that risk-taking behaviour can be modulated through external stimuli, and internal ones. Studies on animals' foraging behaviour lead to a more nuanced perspective, suggesting the role of the physiological state in influencing behaviour in risky situations. A study conducted on dark-eyed juncos, for instance, revealed that these birds show different behaviours in risky situations, based on their body temperature; when facing a lottery between a fixed and variable (around the same mean) option of millet seeds, they prefer the fixed option when they are warm, and the variable option when they are cold (Caraco 1981). This example reveals that as a drop in the temperature leads to switching from risk aversion to risk seeking, any internal states may influence choices and changes of the internal states may lead the subject to change risk-taking behaviour.[7]

Recently, a distinction between decisions from *description* and decisions from *experience* has emerged as a factor influencing risk-taking behaviour (Hertwig *et al.* 2004). Experience refers to learning the outcomes of alternatives by personally living the consequences of the choices; outcomes that represent rewards increase the probability of repeating the choice, while the opposite is true for punishments. Descriptions concern primarily humans and consist in summaries or reports – in different formats - about the consequences of the choices. Investigations report differences in individual decisions in risky situations in the two conditions. In the case of the description, as revealed by studies on prospect theory, subjects overweight small probabilities; when deciding from experience, on the contrary, rare events tend to be underweighted (Weber, Shafir and Blais 2004). The measure *coefficient of variation*

---

[7]The reason why when the temperature is low, birds prefer the risky option is that in cold conditions, the expenditure of energy is high and, therefore, they have to gamble to acquire the necessary resources to survive. On the contrary, when it is warm, energy expenditure is generally lower and the payoff of the fixed option is adequate for the birds' energy needs.

(CV)[8] that provides a relative measure of risk is not a significant better predictor than variance or standard deviation in decisions from description but is a far better predictor in decisions from experience. To this more complex vision of risk taking behaviour, it is worth adding that also the format through which the description is presented is able to modulate risk perception. The framing effect is one example of format presentation that affects risky decisions, as illustrated in the next section.

6.5 Framing effect and neural circuits

In their experiments, Tversky and Kahneman (1981) report the existence of the *framing effect* according to which people react differently to the same problem depending on how it is presented. The same choice, in fact, might be framed in term of gains or losses. For example, in the famous "Asian disease problem", different groups of people are asked to choose between adopting a specific programme and:

a. saving 200 people or
b. saving 600 with one-third probability and 0 with two-thirds probability,

or adopt the programme and observe

c. 400 people die or
d. 0 people die with one-third probability and 600 live with two-thirds probability.

The robust finding in this experiment is that even if options A and C and options B and D are equivalent, people prefer option A for the first gamble and option D for the second gamble. Despite the fact that the problems are equivalent, individuals' behaviour violates systematically from rational behaviour; people choose the sure gains over the probable gains but the probable loss over the sure loss. Summing up, subjects display different behaviours in the gain or loss domains, preferring the certainty for the gains and the uncertainty for the losses, even if the expected values of the options are equivalent. In this perspective, people who buy insurance or those who speculate in financial markets would represent deviations, making it, therefore, interesting to

---

[8] The coefficient of variation is the standard deviation standardised by the expected value. Its formula: $CV(X) = SD(X) / EV(X)$ where X is the lottery, SD the standard deviation and EV the expected value.

explore what drives these outputs. Some researchers have started to explore the link between risk perception and the framing effect. De Martino and colleagues (2006) have studied the framing effect of Kahneman and Tversky in the fMRI scanner, observing that subjects who did not behave in line with prospect theory showed a significant activation of the anterior cingulate cortex and of the prefrontal cortex, while subjects who behave as predicted by prospect theory showed a higher activation of the amygdala. The authors interpreted these findings stating that the bias of the prospect theory, i.e. the preference of certainty for gains and of uncertainty for losses, is driven by emotions regulated by the subcortical structure of the amygdala. When cognitive functions associated to the prefrontal cortex dominate emotional mechanisms, a contrast between cognitive and emotional systems takes place, as revealed by the activation of the anterior cingulate cortex, an area usually associated with conflicts' resolution. The behaviour displayed is, therefore, the result of the interaction between the two systems. Nevertheless, in another study, Tom *et al.* (2007) report different results. Their fMRI analysis does not reveal the activation of the amygdala but an increased activity of ventromedial prefrontal cortex and of the orbitofrontal cortex as potential gains increased, and a decreased activity of the same brain regions for potential losses. These findings lead to hypothesise that the different sensitivity to gains and losses when making decisions is linked to the single neural system that presides over cognitive functions and it is stimulated by expected rewards. Moreover, cognitive functions are activated when the expected gains are larger than expected losses, probably unveiling the neural basis of loss aversion. Even if at a first look the results of the two experiments appear to conflict, a more in-depth analysis might reconcile them. In fact, the source of the conflict may lie in the different protocols. In the second experiments, participants had to accept or reject gambles that offered a 50/50 chance of gains or losses without actually choosing but rather indicating one of the four answers (strongly accept, weakly accept, weakly reject, and strongly reject). The different emotional involvement in the case of making a choice with respect to a mere expression of a preference might explain the absence of activation of the amygdala. These experiments, besides representing the first studies to investigate the neural basis of decision making under risk, make other significant contributions. In essence, they highlight the importance of distinguishing, in economics and finance, among experienced, anticipated, and decision utility; they also underline the difference between risk aversion and loss aversion. Finally, the different sensitivity among individuals to risk and losses may suggest the importance of using an interdisciplinary approach to study disorders, such as pathological gambling, substance abuse, and so on, in risk taking behaviour.

6.6 Ambiguity and Uncertainty

"The mental operations by which ordinary practical decisions are made are very obscure, and it is a matter of surprise that neither logicians nor psychologists have shown much interest in them." (Frank Knight 1921, Chapter 7)

Since this statement, a great deal of progress has been made in the field of decision making under uncertainty. Already in 1921, Knight proposed to detect two different levels of uncertainty where the first refers to the measure of the information and the second to its reliability. Lately, the word *ambiguity* has been introduced to refer to situations of partial information or excess of information from different and conflicting sources. While the word uncertainty refers to the complete lack of knowledge, ambiguity refers to partial, biased, or contradictory information. The recent results in neuroeconomics highlight that this semantic difference is relevant and not associated to empty definitions. In fact, researchers report that decisions under uncertainty and under ambiguity are associated to a different brain activity confirming that the latter is a *sui generis* category rather than a subsample of the former.

Rustichini *et al.* (2005), using the Positron Emission Tomography (PET), aim at studying brain activations during choices under ambiguity, risk and uncertainty.[9] The primary finding of their research is that under conditions of uncertainty and risk, the main brain area activations are located in the parietal lobes, while ambiguous choices involve activations also in the frontal regions. This difference is relevant in that it shows that ambiguity is associated to a greater cognitive effort and implies the involvement of more sophisticated processes. In fact, in risky and uncertainty situations, brain effort is lower since it has to integrate magnitude and probability (risk) or has no computations to make at all (uncertainty). On the contrary, in ambiguous situations, decision making implies approximation, definition of strategies, recourse of mental short cuts and other mental reasoning to overcome the limits of missing information and making a choice. These preliminary results showed that under ambiguity the brain works differently than under risk or uncertainty, revealing that ambiguity represents an independent condition of decision making. This remark is confirmed also by another neuroeconomics' study conducted through fMRI. Hsu *et al.* (2005) report evidence of different brain activations under ambiguity and under

---

[9] Even if the definitions of ambiguity, risk and uncertainty are generally accepted, some researchers use different definitions; the authors use the word partial ambiguity to refer to ambiguity and the word ambiguity to refer to uncertainty.

risk that do not pertain only to cortical structures involved in cognitive functions but also to subcortical structures involved in emotions processing. The authors reveal, in fact, that ambiguous choices are associated to greater activations with respect to risky choices of orbitofrontal cortex and amygdala, while risky choices imply a greater activation of dorsal striatum. Summing up, while Rustichini's team sustains the cognitive dimension of decision making under ambiguity, Hsu's team underlines the emotional involvement of ambiguity perception. Despite these intriguing achievements, there is still much to discover in neuroeconomics to shed light on the brain mechanisms that underlie decision making under ambiguity.

6.7 Regret

Individuals continuously use strategies to avoid negative feelings, such as sadness, frustration, fear, hate, anger, and so on. An unpleasant emotion for humans also is regret, which is the sensation of knowing *ex post* that a different decision *ex ante* would have led to a better result.[10] The different violations of expected utility theory in decision making under uncertainty have led to some new theories we have reviewed above. An alternative explanation of that behaviour has been provided also by Bell in 1982, who proposed introducing anticipated regret in the utility function in order to take into account not only monetary rewards but also the sensation of knowing it would have felt better if a different choice was made. The comparison of the payoff of the chosen alternative with the discarded one (or ones) is possible through counterfactual thinking; this process of reasoning associated to a negative feeling makes the emotion of regret a cognitive-mediated emotion. The feeling of regret differs from that of disappointment since it includes the knowledge about the outcomes of the alternatives, while disappointment is related to an unexpected negative outcome and does not include the component of personal responsibility (Bell 1985). While experimental studies have shown that regret influences behaviours, neuroeconomics has started to investigate neural correlates of regret, confirming a neuroanatomical dissociation of regret versus disappointment and, therefore, confirming the need to distinguish these two emotions in decision making. Researchers report that the main brain areas involved when experiencing regret are the orbitofrontal cortex, anterior cingulate cortex, amygdala and hippocampus. Briefly,

---

[10] Minimisation of regret generally differs from minimisation of losses: the only case in which they are equivalent s when regret is a linear function of the monetary measure of losses.

orbitofrontal cortex is involved in the cognitive dimension of regret, i.e. in the computation of the magnitude of the differences between the obtained outcome and the foregone one; anterior cingulate cortex, as discussed in previous sections, is implicated in conflict resolution and errors perception. Amygdala activations are related to negative emotional components, such as fear, of decision making and, specifically, drive regret avoidance behaviour. Finally, the hippocampus encodes declarative memory that has a key role in an emotion based on a declarative cognitive process, such as the regret (Coricelli *et al.* 2005).

6.8 Conclusions

Understanding which neural structures are involved is crucial in order to map neural systems that, interacting, lead to choices. In particular, these studies have started to elucidate the role of the orbitofrontal cortex in integrating emotional and cognitive mechanisms that shape decision making. Neuroeconomics is a nascent field and despite the fascinating results described above, considerable research will have to be conducted in order to fully describe neural mechanisms that drive (economic) behaviour.

Figures

Figure 1.
The self-stimulation experiment

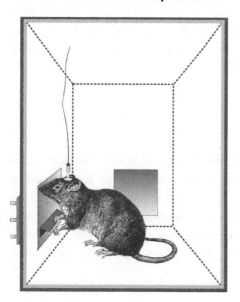

Source: Authors' elaboration.

Figure 3.
Risk response

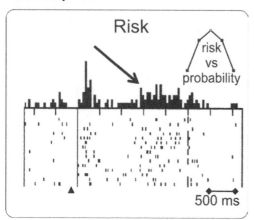

Source: Schultz W., (2010), «Dopamine signals for reward value and risk: basic and recent data», Behavioral and Brain Functions, 6(24).

Figure 2.
Graphical representation of firing rate. The image displays midbrain dopamine neurons phasic activations following primary reward

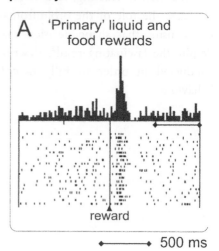

Source: Schultz W., (2010), «Dopamine signals for reward value and risk: basic and recent data», Behavioral and Brain Functions, 6(24).

Figure 4.
The image displays a highly arousing – positive valence picture (a), a highly arousing – negative valence picture (b), and a neutral picture (c)

(a)

(b)

(c)

Source: Authors' elaboration.

References

Bell, D.E., (1982), «Regret in Decision-Making under Uncertainty», *Operations Research*, 30, pp. 961-981.

Bell, D.E., (1985), «Disappointment in Decision-Making under Uncertainty», *Operations Research*, 33, pp. 1-27.

Bernoulli, D., (1954), «Exposition of a New Theory on the Measurement of Risk», *Econometrica*, 22, pp. 23-36 (Translation of Bernoulli, D., (1738) «Specimen Theoriae Novae De Mensura Sortis», *Papers of the Imperial Academy of Sciences in Petersburg*, 5, pp. 175-192).

Bromiley, P. and Curley S.P., (1992), «Individual differences in Risk Taking», in J.F. Yates (Ed.), *Risk-taking behaviour*, Chichester, John Wiley.

Caraco, T., (1981), «Energy Budgets, Risk and Foraging Preferences in Dark-Eyed Juncos (Junco hymelais)», *Behavioural Ecology and Sociobiolology*, 8,   pp. 820-830.

Coricelli, G., Critchley, H.D., Joffily, M., O'Doherty, J.P., Sirigu, A. and Dolan, R.J., (2005), «Regret and its Avoidance: A Neuroimaging Study of Choice Behaviour», *Nature Neuroscience*, 8, pp. 1255-1262.

Cramer, G., (1728), 1975, «Letters to Nicolas Bernoulli», in J. Bernoulli, *Die Werke von Jakob Bernoulli*, v. 3, ed. by van der Waerden B.L., Birkäuser Verlag, pp. 560-63.

De Martino, B., Kumaran, D., Seymour, B. and Dolan, R., (2006), «Frames, Biases, and Rational Decision-Making in the Human Brain», *Science*, 313(5787), pp. 684-687.

Ellsberg, D., (1961), «Risk, Ambiguity, and the Savage Axioms», *Quarterly Journal of Economics*, 75, pp. 643-669.

Fiorillo, C.D., Tobler, P.N. and Schultz, W. (2003), «Discrete Coding of Reward Probability and Uncertainty by Dopamine Neurons», *Science*, 299(5614), pp. 1898-1902.

Glimcher, P.W. and Fehr, E., (edited by), (2014), *Neuroeconomics: Decision Making and the Brain*, 2nd edition, Academic Press.

Hertwig, R., Barron, G., Weber, E.U. and Erev, I., (2004), «Decisions from Experience and the Effect of Rare Events in Risky Choice», *Psychological Science*, 15, pp. 534-539.

Hsu, M., Bhatt, M., Adolphs, R., Tranel, D. and Camerer, C. F., (2005), Neural systems Responding to Degrees of Uncertainty in Human Decision-Making, *Science*, 310, pp. 1680-1683.

Kahneman, D. and Tversky, A., (1979), «Prospect Theory: An Analysis of Decision under Risk», *Econometrica*, 47, pp. 263-91.

Knight, F.H. (1921), *Risk, Uncertainty, and Profit*, New York, Houghton Mifflin.

Knutson, B. and Greer, S.M., (2008), «Anticipatory Affect: Neural Correlates and Consequences for Choice, Philisophical Transactions of the Royal Society B», *Biological Sciences*, 363, pp. 3771-3786.

Knutson, B., Fong, G.W., Bennett, S.M., Adams, C.M. and Hommer, D. (2003), «A Region of Mesial Prefrontal Cortex Tracks Monetarily Rewarding Outcomes: Characterization with Rapid Event-Related fMRI», *Neuroimage*, 18, pp. 263-272.

Knutson, B., Rick, S., Wimmer, G.E., Prelec, D. and Loewenstein, G., (2007), «Neural Predictors of Purchases», *Neuron*, 53(1), pp. 147-156.

Kuhnen, C.M. and Knutson, B., (2005), «The Neural Basis of Financial Risk-Taking», *Neuron*, 47, pp. 763-770.

Kuhnen, C.M. and Knutson, B., (2011), «The Influence of Affect on Beliefs, Preferences, and Financial Decisions», *Journal of Financial and Quantitative Analysis*, 46, pp. 605-626.

Loewenstein, G.F., Weber, E.U., Hsee, C.K. and Welch, N., (2001), «Risk as Feelings», *Psychological Bulletin*, 2, pp. 267-286.

Markowitz, H.M. (1959), *Portfolio Selection: Efficient Diversification of Investments*, Wiley.

Olds, J. and Milner, P.M., (1954), «Positive Reinforcement Produced by Electrical Stimulation of Septal Area and Other Regions of Rat Brain», *Journal of Comparative and Physiological Psychology*, 47, pp. 419 - 427.

Preuschoff, K., Bossaerts, P. and Quartz, S.R., (2006), «Neural Differentiation of Expected Reward and Risk in Human Subcortical Structures», *Neuron*, 51, pp. 381-390.

Rustichini, A., Dickhaut, J., Ghirardato, P., Smith, K. and Pardo, J.V., (2005), «A Brain Imaging Study of the Choice Procedure», *Games and Economic Behaviour*, 52, pp. 257-282.

Schmidt, C., (2013), *Neuroeconomia*, Codice.

Schultz, W., (2006), «Behavioral Theories and the Neurophysiology of Reward», *Annual Review of Psychology*, 57, pp. 87-115.

Schultz W., (2010), «Dopamine Signals for Reward Value and Risk: Basic and Recent Data», *Behavioral and Brain Functions,* 6(24).

Tobler P.N., Fiorillo C.D., Schultz W., (2005), «Adaptive Coding of Reward Value by Dopamine Neurons», *Science*, 307(5715), pp. 1642-1645.

Tom, S.M., Fox, C.R., Trepel, C. and Poldrack, R. A., (2007), «The Neural Basis of Loss Aversion in Decision-Making under Risk», *Science*, 315, pp. 515-518.

Tversky A. and Kahneman D., (1981), «The Framing of Decisions and the Psychology of Choice», *Science*, 211, pp. 453-458.

Tversky, A. and Kahneman, D., (1986), «Rational Choice and the Framing of Decisions», *Journal of Business*, 59, pp. 251-278.

von Neumann, J. and Morgenstern, O., (1947), *Theory of Games and Economic Behavior,* 2nd ed., New York, Princeton University Press.

Watson D., Wiese D., Vaidya J., Tellegen A., (1999). «The Two General Activation Systems of Affect: Structural Findings, Evolutionary Considerations, and Psychobiological Evidence», *Journal of Personality and Social Psychology*, 76, pp. 820–838.

Weber E.U., Shafir S. and Blais A. R., (2004), «Predicting Risk Sensitivity in Humans and Lower Animals: Risk as Variance or Coefficient of Variation», *Psychological Review*, 111, pp. 430-445.

Yacubian, J., Glascher J., Schroeder, K., Sommer, T., Braus, D. F. and Buchel, C. (2006), «Dissociable Systems for Gain - And Loss- Related Value Predictions and Errors of Prediction in the Human Brain», *Journal of Neuroscience*, pp. 9530-9537.

7. The Neuroscience of Human Intertemporal Choice: State-of-the-Art

by Manuela Sellitto, Giuseppe di Pellegrino

Imagine you are on a diet and you are facing two options: You can either eat an apple or a chocolate ice cream for dessert. What would you pick up? To make your choice, you need to consider, among other things, the amount of reward that you can gain from both options as well as the time that these rewards occur. Choosing the apple is considered a prudent choice; it is less tasty than the ice cream but it allows you not to break your diet. In three months, let's say, you will definitely lose weight in this way. If you go for the ice cream instead, you are giving in to temptation of a delicious treat in the immediate present but you are definitely not complying with your diet and, therefore, you will not accomplish your future goal of losing weight. It is considered that you are being impulsive. This is one of the numerous examples of a so-called *intertemporal choice*, a decision between alternatives whose outcomes are different in size and whose occurrences are spread over time (smaller size sooner, larger size later; Sellitto, Ciaramelli and di Pellegrino 2011).

7.1 Intertemporal choice and temporal discounting

Typically, the subjective value of a reward declines as a function of time until its delivery, giving rise to the so-called *temporal or delay discounting* phenomenon (Myerson *et al.* 2003). If you are very young and the time for retirement is far away, you will probably care less about saving money for the future and spend it, instead, on nice holidays. If you are already in your 50s, you will probably think twice before investing a large amount of money to go on a long vacation.

In a typical laboratory setting, intertemporal choice in humans is usually investigated by subjecting participants to a series of decisions between a smaller-sooner amount of money and a larger-later amount of money. However, intertemporal choice behaviour has also been investigated considering commodities like food, abstract objects, and drug abuse, as this kind of paradigm is easily impressionable. The more often one goes for sooner but smaller rewards, foregoing the larger but later outcome, the more one is considered impatient (Frederick, Loewensteing and O'Donoghue 2002). This holds even more if the sooner reward is available in the immediate present. Intertemporal choices are ubiquitous, spanning from savings behaviour to addiction and psychiatric disorders, from quitting smoking to the mortgage and credit card problems and the most recent financial crisis and, over the years, psychology and behavioural neuroscience have dedicated increasing attention to this topic, which has been traditionally under the care of economics' scholars (Story *et al.* 2014; Dalley and Robbins 2017). For a long time, economic models have explained humans' and other animals' intertemporal preference in terms of maximisation of achieved utility (Kalenscher and Pennartz 2008). However, psychology and behavioural neuroscience have more recently revealed inconsistencies in human behaviour (and also in non-human animal behaviour), promoting the idea that irrational behaviour is not simply a deviation from normative prescription (see also Seinstra, Sellitto and Kalenscher 2017). Indeed, during intertemporal choice, it is very common to behave impatiently when the smaller option is immediately available (e.g., by preferring €10 now over €30 in 2 months' time), than to be willing to wait for the larger option when both options are shifted in time by the same front-end delay (e.g., by preferring €30 in 3 months over €10 in 1 month). These so-called "preference reversals" are captured well by hyperbolic models, which put extra weight on short delays, and better than exponential models prescribed by traditional economics (Sellitto, Ciaramelli and di Pellegrino 2011).

As mentioned before, intertemporal choice paradigms are very versatile and especially adopted for investigating issues related to self-control. High delay discount rates are, indeed, usually associated with pathological conditions characterised by poor self-control, which is crucial for achieving long-term plans. Drug addict individuals, for instance, have increased overall impulsivity; namely, not only do they act impatiently towards the object of their desire (i.e., the drug they use to abuse) but they tend to discount more markedly (i.e., they choose more often the smaller-sooner option) than healthy controls or monetary rewards (Bickel *et al.* 2011).

Over the years, several neuroscientific reviews on the topic of intertemporal choice have been published, and it is striking to see the exponential increase in imaging studies explicitly directed at investigating the neural bases of such decisional process, as well as aiming at "change" of intertemporal preference (e.g., Frederick, Loewensteing and O'Donoghue 2002; Berns, Laibson and Loewenstein 2007; Frost and Mcnaughton 2017; Kalenscher and Pennartz 2008; Peters and Büchel 2011; Sellitto, Ciaramelli and di Pellegrino 2011).

More than a decade ago, a first imaging study attempted to unravel the neural underpinning of the intertemporal decision. By scanning volunteers through functional magnetic resonance imaging (fMRI) while they were making a series of monetary intertemporal choices, McClure and colleagues (McClure *et al.* 2004, McClure *et al.* 2007) found activation of two neural networks in agreement with their dual-system model (which determined their imaging analyses). Parts of the limbic system, including the *ventral striatum* (*VS*), the medial prefrontal cortex (MPFC), the medial orbitofrontal cortex (MOFC), and the posterior cingulate cortex (PCC), were preferentially activated by decisions involving immediately available rewards. These brain structures receive strong projections from the midbrain dopamine system and have been commonly implicated in impulsive behaviour (Biederman and Faraone 2002) and drug addiction (Koob and Bloom 1988). In contrast, regions of the dorsolateral prefrontal cortex (DLPFC) and the posterior parietal cortex (PPC), brain areas directly linked to higher level cognitive functions (Miller and Cohen 2001), were engaged uniformly by intertemporal choices irrespective of delay. Furthermore, greater fronto-parietal activity was found when subjects chose longer-term options.

Following McClure *et al.*'s (2004) study, Kable and Glimcher's (2007, 2010) works focused on relating neural activity to subjective value directly (the so-called psychoneurometric approach). By doing so, regions like the *VS*, the MPFC, and the PCC were found to track the subjective value of reward at all delays and independently of participants' choices, giving rise to a single-system approach.

7.2 Lesion studies

However, neuroimaging studies can only inform us of the correlational nature of the involvement of a brain region in a particular task or cognitive process. Lesional studies, on the contrary, can give us more information on the functional role of an area when this is damaged, disconnected, or virtually disrupted by transcranial magnetic stimulation (TMS) or electrical stimulation and, therefore, of the mechanism underlying such cognitive processes. Sellitto, Ciaramelli and di Pellegrino 2010 provided evidence about the causal involvement of MOFC during the processing of intertemporal decisions. The behaviour of a group of patients with selective and almost always bilateral lesion of the MOFC was compared with that of two control groups: healthy controls and patients with brain lesions sparing the frontal cortex, matched on gender, age, education, and general cognitive functioning. All participants underwent a series of intertemporal decisions between an immediate-sooner reward and a larger-later reward. In one task, this reward was hypothetical money, in a second task, the reward was hypothetical food, and in a third task, the reward was a hypothetical coupon for diverse activities. All three tasks followed a titration procedure aimed at measuring the discounting degree of each group for each commodity. MOFC-lesioned participants showed significant increased preference for immediate rewards compared with the two control groups, for each commodity at stake. However, the normal tendency of discounting primary rewards (in this case, food) more steeply than secondary rewards (in this case, money and coupon) remained unaffected by the lesion. The increased impulsivity in MOFC-lesioned subjects relative to monetary reward held true when participants were confronted with real money (i.e., when one of their choices would have been implemented and paid for in reality). In light of the imaging evidence of a neural network consistently activated during intertemporal decisions, the MOFC is hypothesised to compute the subjective value of expected outcomes during choice by integrating different kinds of information and concerns (e.g., magnitude, delays) into a common "neural currency" and, therefore, to represent the value of both immediate and future rewards. When damaged, signals coming from the amygdala and the *VS*, signalling that the immediate pleasure attached to a certain choice would prevail, are no longer subjected to top-down control signals from lateral cortices through MOFC mediation. These data (Sellitto, Ciaramelli and di Pellegrino 2010) were recently replicated on another sample of MOFC patients (Peters and D'Esposito 2016). These subjects were not only more impulsive than healthy matched controls in a task involving a smaller immediate alternative against a larger future alternative, but they also made significantly more impulsive preference reversals as compared to the condition in which a larger-later delayed reward is an alternative to a smaller sooner, but not immediate reward, where the patients did not differ from the controls. Moreover, damage to the MOFC also affected reward valuation ratings when no choice was required, whereby magnitude attractiveness was significantly reduced in the patients, whereas delay sensitivity and valuation of immediate versus delayed rewards were not significantly different. These results corroborate the idea that MOFC is crucially involved in reward valuation as well as in the implementation of control signals coming from the lateral cortices.

Additional to these findings, a 2010 study employed TMS to virtually disrupt the DLPFC to investigate its causal role during intertemporal choice and can, therefore, be deemed a lesional study too (Figner *et al.* 2010). TMS on the left but not on the right DLPFC increased subjects' impatient choices when an immediate option was offered in the choice pair but not when the decision involved only future options. Moreover, this virtual lesion did not affect single valuation of rewards. These findings support the idea that the lateral prefrontal cortex exerts a modulatory (top-down control) role on the activity of areas as MOFC, which compute the final subjective value, during difficult intertemporal decisions (Figner *et al.* 2010).

The investigation of the role of specific brain regions in the processing of intertemporal choice was then followed by another study focusing on the role of the insular cortex (Sellitto *et al.* 2016). The *insula* has been found consistently activated in a series of human studies involving decision making towards money or other goods, such as drugs, as well as involving intertemporal choice. However, its role in such decisions has been unclear for a long time. Using a similar approach, as in Sellitto, Ciaramelli and di Pellegrino (2010), and using a task more similar toPeters and D'Esposito (2016), the behaviour of a group of patients, whose lesions encompassed the insular cortex, was compared with that of a control group of healthy participants as well as with that of a control group of brain-damaged patients whose lesions spared both the insular cortices and the frontal cortex. In this study, participants made a series of choices in two conditions. In one, they chose between smaller-immediate and larger-later monetary rewards, and in the other, both alternatives were delayed in time; namely the choice was between a smaller-sooner, but not immediate, and a larger-later amount of money. Patients with damage to the insular cortex showed reduced preferences for immediate outcomes as compared to the control groups. However, no differences emerged when considering the task in which no immediate alternative was available. Additionally, insular-lesioned patients, who had similar scores at a scale assessing depression as the other two groups, showed reduced activation when rating positive-valenced pictures but no difference with control groups in estimating temporal intervals. The authors speculate that during such choices, the *insula* may anticipate the emotional/bodily effects of different choice options and, specifically, may signal the urge to obtain a reward as soon as possible. Damage to the *insula*, therefore, would diminish the motivation to obtain a reward sooner, allowing patients to wait for larger-later outcomes, thus reducing delay discounting (see also Naqvi *et al.* 2007).

Together, these and previous findings (Sellitto, Ciaramelli and di Pellegrino 2010) allowed refining of the neural circuit underlying intertemporal choice. It has been proposed that the MOFC, along with the adjacent MPFC and the *VS*, take part in a system representing the subjective value of both immediate and delayed outcomes, under the top-down control by DLPFC (Christakou *et al.* 2009; Christakou, Brammer and Rubia 2011; Figner *et al.* 2010; Hare, Camerer and Rangel 2009; Kable and Glimcher 2007, 2010). Within this network, MOFC and adjacent medial prefrontal regions are thought to weight the long-term outcome of choices (Schoenbaum *et al.* 2009; Sellitto, Ciaramelli and di Pellegrino 2010), whereas the *VS* may convey signals of immediate pain or pleasure (Bechara and Damasio 2005; Kringelbach 2005). The *insula* is connected with both the VMPFC and the *VS* (Reynolds and Zahm 2005). Thus, during intertemporal choice, it may relay interoceptive inputs about need states to both systems, determining the strength with which individuals will pursue a reward option or the other (Weller *et al.* 2009). According to this model, damage to the MOFC would impair valuing future outcomes, leading to steep temporal discounting and impulsive choice behaviour, whereas damage to the *insula* would lead to emotionally blunt intertemporal choices based on a heuristic of quantity and, therefore, reduced temporal discounting, which is what has been observed in brain-damaged patients (Sellitto *et al.* 2016).

The data from Sellitto *et al.*'s (2016) study, however, need to be taken cautiously since the insular cortex was damaged only unilaterally and, despite an additional voxel-based lesion-symptom mapping analysis, showed that the insular cortices were only statistically associated with reduced delay discounting, however, other regions were implicated too in the overall brain damage of the patients.

7.3 Intertemporal choice and other clinical populations

Apart from brain-lesioned patients' vs. healthy participants' studies, investigating other pathological populations can also inform us about the functional and neural mechanisms of intertemporal choice and temporal discounting; the gain is double. Not only do we obtain, in this way, further insights about how discounting processes occur but we can also learn how to possibly modulate and bias discounting behaviour towards more optimal courses of action. For instance, multiple sclerosis (MS), a chronic inflammatory disease of the central nervous system that very often affects young adults (Faguy 2016), is known to be responsible for dopaminergic dysfunctioning. Dopaminergic dysregulation is, in turn, known to affect both subcortical and cortical regions of the brain and, therefore, reward sensitivity. Grippa and colleagues (Grippa *et al.* 2017) tested a group of young adults affected by relapsing-remitting MS and a sample of matched controls on an intertemporal choice task. In this task, hypothetical binary monetary choices were submitted to participants. In half of the trials, the smaller option was available immediately whereas, in the other half, it was available after a delay (smaller than that of the larger option). As a result, MS patients favoured the immediate reward less, whereas their discount rate was comparable to that of the control group in the condition involving only delayed rewards. Additionally, MS patients showed lower scores at a scale that assesses responsiveness to rewards. These findings point to a decreased immediacy bias and, therefore, to an apparent increased willingness to wait for future rewards in individuals with MS.

A personality trait that can be found in the normal population with variable intensity is alexithymia. Alexithymic people are characterised by partial elaboration of the emotional content of stimuli and, therefore, impoverished emotions' understanding and regulation (Taylor, Bagby and Parker 1991). Since the ability to anticipate the affective content of a stimulus is crucial for optimal intertemporal choice (for both immediate and later rewards), Scarpazza, Sellitto and di Pellegrino 2017 submitted participants with high and low alexithymia to a monetary intertemporal choice task as well as taking a measure of interoceptive sensitivity (by matching objective heartbeat collected via electrocardiography with concurrent subjective heartbeat counting). In this task, participants faced binary decisions with an immediate option in the choice pair as well as decisions with only delayed rewards. The main finding was high-alexithymic subjects were more impulsive than low-alexithymic ones, particularly when the sooner reward was available immediately. Additionally, the greater their sensitivity to their own visceral sensations (interoceptive sensitivity measure), the greater was their impatience. These findings point to an exaggerated valuation of immediate rewards in high alexithymia and, therefore, suggest that overweighing perceived bodily physiological signals can affect intertemporal choice.

The recent epidemics of obesity in the western world (Haslam and James 2005) due to change in lifestyle has become of great interest and governments are trying to implement policies with the aim of reducing this phenomenon. In a recent study by Schiff and colleagues (Schiff *et al.* 2016), a sample of obese participants (body mass index, BMI > 30 kg/m^2) and a sample of normal-weight participants underwent an extensive neuropsychological assessment to avoid differences between groups and then performed three intertemporal choice tasks. In these tasks, participants chose between hypothetical amounts of food, amounts of money, and hypothetical amounts of coupons, separately. The main finding was obese participants showed selective increased sensitivity for immediate smaller amounts of food (i.e., increased discount rate). This result emerged despite all rewards being hypothetical and cannot be explained by psychopathological and neuropsychological profiles. No difference between the groups emerged when considering money or coupons. Moreover, looking at all participants as a whole, an increased BMI corresponded with increased impulsivity toward food. Knowing this, is there a way to modify such poor behaviour?

7.4   The malleability of intertemporal choice

Borrowing the concept of "malleability of intertemporal choice" from a recent review (Lempert and Phelps 2016), it has been shown often that decisions among alternatives whose outcomes occur at different points in time can be subjected to biases and experimental manipulations. Lempert and Phelps 2016 attempted to categorise the different ways in which the context can influence intertemporal choice and they reached consensus on two, big, broad classes of effects. On the one hand, the so-called "framing effects" entail all the ways in which intertemporal preferences are elicited and that can influence choice. For example, one can explicitly state the default outcomes associated with each choice. For example, instead of offering participants a choice between €9 today and €22 in 30 days, offering instead a choice between an option of €9 today plus €0 in 30 days, and an option of €0 today plus €22 in 30 days. By revealing this usually "hidden-zero", participants show reduced temporal discounting (Zhao *et al.* 2015). On the other hand, the so-called incidental carry-over effects, which refer to the events that occur before the choice and that, despite being peripheral to it, can influence intertemporal preferences. A large body of research has, for instance, focused on the effect of "episodic future thinking", also usually referred as to "mental time travel". By training or priming participants to project themselves into future time, they showed lower discount rates in subsequent or concurrent intertemporal decisions (Benoit, Gilbert and Burgess 2011; Bertossi *et al.* 2016). Beyond this categorisation, intertemporal decisions and, therefore, one's degree of discounting, can be intuitively biased towards any of the two extreme sides of the continuum between impulsivity and self-control.

As discussed above (Schiff *et al.* 2016), there are nowadays increasing incidences of eating disorders, and this has been linked with failure in the implementation of self-control during food decisions and, therefore, to poor intertemporal choice. Any of us has experienced at some point in our life the increased desire for tempting, but very unhealthy, food on the spur of the moment, maybe under the effect of stress. Sellitto and di Pellegrino (2014, 2016) established a protocol aimed to reduce impulsive food choice by healthy women by using a novel procedure. The rationale of this study lies in the idea that the ability to control behaviour is enhanced in contexts in which errors occur more often. Errors, indeed, represent lapses in performance (and utility) and signal the need to increase the on-line control for current and future behaviour, thus contributing to the optimisation of the decision-making performance. After collecting the BMI from a sample of healthy young women — in order to double check that this was in the normal range — participants rated their current hunger level and their willingness to eat several sweet foods at that very moment. Afterwards, the two foods with the highest rating for each participant were selected and used as stimuli in the two following tasks. In the first task, participants were required to give or not give responses. One of the two foods was used as a cue in easy trials, whereby it was not difficult for the subject to refrain from giving a response when a stop signal appeared superimposed on the go signal. The other food, instead, was used in difficult trials; the stop signal requiring participants to refrain from giving a go response appeared superimposed on the go signal but delayed enough so that they would make an error about 50% of the time. After (implicitly) learning the association between one food with a small amount of errors and the other food with a large amount of errors, participants underwent a series of intertemporal choices about the two foods, separately. As a result, participants showed a reduced degree of discounting when making choices towards the food previously associated with a high number of errors in performance. However, this was true only in participants with a low level of hunger at the time of the experiment. These findings reveal that errors, which are motivationally salient events that recruit cognitive control, may be effective in reducing impulsive choice and immediate gratification for the sake of future benefits but only by crucially accounting for strong motivational signals (such as hunger).

7.5 Conclusions

Over the last two decades or so, there has been a substantial increase in the number of laboratory studies that have examined how humans and animals make decisions involving future outcomes, namely intertemporal decisions. One reason for this increased research activity is that steeply discounting the value of delayed outcomes is strongly correlated with poor decision making and substance use (MacKillop *et al.*

2011; Yi, Mitchell and Bickel 2010). There is evidence that abnormal discounting of delayed reward represents a behavioural, or at least an antecedent, marker of various forms of addiction, obesity, problem gambling, and risky sexual behavioural (Bickel *et al.* 2012). With the use of functional magnetic resonance imaging in health individuals, as well as lesion studies in the neurological population, we are now beginning to characterise the neurobiological bases and functional mechanisms of such behaviour in humans, and to link work on this domain from cognitive neuroscience, psychology, and behavioural economics. Although recent work has provided critical insight into the nature of temporal decision making, there are still many questions left unanswered. For example, there is no consensus among researchers about how intertemporal choice preferences actually arise. One intriguing possibility is that optimal temporal decision making requires prospection; the ability to project oneself into the future, which is strongly linked to the functioning of the MOFC (Sellitto, Ciaramelli and di Pellegrino 2010). In view of this, during intertemporal choice, prospection may allow individuals to simulate future experiences associated with rewards and, thus, upregulate valuation of delayed options based on the resulting affective states. Future research investigating these aspects would be most valuable in illuminating the subtleties of intertemporal preferences and temporal discounting.

References

Bechara, A., and Damasio, A.R., (2005), «The Somatic Marker Hypothesis: A Neural Theory of Economic Decision», *Games and Economic Behavior*, 52, pp. 336-372.

Benoit, R.G., Gilbert, S.J., and Burgess, P.W., (2011), «A Neural Mechanism Mediating the Impact of Episodic Prospection on Farsighted Decisions», *The Journal of Neuroscience*, 31(18), pp. 6771-6779.

Berns, G. S., Laibson, D., and Loewenstein, G., (2007), «Intertemporal Choice – Toward an Integrative Framework», *Trends in Cognitive Sciences*, 11(11), pp. 482-488.

Bertossi, E., Tesini, C., Cappelli, A., and Ciaramelli, E., (2016), «Ventromedial Prefrontal Damage Causes a Pervasive Impairment of Episodic Memory And Future Thinking», *Neuropsychologia*, 90, pp. 12-24.

Bickel, W.K., Jarmolowicz, D.P., Mueller, E.T., Koffarnus, M.N., and Gatchalianm, K.M., (2012), «Excessive Discounting of Delayed Reinforcers as a Trans-Disease Process Contributing to Addiction and other Disease-Related Vulnerabilities: Emerging Evidence», *Pharmacology & Therapeutics*, 134, pp. 287-297.

Bickel, W.K., Landes, R.D., Christensen, D.R., Jackson, L., Jones, B.A., Kurth-nelson, Z., and Redish, A.D., (2011), «Single- and Cross-Commodity Discounting Among Cocaine Addicts: The Commodity and its Temporal Location Determine Discounting Rate», *Psychopharmacology*, 217(2), pp. 177-187.

Biederman, J. and Faraone, S.V. (2002), «Current Concepts on The Neurobiology of Attention-Deficit/Hyperactivity Disorder», *Journal of Attention Disorders*, 6(1), S7-16.

Christakou, A., Brammer, M., and Rubia, K., (2011), «Maturation of Limbic Corticostriatal Activation and Connectivity Associated with Developmental Changes in Temporal Discounting», *Neuroimage*, 54, pp. 1344-1354.

Christakou, A., Brammer, M., Giampietro, V., and Rubia, K., (2009), «Right Ventromedial and Dorsolateral Prefrontal Cortices Mediate Adaptive Decisions Under Ambiguity by Integrating Choice Utility And Outcome Evaluation», *The Journal of Neuroscience*, 29, pp. 11020-11028.

Dalley, J.W., and Robbins, T.W., (2017), «Fractionating Impulsivity: Neuropsychiatric Implications», *Nature Publishing Group*, 18(3), pp. 158-171.

Faguy, K. (2016), «Multiple Sclerosis: An Update», *Radiologic Technology*, 87, pp. 529-550.

Figner, B., Knoch, D., Johnson, E.J., Krosch, A.R., Lisanby, S.H., Fehr, E., and Weber, E.U, (2010), «Lateral Prefrontal Cortex and Self-Control in Intertemporal Choice», *Nature Neuroscience,* 13(5), pp. 538-539

Frederick, S., Loewenstein, G., and O'Donoghue, T., (2002), «Time Discounting and Time Preference: A Critical Review». *Journal of Economic Literature,* 40(2), pp. 351-401.

Frost, R., and Mcnaughton, N., (2017), «The Neural Basis of Delay Discounting: A Review and Preliminary Model», *Neuroscience and Biobehavioral Reviews,* 79, pp. 48-65.

Grippa, E., Sellitto, M., Scarpazza, C., Mattioli, F., and di Pellegrino, G., (2017), «Multiple Sclerosis Reduces Sensitivity to Immediate Reward During Decision Making» *Behavioral Neuroscience,* 131(4), pp. 325-336.

Hare, T.A., Camerer, C.F., and Rangel, A., (2009), «Self-control in Decision-Making Involves Modulation of the Vmpfc Valuation System», *Science,* 324, pp. 646-648.

Haslam, D.W., and James, W.P., (2005), «Obesity», *Lancet,* 366 (9492), pp. 1197-1209.

Kable, J.W., and Glimcher, P.W., (2007), «The Neural Correlates of Subjective Value During Intertemporal Choice», *Nature Neuroscience,* 10(12), pp. 1625-1633.

Kable, J.W., and Glimcher, P.W. (2010), «An "As Soon As Possible" Effect in Human Intertemporal Decision Making: Behavioral Evidence and Neural Mechanisms», *Journal of Neurophysiology,* 103, pp. 2513-2531.

Kalenscher, T., and Pennartz, C.M.A., (2008), «Is a Bird in the Hand Worth Two in the Future? The Neuroeconomics of Intertemporal Decision-Making», *Progress in Neurobiology,* 84, pp. 284-315.

Koob, G.F., and Bloom, F.E. (1988), «Cellular and Molecular Mechanisms of Drug Dependence», *Science,* 242(4879), pp. 715-723.

Kringelbach, M.L., (2005), «The Human Orbitofrontal Cortex: Linking Reward to Hedonic Experience», *Nature Reviews Neuroscience,* 6, pp. 691-702.

Lempert, K.M., and Phelps, E.A., (2016), «The Malleability of Intertemporal Choice», *Trends in Cognitive Sciences,* 20(1), pp. 64-74.

MacKillop, J., Amlung, M.T., Few, L.R., Ray, L.A., Sweet, L.H., and Munafò, M.R. (2011), «Delayed Reward Discounting and Addictive Behavior: A Meta-Analysis», *Psychopharmacology,* 216, pp. 305-321.

McClure, S.M., Laibson, D.I., Loewenstein, G., and Cohen, J.D., (2004), «Separate Neural Systems Value Immediate and Delayed Monetary Rewards», *Science*, 306(5695), pp. 503-507.

McClure, S.M., Ericson, K.M., Laibson, D.I., Loewenstein, G., and Cohen, J.D., (2007), «Time Discounting for Primary Rewards», *The Journal of Neuroscience*, 27(21), pp. 5796-5804.

Miller, E.K. and Cohen, J.D., (2001), «An Integrative Theory of Prefrontal Cortex Function», *Annual Review of Neuroscience*, 24, pp. 167-202.

Myerson, J., Green, L., Hanson, J.S., Holt, D.D., and Estle, S.J., (2003), «Discounting Delayed and Probabilistic Rewards: Processes and Traits», *Journal of Economic Psychology*, 24, pp. 619-635.

Naqvi, N.H., Rudrauf, D., Damasio, H., and Bechara, A., (2007), «Damage to the Insula Disrupts Addiction to Cigarette Smoking», *Science*, 315(531), pp. 531-534.

Peters, J., and Büchel, C., (2011), «The Neural Mechanisms of Inter-Temporal Decision-Making: Understanding Variability», *Trends in Cognitive Sciences*, 15(5), pp. 1-13.

Peters, J., and Esposito, M.D., (2016), «Effects of Medial Orbitofrontal Cortex Lesions on Self-Control in Intertemporal Choice Report Effects of Medial Orbitofrontal Cortex Lesions on Self-Control in Intertemporal Choice», *Current Biology*, 26, pp. 2625-2628.

Reynolds, S.M., and Zahm, D.S. (2005), «Specificity in the Projections of Prefrontal And Insular Cortex To Ventral Striatopallidum And The Extended Amygdala», *The Journal of Neuroscience*, 25, pp. 11757-11767.

Scarpazza, C., Sellitto, M., and di Pellegrino, G., (2017), «Now or Not-Now? The Influence of Alexithymia On Intertemporal Decision-Making», *Brain and Cognition*, 114, pp. 20-28.

Schiff, S., Amodio, P., Testa, G., Nardi, M., Montagnese, S., Caregaro, L., di Pellegrino, D., and Sellitto, M., (2016), «Impulsivity Toward Food Reward Is Related to BMI: Evidence From Intertemporal Choice In Obese And Normal-Weight Individuals», *Brain and Cognition*, 110, pp. 112-119.

Schoenbaum, G., Roesch, M.R., Stalnaker, T.A., and Takahashi, Y.K., (2009), «A New Perspective on the Role of the Orbitofrontal Cortex in Adaptive Behavior», *Nature Reviews Neuroscience*, 10, pp. 885-92.

Seinstra, M.S., Sellitto, M., and Kalenscher, T., (2017), «Rate Maximization and Hyperbolic Discounting in Human Experiential Intertemporal Decision Making», *Behavioral Ecology*, 29(1), pp. 193-203.

Sellitto, M., and di Pellegrino, G. (2014), «Errors Affect Hypothetical Intertemporal Food Choice in Women», *PLOS ONE*, 9(9), e108422.

Sellitto, M., and di Pellegrino, G. (2016), «Errors as a Means of Reducing Impulsive Food Choice», *Journal of Visualized Experiments*, 112, e53283.

Sellitto, M., Ciaramelli, E., and di Pellegrino, G. (2010), «Myopic Discounting of Future Rewards After Medial Orbitofrontal Damage in Humans», *The Journal of Neuroscience*, 30(49), pp. 16429 -16436.

Sellitto, M., Ciaramelli, E., and di Pellegrino, G. (2011), «The Neurobiology of Intertemporal Choice: Insight From Imaging and Lesion Studies», *Reviews in the Neurosciences*, 22(5), pp. 565-574.

Sellitto, M., Ciaramelli, E., Mattioli, F., and di Pellegrino, G., (2016), «Reduced sensitivity To Sooner Reward During Intertemporal Decision-Making Following Insula Damage In Humans», *Frontiers in Behavioral Neuroscience*, 9(367).

Story, G.W., Vlaev, I., Seymour, B., Darzi, A., and Dolan, R.J., (2014), «Does Temporal Discounting Explain Unhealthy Behavior? A Systematic Review and Reinforcement Learning Perspective», *Frontiers in Behavioral Neuroscience*, 8, pp. 1-20.

Taylor, G.J., Bagby, R.M., and Parker, J.D. (1991), «The Alexithymia Construct. A Potential Paradigm For Psychosomatic Medicine», *Psychosomatics*, 32, pp. 153-164.

Weller, J.A., Levin, I.P., Shiv, B., and Bechara, A., (2009), «The Effects of Insula Damage on Decision-Making for Risky Gains and Losses», *Society for Neuroscience*, 4, pp. 347-358.

Yi, R., Mitchell, S.H., and Bickel, W.K. (2010). «Delay Discounting and Substance Abuse-Dependence», in G.J. Madden and W.K. Bickel (Eds.), *Impulsivity: The Behavioral and Neurological Science of Discounting*, pp. 191-211.

Zhao, C., Jiang, C., Zhou, L., Li, S., Rao, L., Zheng, R., and Davelaar, E.J. (2015), «The Hidden Opportunity Cost of Time Effect on Intertemporal Choice», *Frontiers in Psychology*, 6, pp. 1-7.

Part III
The Brain in Economics

8. From Mental Accounting to Neuroaccounting
by Frank G.H. Hartmann

It is wrongly assumed by many that accounting as a discipline is a relatively recent development in human history. This may be the case for accounting as an *academic* discipline but accounting as a practical and even professional discipline is amongst the oldest of human faculties or, at least, amongst the oldest recorded ones (Carmona and Ezzamel 2007). Indeed, the relationship between accounting and the development of humanity at large is well documented across the academic literature, recently even leading to speculation about the way in which the development of accounting and human evolution may or even must have interacted (Dickhaut *et al.* 2010). Despite such quite convincing arguments concerning the intense relationship between accounting and *humanities*, the contemporary associations of many academics, practitioners and the general public with 'accounting' as a field of human interest are mainly technical and toolbox in nature. A simple Google-search on the term 'accounting' suffices to confirm this orientation in popular thought. A similar Google-search on the term 'accountant' also returns disappointing results, with stereotypes on accountants' alleged physiognomy and mental and social capacities (and limitations thereof) dominating the scene (see for interesting discussions and examples, among others: Beard 1994; Carnegie and Napier 2010).

I think this equation of accounting with a set of technical standards and instruments is a serious pity for a variety of reasons. First of all, I think it has led to an unbalance between the academic thrust in contemporary accounting research and the societal and individual desires and needs for accounting knowledge. Take the role of accounting within business firms as an example. Throughout the last decades of increased industrialisation, the increasing gaps between ownership and management of firms, and between top- and secondary levels within the firm have aggravated the problems of 'controlling' the decentralised firm. The 'crises' that occur from time to time serve to illustrate not only the crucial role of accounting systems in firms and societies but also the problems such systems face, as well as the needs policy makers, owners, managers and the common public have for better accounting. The Enron crisis that occurred at the start of this millennium, as well as the more recent world financial crisis, have both been directly connected with the role of accounting (see, among many others, for example, Gordon 2002; Bezemer 2010). Second, and paradoxically, it has led to what could be called a 'marginalisation' of accounting in current business practice. Accounting is not seen by most for what I believe it is, namely, a language to depict and communicate the economic reality of firms and their subparts to stakeholders. Rather, the technical toolbox-orientation in many practical understandings of accounting has made it a discipline of *ex-post* control, regulation and audit. It is, thus, as some have commented, wrongly seen as merely a restricting ('coercive') practice rather than a supporting ('enabling') one (Adler and Borys 1996).

In this paper, I identify and address some issues in current academic accounting research to support a plea that I will make towards the adoption of neuroscience methods in accounting research. I will briefly sketch the main current theoretical streams in accounting research, necessarily in broad, coarse and biased strokes, and argue how these streams contribute to accounting knowledge. I will also argue that each of these streams has specific challenges when it comes to informing accounting practice. Finally, I will draw some conclusions that aim to show that adopting neuroscience methods has theoretical rather than simply methodological implications.

8.1 Accounting, accountants and accounting research[1]

Empirical accounting research has developed over the last decades at an enormous rate when considering the quantity of both accounting journals and papers. Also in qualitative terms, the growth and development has been impressive. When focusing on empirical work in accounting, even a short glance at the statistical sections of typical accounting papers today suffices when compared to similar papers some decades ago. I believe this growth is easily observable within the accounting discipline but, when compared to other disciplines, accounting is still a 'net consumer' of theories, concepts and insights from disciplines higher up in the pecking order.

---

[1] A previous version of this and the next sections appeared in Hartmann (2017).

Economics including its behavioural branch and psychology seem to be the theoretical drivers of accounting research, with sociology in a firm third position. Reversely, there seems to be very little interest in accounting research in these disciplines. Thus, although accounting may be seen by accounting researchers to have fundamental relationships with humanity, this does not reflect in a knowledge transfer from accounting to humanities. Overall, these and other considerations have led to worries that academic accounting research is stagnant (Basu 2012; Moser 2012; Waymire 2012) and locked-in in a position of an applied science at best. I feel this poor position is undeserved.

I think it would not harm us to understand the need for accounting knowledge from the perspective of the accountant-practitioner. Suppose (s)he seeks knowledge and explores the academic accounting literature. What would s(he) see? What must be striking is an apparent overall low interest in the accountant-practitioner and his or her worries. Despite being an applied science, accounting research tends to be about more or less abstract phenomena and less about the issues that real actors in real situations face and can address. This divergence has three strongly related causes. First, the growth in accounting research's sophistication has mainly made the content matter presented in a format unattractive to the accountant-practitioner. I always like to illustrate this issue with a comment by Rothbard (1973, p. 31) on the status of academic *economics*:

> Let the nonspecialist in economics pick up a journal article or monograph today and contrast it with one of a generation ago, and the first thing that will strike him is the incomprehensibility of the modern product. The older work was written in ordinary language and, with moderate effort, was comprehensible to the layman; the current work is virtually all mathematics, algebraic or geometric.

Of course, accounting research is not economic theory, even if it is a big consumer of the same, but I believe it would be a fair statement about the accountant-practitioners' current state of accounting research, if the quote above were rewritten to read 'accounting' where it now says 'economics'.

This is not merely a matter of problems of interpretation of statistics and mathematics but goes deeper. The second reason, or so I would like to argue, is, therefore, the decreasing ability – or at least inclination – of academic researchers to conduct their analyses with the human actor in mind. This means that much of our current academic work disregards the agency implications of research questions and answers. This could be addressed by acknowledging how accounting knowledge could add to an agent's behavioural or cognitive repertoire. Let me fine-tune this statement by pointing out the third cause of the divergence of academic accounting research with accounting practice, which relates to the question whether economics (or psychology, or sociology) should be seen as a natural science, following the naturalistic methods and language of these sciences, or as a social science (which wrongly mimics the methods and language of the natural sciences).

For accounting, I propose that this question is not so much rooted in the methods but rather in the level of analyses of the theories we develop and test.

8.2 Levels of analysis in accounting research

The term 'level of analysis' has various meanings from which it is indicated at what level (atoms, molecules, brain processes, humans, social systems, etc.) we collect our *empirical* data. However, a more fundamental, though related, conceptualisation of such levels specifies at which *theoretical* level we aim to discover patterns or, in other words, in what conceptual networks our data interpretation takes place. By choosing a level of analysis, researchers fixate the phenomena they are interested in, as well as specify in which causal network of antecedents and consequences they consider this phenomenon worthy of interpretation. Let us return to the accounting practitioner; how could we specify how (s)he profits from current accounting research? Distinguishing between at least three levels of analyses in current accounting research may help to understand better how to define practical accounting knowledge or obstacles to such knowledge in current mainstream academic accounting literature. The three levels of analysis that make sense in my view relate to the personal level, the sub-personal level, and the supra-personal level.

At the personal level of analysis (the accountant as free agent), we would expect to find studies where the outcome immediately informs accountants about practical solutions to practical problems. Moreover, at this level of analysis, knowledge is cast in terms that are meaningful, interpretable, and actionable to the agent. Although this relates, in a literal sense, to trivial (i.e. day-to-day applicable) knowledge, these characteristics are not trivial themselves. In fact, such simple terms as 'meaningfulness' and 'usefulness' are themselves a matter of deep philosophical debate in the social sciences. An example may help understand the issues at hand. For instance, it is one thing to conclude that accountants may suffer from social bias in decision-making settings (see Hartmann and Maas 2010)[2] and quite another thing to help accountants solve, evade or avoid settings in which social bias may happen. In fact, the distinction between having knowledge *about an agent* and knowledge *that is useful to the agent* is fundamental, and far from trivial. At the very least, it requires alignment between the accountants' and academic researchers' conceptualisation of the accountants' work, which I believe can be done. Although practitioners talk about their work in trivial, 'folk' terms and academic researchers seem uneasy to deal with that, the level of analysis that considers the accountant-professional as both an actor and a user of academic texts seems to hold most promised for an applied discipline. Here, the contribution of academic accounting lies in developing the accountant's folk theory (i.e. theory in use) of his or her own behaviour.

At the supra-personal level of analysis (the accountant as part of a larger system), we find academic output showing how accountants' behaviours operate in larger structures, such as (economic) markets. Typical examples include economic models of organisations or markets in which accountants or auditors function as point-masses that follow certain micro-economic laws, and in their interactions with other such point-masses to reach certain equilibria. These studies can be considered the 'as-if' type, meaning that behaviour of organisations and markets is explained through the agency of accountants, 'as-if' they were maximising utility, averting risks, and avoiding losses. In behavioural economics, the agent acts 'as-if' (s)he is doing *mental accounting*, which is a specific bias in the way monetary amounts from different sources are assigned different value (see, e.g., Bonner, Clor-Proell and Koonce 2014). The metaphor of the accountant as 'point-mass' signifies that, rather than being a free actor, the accountant behaves in line with certain law-like principles. Here the barrier between the academic analyses and the folk theory of the practitioner becomes most visible, not merely because of a fundamental difference in vocabulary, but rather in the outright denial of the accountant as an individual free-willed agent. The question here is how larger-system optimal structures can inform individual agents and, if they can, whether they should. Again, the question comes up: what counts as true accounting knowledge here? No short answer exists but it is important to take care in translating

---

[2] Hartmann and Maas (2010) investigated under what conditions business unit (BU) controllers engaged in the creation of budgetary slack under social pressure. They found evidence of an interactive effect of personality (Machiavellianism) involvement in decision making. This may be seen as having practical consequences in terms of what people to hire, the way to design roles and functions, and how to assess and evaluate individual performance, for example, yet those consequences depend on a variety of other factors not researched in this study.

this type of knowledge to the type of knowledge that adds to the accountant's folk theory.

Most recently, a third level of analysis has been introduced to the accounting literature, which lies at the sub-personal level of analysis (the accountant as a collection of internal cognitive programmes or automatic, behavioural processes). Under the explosive growth of cognitive and social neuroscience elsewhere, some early adopter papers have investigated neural, biological, drivers of the accountant's agency. Eskenazi, Hartmann and Rietdijk (2016) form a good example. They build on Hartmann and Maas (2010), predicting that the effect of social pressure can be explained by the accountant's biological make-up. Mirror neuron system functionality is used to explain the vulnerability of accountants. Different from the personal level of analysis and similar to the supra-personal level of analysis, this sub-personal level of analysis does not provide immediate input for agency. In other words, and to give a practical example, it is simply impossible for an accountant to change the biological structure that, apparently, (co-)determines behaviour. However, the difference between sub- and supra-personal levels of analysis is fundamental. The sub-personal aims to discover drivers of behaviour of the person, including such 'mystical' drivers as 'biases', 'preferences' and 'moods', and are, therefore, best understood as real constituents of personal behaviour. Supra-personal knowledge lacks this quality, both because of its 'as-if' nature and because of its (implicit) denial of individual agency. Overall, the knowledge consequences of this level for individual accounting agents also deserves fundamental scrutiny, even if the outcome is that true accounting knowledge cannot be defined as this level. Currently, the problematic relationship between folk concepts, part of the vocabulary in which the practitioner conceptualises his or her actions and practices, and fundamental neuroscience start to be acknowledged. For example, Francken and Slors (2014) point to difficulties in mapping concepts across these levels of analyses for not merely empirical but rather conceptual reasons. It is, therefore, that I believe more attention is needed to such mappings and more vigilance is required in translating sub-personal patterns to the personal level of action. In any case, this means that I believe that neuroscience is wrongly assumed to give us 'just better methods', but rather, it gives us potentially more fundamental explanations. These occur at the theoretical level, not at the methodological and, ultimately, may or may not affect accountants' folk-theoretic repertoire.

8.3 Conclusions

It is easier to speculate than to document about the way in which accounting research and accounting researchers are going or should go, as researchers and their research differ substantially in terms of scope, intellectual orientation, and research topic. However, the mere existence of groups of accounting academics as well as academic accounting journals, both suggest that accounting is a topic of academic work that has, at least, some common characteristics in the large variety of accounting streams, themes and researchers.

In this paper I have tried to establish a preliminary argument for a further understanding of the divide between accounting theory and accounting practice based on the explicit recognition of the various levels of analyses, of which I have elaborated only three now. Much of this is very sketchy, potentially misguided, and certainly open for further analysis and discussion. However, recognising the levels, their meaning and their (limited) significance to address practical concerns by practical accountants may be a way to structure any discussion about the future of our discipline. As such, these levels of analysis in contemporary accounting research may point to three distinct barriers between theory and practice, which may serve as clear targets for reconciliation. This may help to take away the feeling of stagnation in the intellectual debate, which accounting as a fundamental part of humanity cannot afford (cf. Basu 2012; Moser 2012; Waymire 2012).

References

Adler, P. S., & Borys, B., (1996), «Two Types of Bureaucracy: Enabling and Coercive», *Administrative Science Quarterly*, pp. 61-89.

Basu, S., (2012), «How Can Accounting Researchers Become More Innovative?», *Accounting Horizons*, 26, pp. 851-870.

Beard, V. (1994), «Popular Culture and Professional Identity: Accountants in the Movies», *Accounting, Organizations and Society*, 19(3), pp. 303-318.

Bezemer, D. J. (2010), «Understanding Financial Crisis Through Accounting Models», *Accounting, Organizations and Society*, 35(7), pp. 676-688.

Bonner, S. E., Clor-Proell, S. M., & Koonce, L. (2014), «Mental Accounting And Disaggregation Based on the Sign and Relative Magnitude of Income Statement Items», *The Accounting Review*, 89(6), pp. 2087-2114.

Carmona, S., & Ezzamel, M. (2007), «Accounting and Accountability in Ancient Civilizations: Mesopotamia and Ancient Egypt», *Accounting, Auditing & Accountability Journal*, 20(2), pp. 177-209.

Carnegie, G. D., & Napier, C. J. (2010), «Traditional Accountants and Business Professionals: Portraying the Accounting Profession After Enron», *Accounting, Organizations and Society*, 35(3), pp. 360-376.

Dickhaut, J., Basu, S., McCabe, K., & Waymire, G. (2010), «Neuroaccounting: Consilience Between the Biologically Evolved Brain and Culturally Evolved Accounting Principles», *Accounting Horizons*, 24(2), pp. 221-255.

Eskenazi, P. I., Hartmann, F. G., & Rietdijk, W. J. (2016), «Why Controllers Compromise on Their Fiduciary Duties: EEG Evidence on the Role of The Human Mirror Neuron System», *Accounting, Organizations and Society*, 50, pp. 41-50.

Francken, J. C., & Slors, M. (2014), «From Commonsense to Science, and Back: The Use of Cognitive Concepts in Neuroscience», *Consciousness and Cognition*, 29, pp. 248-258.

Gordon, J. N. (2002), «What Enron Means for the Management and Control of the Modern Business Corporation: Some Initial Reflections», *The University of Chicago Law Review*, pp. 1233-1250.

Hartmann, F. G. (2017), «Accounting Research: Between Natural Science and Practice», *Revista Contabilidade & Finanças*, 28(73), pp. 7-10.

Hartmann, F. G., & Maas, V. S. (2010), «Why Business Unit Controllers Create Budget Slack: Involvement in Management, Social Pressure, and Machiavellianism», *Behavioral Research in Accounting*, 22(2), pp. 27-49.

Moser, D., (2012), «Is Accounting Research Stagnant?», *Accounting Horizons*, 26, pp. 845-850.

Rothbard, M. N. (1973), «Praxeology as the Method of the Social Sciences», *Phenomenology and the Social Sciences*, 2, pp. 323-35.

Waymire, G., (2012), «Introduction for Essays on the State of Accounting Scholarship», *Accounting Horizons*, 26, pp. 817-819.

9. Neuromarketing: a Scientific Frontier for Marketing Research
by Gianpiero Lugli

Although firms invested as much as $40 billion in marketing research in the year 2015, they still pursued the wrong course of action in their relationships with consumers. The importance of these mistakes may be better conceived taking into account that:

- Only 10% of new grocery products survived in the market beyond one year after their launch;
- Many advertising campaigns have a low efficacy score in terms of engagement, arousal and shared emotions;
- Product proliferation and consequent choice overload may negatively influence the buying process.

The reason for these shortcomings of the actual marketing research is to be found in its target; being based on interviews and focus groups; marketing research addresses the cognitive mind while 95% of shopping decisions are taken through the activation of our limbic system. To reduce marketing mistakes, we need, therefore, to change marketing research.

9.1 How to improve marketing research

It is not enough to study shopping behaviour *ex post*, as well as how and what consumers purchased; we have also to investigate how consumers take their decision and why they purchase product A instead of product B. If we want to improve our marketing decisions, we have to reject the Neoclassical Economic axioms of consumer preferences that are given, stable, insensible to framing and revealed through the actual choices. What is needed is a cross fertilisation of marketing with neuroscience and cognitive psychology; only going out of the boundaries of a single discipline is it possible to improve our understanding of economic behaviour and so help firms in their decision making. We do not have to abandon traditional marketing research but rather complete it with a new approach that focuses on biometric indicators; physical reactions to a stimulus are in fact automatic and, therefore, cannot be biased. There are many neuroscientific technologies of different complexity and costs that may be used to improve our knowledge of consumer behaviour.

According to Neuroscience and Behavioural Economics, buying decisions are taken by combining automatic mental processes with controlled mental processes; i.e., emotions with cognition. Our buying decisions are also influenced by our relationships with other consumers because our mirror neurons make us capable of perceiving emotions felt by others. To minimise our regret in buying, we are also prone to imitate others' choices; this socialisation of the buying process may well drive us to select products different to the ones we prefer. The framing of choice by clustering the assortment in categories, improving access and visibility by merchandising, anchoring price to enhance product value and showing pricing alternatives according our loss aversion, are all suitable ways to direct our buying behaviour according to the seller's benefit.

9.2 Information and choice

To choose, we need information about the available alternatives but this does not mean that the more information we have, the better our choices will be. Our cognitive mind may process only a very limited amount of information; therefore, plentiful information reduces our attention and, in the case of information overload, we simply cannot take any decision. Information processed by our cognitive mind plays a marginal role in our choices; there is in fact much more information that we are not aware of that plays an important role in our decision making. Evolution and our experiences have stored information in our limbic system and drive our choices before the involvement of the cognitive mind that simply confirms and justifies emotional decisions already taken. More than rational human beings, we are human beings always engaged in rationalising our emotional choices.

Our subliminal mind does process information and take decisions without any effort and cognition, automatically; it works by association, confronting the actual situation we are in with the genetic and personal experience. The limbic system processes information by neuron firing and hormone release (cortisol, dopamine, oxitocine, …) that produce primary emotion, such as anger, fear, disgust, happiness, sadness, surprise, and contempt.

9.3 Emotions and choice

It is the trade-off between positive and negative emotions that drives our decision to buy. When we see a product that we like, we anticipate the pleasure to use it through an activation of our reward system (nucleus *accumbens*). The forecasted pleasure is then matched with the pain we feel when we see the price we ought to pay to get the desired product; this neuron conflict may lead to a purchase or not, depending on the prevailing emotions. Firms have learned by market experience how to bend the neuron conflict towards the buying option. Product innovation, as well as an artificial scarcity, can sustain our desire exciting the nucleus *accumbens*. It is also possible to manage the neuron trade off, reducing the pain perceived in the payment process by allowing the use of credit cards or by instalment payments with zero interest rate. Because our limbic system cannot anticipate future emotions, payment by credit card is emotionally equivalent to a gift. As for the zero interest rate applied for instalment payments, it is clearly an oxymoron; you do not need to explain the interest rate to make the buyer pay it. All you have to do to minimise the *insula* activation, is to embed the interest rate in the price and say there is no interest to pay.

Manufacturers and retailers alike have learned to stimulate emotions in order to drive the buying process. By claiming that a product is free from harmful ingredients, or that they contain pharmaceutical substances that prevent / cure certain illnesses, firms create a kind of fear that may help their sales. Again, by offering so called fair trade products, firms rely on our empathy in order to drive the buying process. When retailers say their brand is as good as the industrial one but costs less, they aim to create a feeling of regret in those buyers who insist on purchasing industrial brands. The regret is an emotion driven by our cognitive mind; it is the doubt that we are taking the wrong decision. Some consumers that feel regret while listening to the retailer's claim may decide to shift their choice to the retailer's brand.

However, the most important tool that firms use to drive our purchase process is price promotion. The saving desire is very strong in all segments of the population and, sometimes, a promotion may be framed to be irresistible. Offers of more quantity for free or take three and pay for two reduce the *insula* activation and make consumers buy products that are far from their preferences; when you accept a promotion, you "buy" the price, not the product. Again, you would not buy the same discounted product at a full price equal to the discounted one.

9.4 How to improve advertising with the help of affective computing technology

In their relationships, human beings employ different channels of different importance; content may be channelled through:

- Words, which account for 7%;
- Voice modulation (height, tone, time, rhythm, pause), which accounts for 38%;
- Facial expressions and posture, which account for 55%.

Facial expressions are not learned because they are a product of evolution; therefore, it is possible to detect emotions reading facial expression all over the world. The only difference provided by culture is the intensity of emotions shown by facial expressions. When we relate to other people, we pay attention to the words and not to voice modulation or facial expressions. Our cognitive mind cannot process facial expressions because it functions in series and, if we pay attention to the words, there is no spare capacity to process facial expressions. We also cannot read the facial expression of people we are talking to because they last for too short a time, less than half a second. To read and measure emotions driven by a stimulus, we need software that can detect even the shortest micro-expressions. This is the role of affecting computing technology. The biologic reaction to a marketing stimulus may, thus, be measured in order to help firms in their decision making. The Economic Department of Parma University has conducted some experiments in the optimisation of advertising. We observed facial expressions of people watching an advertising campaign in order to develop performance indicators; of course, firms should apply this technology before going out with their message in order to choose between different alternatives according to their performance. What follows concerns an advertising campaign by Dash, which mixes emotional and rational content as well as famous testimonials with ordinary people.

Affecting computing technology allows computing of many performance indicators; in the case of Dash, we have computed:

- The engagement, measured as a total amount of emotions felt;
- The valence, measured as the prevalence of positive/negative emotions;
- The arousal, measured as the intensity (from 0 to 1) of the emotions felt;
- The emotional sharing, measured as the overlapping of testimonial facial expressions with viewers' facial expressions.

Of course, these indicators have to be computed second by second as well as for the entire slot.

The engagement is a general indicator of performance; an advertising campaign with a high engagement ratio means that it has been able to break consumer barriers and catch people's attention. The valence ratio should be considered with regard to the emotions the firm wants to generate, which may be positive or negative. The arousal is an indicator that might be used to detect content that will be more/less easily memorised and, therefore, to select content that might be eliminated in order to reduce the length without significantly reducing performance. The arousal might also be used to decide the positioning of the brand, which should be the furthest possible from content with a high score in this indicator. Finally, the overlapping of facial expressions is an indicator that the content has been understood; the emotion sharing is a form of brain communication by mirror neurons that means success at a limbic level. In Tab.1 are some results of the Dash experiment.

9.5 How to improve price promotion with the help of affective computing technology

In order to sustain the efficacy of a discounted price, retailers know they have to frame the promotion with the full price. In fact, our cognitive mind needs an anchor to assess the value of the promotion. The anchoring of the promotional price to the full price shows a limit of our rationality; assessing only in relative terms means that the retailer could (and does) increase the full price just before the promotion to improve our value assessment. Nevertheless, it is not just our cognitive mind that is activated by a promotion; also the limbic system comes into play to assess the cheapness of a product. Perception of cheapness may change according to the typestyle fonts of the promotional price and full price. Retailers use a small font for the full price and a larger font for the promotional price; we think they should do the opposite in order to improve our perception of cheapness. Our limbic system works by association and, therefore, a small price is perceived as a reduced price (Tab.2)

Again, the perception of cheapness may be managed through the positioning of the two prices. Retailers put the full price high on the left and the discounted price low on the right, while the best solution would be to write the two prices on the same line. In fact, if we consider the lateralisation of our brain, a stimulus shown low on the right is processed slowly by the left hemisphere where our cognitive mind is located. On the contrary, a stimulus shown high on the left is processed by the right hemisphere where our emotional mind is located. In the case of a vertical portrayal of cheapness, retailers should do the opposite of what they actually do.

However, we suspect that a vertical portrayal of cheapness is not the best solution. Neuroscience makes us believe that the best solution is to write the two prices on the same line with different fonts. With this second portrayal, a perception of cheapness may automatically arise from the fonts' size difference as well as from the distance between the two prices that are written on the same line (Tab.3).

We have tested our hypothesis with the affective computing technique. The emotional response to the different portrayals of price promotion have confirmed that the best solution is writing the two prices on the same line but portraying the full price in a larger font. We hope to confirm this result in the near future using more reliable neuroscientific techniques (fMRI, EEG, and eye tracking).

9.6 How to improve product innovation with the help of brain imaging technology

The functional magnetic resonance imaging technique (fMRI) may help firms improve their forecast of market success of new products. The fMRI allows seeing brain areas activated by simple observation of a product or an advertising campaign as well as brain areas being activated by a decision process. Because different brain areas have different functions with regard to our behaviour, neuroscientists may understand our preferences and forecast our behaviour simply by looking into brain imaging.

The department of Neuroscience and the department of Economics of Parma University have made a fMRI experiment at the request of a firm that was about to launch a new product; they wanted to know if such a technique gave information coherent (or not) with that of traditional marketing research. When we made the experiment, we had no knowledge whatsoever of the data produced by the traditional marketing research. We have been asked to give insights on the success probability of the new product (a cracker sandwich) as well as on the attraction of the packaging, price and story board. Here, we will focus only on the product experiment. As for the architecture of the fMRI experiment, we have:

- Engaged 66 females, aged between 19 and 50 years that normally bought from the cracker category;
- Detected brain areas sensitive to taste asking our subjects to drink different liquids while in the fMRI machine;
- Observed brain areas sensitive to taste (hypothalamus, nucleus *accumbens*, nucleus *caudate*) while subjects observed different images of the product as well as being asked to decide to buy (or not) the product.

Regarding the different product images, we have shown the real image (target), a better image taken from the package, an out-of-focus (worse) image, and a control image (a rubber). As for the inter-subjects conditions, we divided the group in two clusters: the first one was asked to taste the product before entering the fMRI machine, while the second one tasted the product after the experiment. The main experiment results indicate: the red (higher) line shows the brain resonance in those people that have not tasted the new product before entering the fMRI machine, while the green (lower) line shows the brain resonance of subjects who, indeed, have tasted the new product before entering the fMRI machine. As for the histogram, the "target" shows the average resonance in the observation of the real product, while the "VarOpt" shows the average resonance in the observation of product depicted in the package, and "VarBad" shows the average resonance in the observation of an out-of-focus image of the product. The "control" histogram shows the average resonance in the observation of the rubber. In the figure, you can see that the brain resonance was higher for the better image and the target image than the out-of-focus and the control images. However, what was most interesting is the difference of brain resonance between the two clusters: those who tasted before entering the fMRI machine and those who tasted afterwards. What we found is a very significant difference in brain resonance between the two clusters. The brain resonance of those who tasted the product before entering the fMRI machine was much lower, especially in the hypothalamus, than the brain resonance of those who tasted the product afterwards (Figure 1). This result may be explained in two ways, which do not exclude each, either:

- The experience of tasting has been less satisfactory than what was expected;
- The consumption of just one cracker sandwich was enough to feel sated.

The first explanation means that the firm will reach good market penetration easily because people like the concept of a cracker filled with cheese but, after trying the product, they will not buy it anymore because their experience was far less satisfactory than they expected. The second explanation means that the firm should offer a multi-pack alternative with different tastes in order to stimulate consumption of more than one product at a time.

In traditional marketing research, the manufacturer receives the appreciation of consumers who tasted the product and a statement that they would have purchased the product at the price suggested by the firm. In view of the differences between our neuromarketing experiment results and insights obtained from traditional marketing research, we suggested the firm refrains from launching the product. In spite of our suggestion, the product was launched but it had to be withdrawn two years later for failing to obtain its sales target.

9.7 How to improve nutrition communication with the help of brain imaging technology

Obesity (and being overweight) is increasing all over the world; illnesses and low productivity associated to the obesity conditions cost about 2.8% of the global Gross Domestic Product. To address this problem, we ought to ask ourselves why we eat frequently *hyper-caloric* food in excessive quantities with regard to our energy consumption. The main entity responsible of our eating habits is food manufacturers that compete for our taste, which may be improved by increasing the amount of salt, sugar and fat. Such hyper-caloric food becomes irresistible because we are genetically sensitive to salt, sugar and fat. Neuroscience research has also produced evidence of hyper activation of a brain reward area (nucleus *accumbens*) when obese people observe hyper-caloric food. Since food is consumed by our mind before our stomach, the expectation of taste becomes irresistible in the overweight-obese segment of the population. Of course, obesity may be due also to a metabolic disorder or genetic causes, such as a leptin deficit, but these cases account only for 10% of those affected by this condition; obesity is, therefore, a mind phenomenon to be treated by neuroscience knowledge. Besides improving taste, manufacturers are accountable for:

- Increasing formats, because people eat more when they take their food from a larger package and drink more when they drink from a larger bottle;
- Promoting sales by offering a quantity for free or a larger package at a lower unit price because people consider savings before their weight control target;
- Making products easily available everywhere and all the time because accessibility fosters consumption and preparation time is shortened.

Retailers are also accountable for the obesity epidemic because they have done next to nothing to inform consumers of alternative choices in terms of nutritional ingredients and calories, whilst assuring greater accessibility and visibility to hyper-caloric food. Last, but not least, the Government has largely failed in assuring public health and a good quality of life through promoting hypo-caloric diets; their fiscal policy, as well as their communication policy, has both failed in stopping/reversing the obesity trend.

To suggest ways for increasing *hypo-caloric* food consumption, first we have to understand what makes our taste as well as how the taste may be changed. People expect hyper-caloric food to be tastier and, therefore, it is not easy to devise ways to orient choices towards hypo-caloric alternatives. First, we have to acknowledge that the ancient Roman proverb (*de gustibus non disputandum est*) is not correct. We have thousands of receptors on the tongue that detect salt, sugar, bitter, sour and umami; these receptors send a signal to the brain that decides whether we like, or not, a certain food. This is because it is the brain that makes our preferences; taste is not only due to the food we put in our stomach but also to the culture and communication we are exposed to. Taste is, therefore, made of flavour and knowledge and, hence, it may be changed. It is then possible to make people like hypo-caloric food more than hyper-caloric food. If we are hypertensive and the doctor advises us to drastically reduce the amount of salt we eat, we will follow a low salt diet. If we have the willpower to maintain such a low salt diet for a while, we will appreciate insipid food the more we follow the regime. The frequency of consumption does account for our taste because our cognitive mind needs an anchor to assess the food we are eating and, if comparisons are made with the same kind of food, we will eventually appreciate it. It is, therefore, possible to orient people towards buying hypo-caloric food through communication with information that activates the limbic system and promotion that reduces prices as long as consumers repurchase the same hypo-caloric product; in this way firms may sustain consumer health and their sales at the same time.

With the increase of the obesity epidemic, the awareness of the importance of food for a healthy life has also increased; so, despite differences among countries with regard to obesity in the population, there is now a strong segment of consumers who prefer hypo-caloric and nutrient food[1]. There is also strong evidence that people eat more and are prepared to pay more when they buy hypo-caloric food. These new market conditions have prompted many firms to change their business strategy in order to increase their sales and profits; this means enlarging their product portfolio offering hypo-caloric alternatives as well as products free from some harmful ingredients, or products with pharmaceutical substances that cure or prevent some illnesses. Retailers have also started to implement policies to satisfy the demand for healthy diets by changing their assortment, merchandising, branding, and communication policies. Last, but not least, some governments have re- oriented their fiscal policy in order to reduce hyper-caloric food consumption and changed their communication and labelling requirements in order to influence consumers in their food choices.

In this study, we focus on communication, a marketing policy that pertains to manufacturers as well as to retailers and governments. Communication is important because it may affect people with a wish for a certain food, the satisfaction in consumption and the feeling of being replete. In particular, our study focuses on the alternative labels that may be used to communicate the nutritional appropriateness of alternative food one may choose when buying at the supermarket. We start our analysis by stressing the mistakes of nutrition communication based on the assumption of cognitive (rational) choices. Actually, food labels are in a text format and on the back of a pack. Comparing the nutrition content of different food alternatives is very difficult because of label on the back of the pack, and also because information on the label is too detailed and too technical to be understood by the general public. Only a few read the label's text and, of those who read, only some understand its significance and react accordingly. However, for those few who read and understand, the text on the label may be not appropriate for changing their calorie intake. There are neuroscientific studies that compare the behaviour of obese people who follow a diet versus the obese that do not follow a diet when, during their buying process, they are exposed to a textual label on hyper-caloric and hypo-caloric food. Obese people not following a diet buy the food with a hyper caloric label but feel full in a short time because of a cognitive brake. Obese people following a diet and buying food with a hypo-caloric label eat more because of the absence of a cognitive brake. In other words, the positive choice of hypo-caloric food is matched with the negative behaviour of an increased consumption. Therefore, if we want to tackle the obesity epidemic and help those people who are aware of their condition and have chosen to follow a diet, we have to avoid textual labels that speak to the cognitive mind and use labels that speak to the

---

[1] Light Coca-Cola accounts for 32% in USA, 20% in Europe and 6% in South America.

emotive mind, fostering associative learning and automatic reactions. We have, therefore, conducted a fMRI study to compare textual (list) labels with:

- Health star rating labels that are actually tested in Australia and New Zealand;
- Traffic light labels that are actually tested in the UK and by some manufacturers on a voluntary basis;
- Silhouette labels (body), which are not tested anywhere but we think are the most effective because our brain processes images more than words or colours.

We have manipulated the four labels in order to reduce content overlap and have, therefore, a clearer result of the different performances of the various formats of nutrition communication. The greater the brain resonance at label observation, the higher is the probability that the nutritional information may accomplish the task of changing behaviour for weight control. We have observed brain resonance with regard to brain areas mainly involved in taste: *insula*, putamen, cingulum, hypothalamus, and prefrontal cortex. Our experiment has aimed to reject/confirm, in observations as well as in choice conditions, the following hypotheses:

- Labels that target the limbic system (traffic light and silhouette) are more efficient than those that target the cognitive mind (list and star rating);
- Among labels that target the cognitive mind, the star rating is more efficient than lists;
- Among labels that target the limbic system, silhouettes are more efficient than the traffic lights;
- Among the four labels tested, the silhouettes are the most efficient (Figure 2)

We examined 32 people using the fMRI technique: 16 obese and 16 normal weight of both gender. In our experiment, we used four foods and four beverages of a light/regular packaging variants for a total of 128 stimuli. To avoid overlapping of brain resonance to labels and packages, we have manipulated the colour of the two packages (light vs regular) in a way to eliminate any differences besides the format of the label.

Our hypothesis has been confirmed with a high degree of statistical significance. In the following charts, we show some details of the main experiment results for the different brain areas examined. In Figure 3, you can see the performance of the four labels as far as the *insula* activation in an observation condition is concerned; the 'body' label is the more efficient at stirring up the desire in obese people to buy the light variant while no substantial differences have been detected between the four labels in discouraging the regular variant. In Figure 4, you can see that the body label has, instead, not had an effect in rousing the desire in normal weight people to buy the light variant as far as the *insula* is concerned; this may be explained by the non-relevance of calorie communication for people of normal weight that have not followed a diet. In Figure 5, you can see that the body label is, again, the more efficient in stimulating the desire for the light product in a choice condition among obese people as far as the *insula* is concerned; on the contrary, the same body label cannot encourage normal weight people to buy the light product because they do not need to control their weight and, therefore, such a nutrition communication has no relevance to them. In Figure 6, you can see that the body label again is the more efficient in stirring up the desire for the light product in a choice condition among obese people as far as the Putamen is concerned. Figure 7 shows the clearest results of all. The body label is the more efficient in rousing the desire for the light product in a choice condition among obese people as far as the Hypothalamus is concerned; the same body label is also the more efficient in discouraging the buying of regular products among obese people. Finally, Figure 8 illustrates the performance of the four different labels in rousing the buying desire for light/regular products as far as the prefrontal cortex is concerned. The most efficient label in activating the prefrontal cortex for the light product in a choice condition has been the star ranking; this means:

- The star ranking targets the cognitive mind;
- The star ranking is able to activate the prefrontal cortex in a choice condition but not in an observation condition;
- Nutritional contents shown with a star ranking label are easily processed by our cognitive mind while the same contents communicated with a list label are simply rejected.

To test the knowledge produced with the fMRI experiment, we applied, in a laboratory setting, the two most efficient labels in the biscuit category on the basis of using the Coop Liguria assortment. First, we positioned the 134 biscuits referenced according to New Zealand Health Star Rating Calculator (HSRC), which takes into account not only calories but also the most important nutrition elements. In this way, we obtained four clusters of different nutritional quality that we labelled with 1-4 stars to target the cognitive mind, and silhouettes differentiated by weight and colours to target the emotional mind (Tab.4). The display of the four segments was then organised in a vertical setting to show the higher nutritional quality first on the shopper's journey (Figure 9). In this way, the consumer was able to compare products with different nutritional quality while shopping; those who knows they have to control their weight cannot avoid paying attention. Both labels have succeeded in changing the behaviour of obese people.

Figures and tables

Figure 1. Activation of area sensitives to taste while product is observed

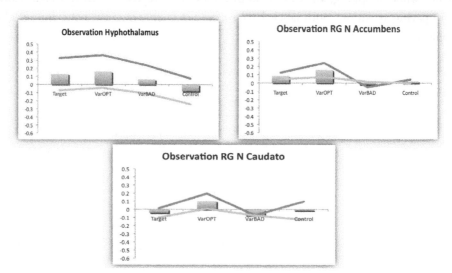

Source: Authors' elaboration.

Figure 2. New labels tested against list labels

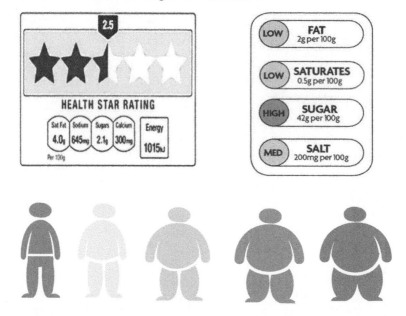

Source: Authors' elaboration.

Figure 3.
Insula activation of obese people while observing four different labels of regular/light products

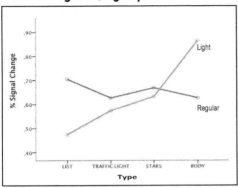

Source: Authors' elaboration.

Figure 4.
Insula activation of normal weight people while observing four different labels of regular/light products

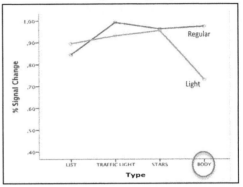

Source: Authors' elaboration.

Figure 5.
Insula activation of obese/normal weight people when asked to choose between regular/light products according to four different labels

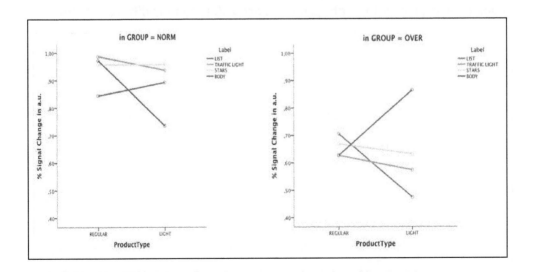

Source: Authors' elaboration.

Figure 6.

Putamen activation of obese/normal weight people when asked to choose between regular/light products according to four different labels

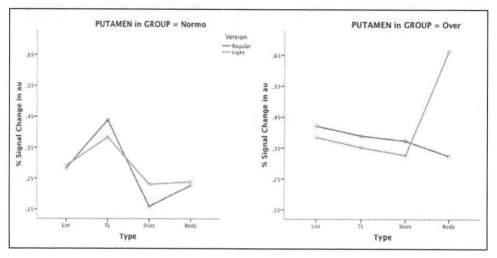

Source: Authors' elaboration.

Figure 7.

Hypothalamus activation of obese/normal weight people when asked to choose between regular/light products according to four different labels

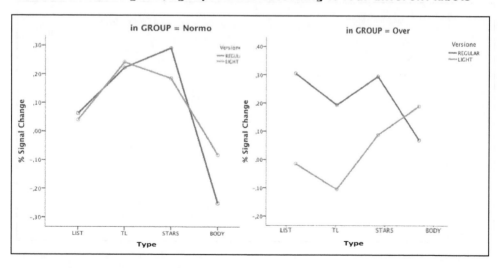

Source: Authors' elaboration.

Figure 8.
Prefrontal cortex activation of obese/normal weight people when asked to choose between regular/light products according to four different labels

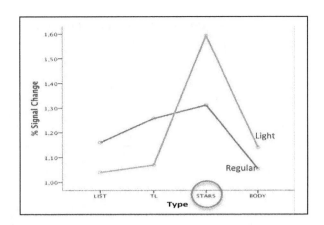

Source: Authors' elaboration.

Figure 9.
Merchandising of biscuit nutrition quality

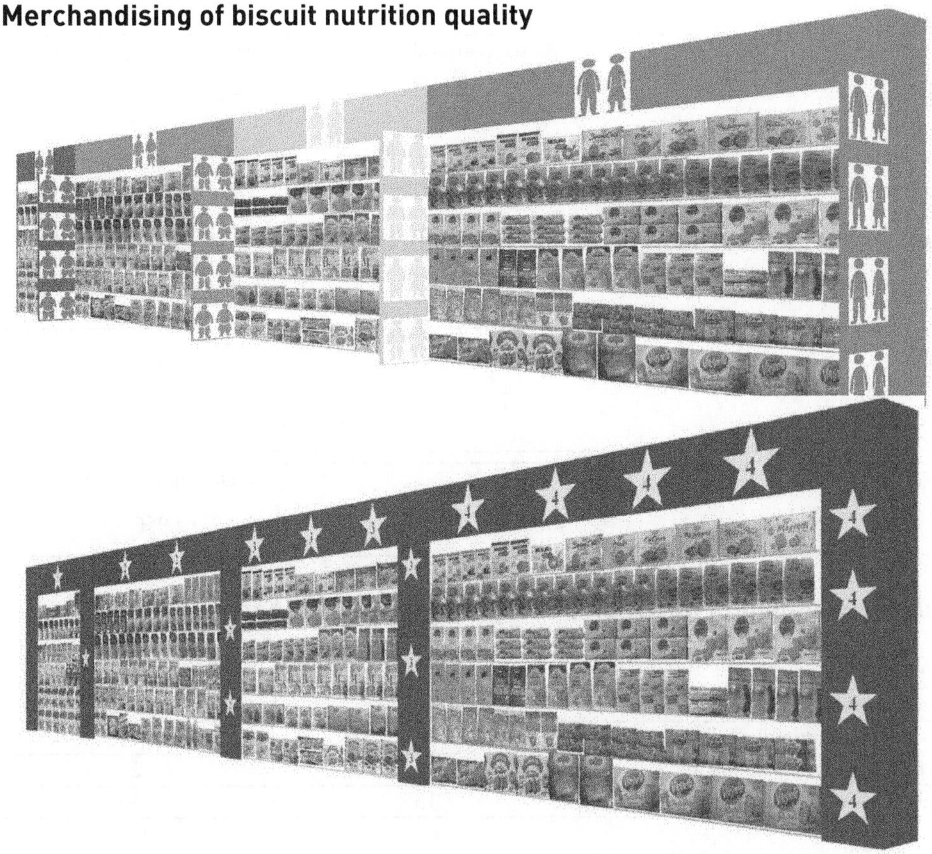

Source: Authors' elaboration.

Tab.1 - Engagement, valence and arousal by students viewing a Dash advertising

	engagement	valence	arousal					
			happiness	sadness	anger	surprise	fear	disgust
total	0,43	-0,02	0,119	0,108	0,033	0,004	0,002	0,018
male	0,44	-0,03	0,114	0,105	0,043	0,004	0,001	0,026
female	0,40	+0,01	0,126	0,112	0,019	0,003	0,003	0,006
20-30	0,33	-0,11	0,052	0,133	0,039	0,003	0,000	0,008
30-40	0,54	+0,01	0,132	0,11	0,029	0,004	0,003	0,006
<40	0,37	+0,20	0,245	0,046	0,006	0,004	0,005	0,005

Tab. 2 - Actual versus recommended price portrayal

	Actual portrayal	Recommended portrayal
Full price	5€	5€
Discounted price	2.95€	2.95€

Tab. 3 - Vertical versus horizontal price portrayal with a smaller font for discounted price

Full price	5€
Discounted price	2.95€

Full price	Discounted price
5€	2.95€

Tab. 4 - Segment of nutrition quality in a biscuit category

	brands	references
Low nutrition quality	9	21
Low–average nutrition quality	16	49
Average–high nutrition quality	13	25
High nutrition quality	13	39

References

Lugli, G., (2010), *Neuroshopping: Come e perché acquistiamo*, 2a edizione, Apogeo.

Lugli, G., (2012), *Troppa scelta: Difficoltà e fatica dell'acquistare*, Apogeo.

Lugli, G., (2014), *Emotions Tracking: Come rispondiamo agli stimoli di marketing*, Apogeo.

Lugli, G., (2015), *Cibo, Salute e Business: Neuroscienze e Marketing Nutrizionale*, 1a edizione, Cultura E Società, Egea.

Kahneman D. and Tversky A. (1979), «Prospect Theory: An Analysis of Decisions under Risk», *Econometrica*, 47(2), pp. 263-291.

Kahneman D., (2011), *Thinking, Fast and Slow*, Farrar, Strauss & Giroux.

Rizzolatti, G., Fogassi, L. and Gallese V., (2001), «Neurophysiological Mechanism Underlying the Understanding and Imitation of Action», *Nature Neuroscience Reviews*, 2, pp. 661-670.

Rizzolatti, G. and Craighero L., (2004), «The Mirror Neuron System», *Annual Review of Neuroscience*, 27, pp. 169-192.

Thaler, R. and Sunstein, C., (2008), «Nudge: Improving Decisions about Health, Wealth, and Happiness», *Choice Reviews Online*, 46(02), pp. 46-0977-46-0977.

Wansink, B., (2017), «Healthy Profits: An Interdisciplinary Retail Framework That Increases the Sales of Healthy Foods», *Journal of Retailing*, 93 (1), pp. 65-78.

Wansink, B., (2017), «Healthy Profits: An Interdisciplinary Retail Framework That Increases the Sales of Healthy Foods», *Journal of Retailing*, 93 (1), pp. 65-78.

10. Neurofinance: New Frontiers and Further Perspectives

by Lucrezia Fattobene, Maria Gabriella Ceravolo [1]

The influence of emotion on individual choice has usually been considered as a factor of irrationality and source of negative results. Over time, different expressions, such *as "keep a cool head"* or *"don't let your heart rule your head",* have spread and consolidated this negative vision. In 1772, Benjamin Franklin suggested to Mr. Joseph Priestley that he list pros and cons and evaluate them to make a decision about his marriage. Franklin's Moral Algebra to evaluate a wedding proposal became the bastion of rational thinking. This negative perception of the role of emotions on decision making has pervaded economics and finance leading to normative theories that assume a decision maker is always rational and able to evaluate advantages and disadvantages objectively before taking the decision, exclusively relying on cognitive processes.

While it might be common wisdom that excluding emotions is conducive to the best and most logical decisions, evidence in neuroscience reveals that merely applying formulae and logic does not imply optimal decision making and that emotions are essential for quality decisions.

In this paper, we will discuss the hypothesis by which effective decision making can be best performed through the balanced processing of internal and external afferent inputs, exploiting emotional memories of previous experience as a reference to pursue rewarding outcomes.

[1] We would like to thank Professor G.M. Raggetti for his precious comments and suggestions and for fostering the interdisciplinary collaboration in Neuroeconomics.

10.1 Affective processes and financial decision making

Several studies using the gambling task, have demonstrated that individuals with damage in emotional neural circuitry perform worse than those whose emotional systems are intact (Bechara *et al.* 1997; Damasio 1994). Some researchers, on the other hand, have observed that in some cases, subjects deprived of emotional reactions may take more advantageous choices than healthy individuals. For instance, investors suffer from *myopic loss aversion;* they adopt a very short-term perspective and put more weight on losses than equivalent gains, originating, at an aggregate level, the *equity premium puzzle.*[2]

An important study that highlights the importance of considering affective processes in financial decision making has been conducted by Shiv *et al.* (2005). The authors hypothesise that if the origin of myopic loss aversion is an emotional substrate (Loewenstein *et al.* 2001) and it leads to suboptimal decisions, then any damage in the emotional circuitry should be translated into more profitable choices. In other words, they aim at investigating if a dysfunction in the emotional neural circuit leads to more advantageous decisions. In order to test their intuition, the authors conduct an experiment which involved patients with damage in the amygdala, the orbitofrontal cortex and the right insular or somatosensory cortex, which are the brain portions known to be crucial in emotion processing.[3] The other participants recruited to perform the experiment were control patients – patients with focal lesions but in areas not related with affective processing – and healthy individuals.

The subjects were initially endowed with $20 of *experimental* money of which the part left at the end of the session would be transformed into a gift certificate. The procedure was articulated over 20 rounds. For each round, the subject had to choose to invest, or not, $1, gambling on the toss of a coin that paid $2.50 in case of tails and $0 in case of heads. In the winning case, the $1 is returned, while it is lost in the losing case. The expected value (EV) of this gamble is always positive (EV= 0.5 ($2.5 + $1) + 0.5 (-$1) = $1.25) and higher than not investing (EV= 1 ($1) = $1). Therefore, the optimal decision is to invest at each round. Results reveal that participants did not

---

[2] The equity premium puzzle is the phenomenon observed in the financial market of anomalously higher returns of stock over government bonds (Mehra and Prescott 1985).

[3] Lesion studies are very important in neuroscience and neuroeconomics because they allow making *causal* inference about brain functions. In fact, while fMRI studies are generally correlational studies, the use of focal and stable lesions permits inferring a causal-effect relationship between brain functions and behaviour.

always invest and exhibit different patterns of behaviour across the three different groups.

Results revealed that the percentage of decisions to invest is higher for target patients; they invested on average 8 times out of 10 (83.7%), compared with about 6 for the controls and normal subjects (60.7% and 57.6%, respectively).

Figure 1 displays the pattern of decisions, splitting the rounds of investment into five blocks.

As shown in Figure 1, at the beginning, all the participants follow the ideal benchmark but as the rounds go forward, target patients keep investing while normal and control ones assume a more conservative behaviour and invest in a lower number of cases, revealing myopic loss aversion.

This study is relevant in neurofinance in that it shows the importance of considering emotions and brain function during risk perception, risk taking, and investing behaviour. The results of this paper suggest also the importance of distinguishing between uncertainty and ambiguity in economics and finance. In fact, while in this experiment, conducted in an uncertain situation - the probability of the outcome is known (50-50) - emotions have a negative role for optimal decision making, and in a situation of ambiguity, other studies reveal a positive influence of affective processes for quality choices (Bechara *et al.* 1997). Neuroscience informs us about the complexity of automatic and affective, on the one side, and controlled and cognitive processes, on the other side. Their functioning is modulated by many and different factors. Moreover, these processes rarely work singularly, without interacting. If this complexity exists, economics and finance should not elaborate models or formulate hypothesis without considering it.

10.2 Neuroscience and the possibility to test hypotheses in finance: the realization utility

The revolution sparked off by neurofinance relies also on the possibility of testing theories that otherwise would not be possible to test. Generally, methodologies have limitations. Beside their own limitations, the neuroscience techniques permit evaluating intuitions and hypothesis overcoming the obstacles of traditional methods in economics and finance. In this sense, an exemplar study has been conducted by Frydman *et al.* (2014) who use fMRI to test the *"realization utility"* hypothesis. Empirical evidence has noticed the existence of a "disposition effect", the tendency of investors to hold loser assets too long and sell winning assets too soon. This phenomenon has been explained through different behavioural elements: i) prospect theory, ii) regret avoidance, iii) mental accounting, and iv) self-control (Shefrin and Statman 1985). All together these factors, combined, generate the observed behaviour in the financial market of not selling losing investments sooner and keeping winner ones longer, contrary to what normative theory states. One possible explanation promoted for this tendency is the realization utility theory: individuals, in addition to the pleasure associated with the consumption, perceive pleasure from the act itself of selling a gaining asset. In other words, investors derive *utility* from the gain and from the action that is conducted to *realize* that gain. This hypothesis has been advanced firstly in 1985 (Shefrin and Statman), and lately in 2012 (Barberis and Xiong) and 2013 (Ingersoll and Jin). Nevertheless, the authors did not have the possibility to actually test this intuition due to the absence of instruments to test a "burst of pleasure". The available methodologies of questionnaires, interviews and focus groups might try to detect if people experience some excitement but compelling evidence shows that affective processes can be automatic, unconscious, and uncontrolled; this means they occur in parallel, are effortless and not accessible to the consciousness (Camerer 2005). Therefore, asking participants to share with the researchers if they experience an affective process that might have occurred unconsciously can lead to wrong conclusions. On the contrary, the neurobiology of emotions has clarified the brain regions generally involved with emotional processing, some of which are nucleus *accumbens* and *insula*. The nucleus *accumbens*, also called the "pleasure centre", together with the olfactory tubercle, constitute the *ventral striatum*, and codify *reward probability* and *reward magnitude* that result in the *expected value*. The neurotransmitter dopamine, produced in the tegmental ventral area and in the *substantia nigra*, spread to the different structures including the nucleus *accumbens* that, therefore, represents a core element in the dopaminergic pathway. This route is involved with reward, pleasure, motivation, addiction, learning, and so on.

A second structure, crucial in emotional decision making, is the above-mentioned *insula*, a cortical area within the limbic lobe that, receiving interoceptive inputs from the body and connecting with prefrontal areas, is involved in representing the emotional experience. In particular, it serves a critical role in emotional awareness that occurs during the supraliminal elaboration of emotional stimuli.

On these premises, one of Frydman *et al.*'s (2014) assumptions is that if individuals experience the realization utility and there is a burst of pleasure related to the sale of a gaining asset, then the activity in the *ventral striatum* should be greater when they take the decision to sell the asset, compared to holding the asset and controlling for the size of the capital gain.

To test their hypothesis, they follow the experimental design of Weber and Camerer (1998) in which the subjects could trade three different stocks, in an experimental market provided with experimental money. Each stock can be in a good state or in a bad state (two-state Markov chain). If the stock is in a good state, the value can increase with probability 0.55 and decrease with probability 0.45, and vice versa if the stock is in a bad state. Stocks are positively auto-correlated: they keep their good or bad state in 80% of the cases. Subjects were given the opportunity to trade for 25 trials during which the researchers could record both experimental data and neural data, to observe the patterns of the disposition effect and brain activations.

Behavioural results reveal that participants exhibit disposition effect and do not negotiate stocks in an optimal way and neural data confirm the realization utility. In particular, Figure 2 shows this greater activity in the *ventral striatum*.

When looking at the time-course of activity in the *ventral striatum* (Figure 3), it is possible to observe that the percentage variation of *ventral striatum* change reaches a peak two seconds after the decision to sell gains is entered and its absolute value is four times that relative to the held gains.

The x-axis indicates the second after the decision is taken and the y-axis is the percentage change of the *ventral striatum* activity. As revealed by Figure 3, the blue line that plots the decision to sell the gaining asset has peaked two seconds after the decision to sell the stock, compared with the decision to keep it in the portfolio. According to the rational model, since utility derives exclusively from the gain, the decision of selling or holding a gaining security should be equivalent. This experiment reveals instead that pleasure is not only related with *consumption* but with the *act* itself of selling the gaining asset and, therefore, *realizing* the gain.

This study is important for different reasons. Firstly, it tests the realization utility hypothesis and confirms its importance in explaining the disposition effect, a well-known and documented phenomenon in the financial market, unexplained by standard theory. Secondly, it demonstrates the revolutionary character of neuroeconomics that provides neural data to test hypotheses otherwise impossible to test because of their specific nature related with the delicacy of internal feelings.

10.3 Traders' behaviour in an ecological setting

The study conducted by Frydman *et al.* (2014) enriches the knowledge about investors' behaviour and verifies the existence of a specific bias in trading decisions. The subjects involved in their experiment are students endowed with *play money*. Several studies have highlighted that results obtained in virtual contexts are different from those in real contexts where also real money is used (Camerer and Hogarth 1999; Hensher 2010; Vlaev 2012). Moreover, involvement is different if the subject is externally endowed with money or he uses his *own* money. In order to overcome the limitations of previous studies, Raggetti *et al.* (2017) conducted an experiment implementing an ecological, reliable investigation protocol, which aims to investigate the neural correlates of financial decisions of *professional* traders that negotiate in a *real market*, using their *own real money*. In particular, the authors explore, in a real scenario:

1. The neural correlates of traders' decisions
2. The existence of specialised neural circuits to handle financial decisions
3. The demographic and contextual variables that modulate the final output

To answer these questions, 20 traders underwent fMRI and were allowed to negotiate using their favorite Direct Access Trading (DAT) platform. This feature complicated data processing but, on the other hand, contributed to recreating the real environment in which the traders work daily. One of the main results of the study concerns the fact that neural data reveal the activations of several *subcortical* brain areas. In classical and normative models, professional traders and investors are assumed to negotiate relying on cognitive processes. More specifically, investing decisions are generally considered the results of thoughtful and informed processes during which advantages and disadvantages of each alternative are carefully weighted. This study, on the contrary, reveals a relevant presence of automatic, affective and unconscious processes, which challenges the traditional hypothesis. In fact, significant activations have been found for nucleus *accumbens* and nucleus *caudatus*, in the pre-decisional phase, confirming the important role of the affective process in the few seconds that precede the awareness of the decision. These results challenge also the *consequentialist* view of the traditional model in economics and finance, according to which feelings and emotional states *follow* the outcome of the decision; the increased activity in the limbic system before the decision is taken confirms, on the contrary, the role of emotions in actually leading the decision-making process, as stated by the affective anticipatory model (Knutson and Greer 2008).

To understand if financial decisions are handled by specialised circuits, the authors observe if the neural correlates activated express similar characteristics and can, therefore, be grouped. The factorial analysis revealed the existence of at least two different specialised circuits. The first one includes cortical and subcortical areas that codify the subjective values of the different options and continuously update them on the basis of traders' results. This circuit is responsible for modulating the arousal and the emotions linked to the trading activity and, therefore, plays a motivational function. The second circuit includes the cortical structures, which integrate, compute, and process information coming from the different sources. This last circuit is responsible for the computational and executive phases and for selecting the final decision.

The authors individuate different trading behaviours through a questionnaire administered after the fMRI recording. The answers collected allowed distinguishing two subgroups of traders. Profile 1, the risk-averse and methodical traders, stick to the rules and are more involved in the information processing and computational phases. Profile 2, the risk-seeker and creative traders, use heuristics, are driven by intuitions and temporary impulses and are particularly involved in the phase of selecting the operation of buying, selling or holding. The main variables that modulate trading decisions were found to be age, experience, and behavioral trading stile. In particular, the younger the trader, the stronger the emotional involvement is during the trading activity. The professional age of the traders, on the other hand, reduces the computational involvement and the counterfactual thinking and leads to rely more on automatic and unconscious processes. Finally, behavioural traders' attitude reveals some more interesting results. Traders of Profile 1, compared to those of Profile 2, display a greater activation of brain areas generally involved in assigning value to the different options. They also display a greater activation of some cortical areas involved in information processing and selecting the final output, independent of age and experience. These traders exhibit stronger interest in informative aspects and a stronger effort in the decisional phase. On the contrary, Profile 2 traders are less emotionally involved; probably, the use of heuristics and intuition lead them to take decisions without the excessive recourse of cognitive processes. This interpretation of data is also confirmed by their faster decisional activity and the lower value of latency registered, i.e. the short time interval between two subsequent decisions.

10.4 The predictive power of neurofinance: theory of mind and financial bubbles

One of the studies showing how neuroscience can inform financial decision theory is that by De Martino *et al.* (2013), who investigate the mechanism underlying the formation of financial bubbles. An accepted definition of bubble is the rapid increase of prices followed by a crash (Brunnermeier 2008), i.e. the phase of burst subsequent that of a boom. The difficulty with this definition consists in the impossibility of identifying the bubble phenomenon in advance, since it implies the phase of the crash. This absence of predictive power of the definition makes the study of bubble formation challenging. One more obstacle comes from the fact that evaluating the phase of price appreciation implies knowing the exact fundamental value of the asset that is rarely known with extreme precision. The first interesting aspect of that paper relies in the study of the bubble formation mechanism in an experimental setting that allows researchers to artificially create fundamental value, appreciation and depreciation and, therefore, manipulate these interesting variables. Secondly, the authors try to understand the neural mechanism underpinning traders' behaviour during financial bubbles.

The authors focus on the two important brain areas: ventromedial prefrontal cortex and dorsomedial prefrontal cortex (Figure 4). Ventromedial prefrontal cortex is generally involved in representing goal value and in reward-related computations (Winecoff *et al.* 2013). In particular, its activity has been found to reflect the subjective value of the options (Kable and Glimcher 2007) and it permits alternatives' comparison by creating a "common neural currency" for reward (Montague and Berns 2002). Dorsomedial prefrontal cortex is a brain region that, together with the temporoparietal junction, is implicated in the process of *mentalising*, or the Theory of Mind (ToM) (Mitchell, Banaji and Macrae 2005), which is the ability to understand the mental state of others and is an important element of social functions (Frith and Frith 1999).

On these premises, they hypothesise that the appreciation observed during the bubble market is associated with an inflated representation of fundamental value in the ventromedial prefrontal cortex that, in turn, increases the susceptibility to buy assets at prices higher than their fundamental value. Moreover, they hypothesise that this inflated representation in the ventromedial prefrontal cortex is the result of an attempt to predict other subjects' intentions, involving the dorsomedial prefrontal cortex.

To test these hypotheses the authors created an experimental setting where students underwent fMRI while trading in an experimental financial market composed of six sessions, of which three were bubble and three non-bubble. The subjects were endowed with some play money and were asked to stay, buy or sell different shares at the market price. To observe if the formation of a bubble is the result of an inflated mental representation, the authors construct a variable, the Current Portfolio Value (CPV), which combines value in cash and value in shares at each time instant, and insert it as a regressor in the model; this permits observing a change in the Blood Oxygenation Level Dependent (BOLD) signal, distinguishing between the bubble and non-bubble market.

The analysis focuses on brain response to changes of the CPV in the bubble market versus non-bubble market and reveals that the activation of the ventromedial prefrontal cortex is positively modulated during the bubble market. In other words, it reveals that when the CPV value is high, there is a positive percentage signal changes in the ventromedial prefrontal cortex, i.e. trading value representation is positively modulated in the bubble market. This result confirms the hypothesis that in bubble markets the mental representation of the portfolio value is inflated. Starting from this outcome, the authors try to test if the ventromedial prefrontal cortex activity is, therefore, able to predict the behavioural tendency to buy inflated stocks, i.e. shares whose prices are above their fundamental values; they call this extra price "bubble susceptibility" and create an index able to capture this tendency to ride the bubble.

The analysis reveals that the activation of ventromedial prefrontal cortex is positively modulated by the subject's propensity to pay an extra price to trade. In other words, activity in the ventromedial prefrontal cortex is able to predict the behaviour of riding the bubble. What is revolutionary about these results is the *predictive* power of a brain region for a specific financial behaviour.

Through this study, the researchers aim also to verify if this inflated representation of values in the ventromedial prefrontal cortex is a consequence of traders' attempts to infer other traders' intentions. They test the ToM skill of the participants through an eye-gaze task (Baron-Cohen *et al.* 2001), which allows constructing an index for each participant that tries to resume their attitude to infer other people's state of mind by looking at their gaze (Figure 5).

Interestingly, the analysis shows that in the bubble market, dorsomedial prefrontal cortex is positively modulated and that the percentage of signal change in the dorsomedial prefrontal cortex related to CPV correlates with the individual's ToM index. The interpretation of these results is that during trading decision making, participants try to make inference about other market participants. It might be also possible that all the other market players are perceived as a unique agent and that people assign intentionality to the markets managing, in this way, to reduce and simplify a complex environment. Finally, the psychophysiological interaction (PPI) analysis between ventromedial prefrontal cortex and dorsomedial prefrontal cortex shows that during the financial bubble, the functional coupling between these two brain areas increases. This outcome might mean that subjects take into account other subjects' intentions to update their trading values and this behaviour is mediated by the interaction between ventromedial prefrontal cortex and dorsomedial prefrontal cortex.

10.5 Ocular movements to test hypotheses in finance: the eye tracking methodology

Many of the studies mentioned above have been conducted using fMRI. Another useful tool in neurofinance that helps to shed light on underlying mechanisms of subjects' judgments and decision making is the eye tracking. Figure 6 displays the Neurofinance Lab at the Polytechnic University of Marche – School of Medicine - Management Department – Experimental and Clinical Medicine Department. It shows a setting made up of an Eye Link 1000 (SR Research) Desktop Mount with head stabilization, display computer, host computer and eye tracking monitor. This eye tracking camera has a sample rate of 1000 Hz monocular or 500 Hz binocular.

In short, eye tracking methodology allows registering eye movement variables, such as the ocular pattern of the participant or the time spent looking at a specific piece of information, and so on. Shavit et al. (2010) employ this technique to examine investors' behavioural biases in an investment task; more specifically, they investigate investors' behaviour with respect to some biases as loss aversion, mental accounting, and value changes' presentation.

The first hypothesis they test is related to loss aversion. According to this theory, people have a tendency to feel more pain when they lose than the pleasure associated with an equivalent gain (Kahneman and Tversky 1979). Based on this assumption, individuals should limit their exposure to losing investments and dedicate more time to gaining them. At the same time, it is well documented that negative information attracts more attention than positive ones (Fiske, 1980; Baumeister et al., 2001). It follows that it is difficult to assert if people dedicate more time to negative stimuli that generally have been found to attract more attention, or they prefer to avoid that exposure to limit their pain; and vice versa for positive information. It is important to better understand this psychological mechanism since outcome is strictly related to the way information is processed; an increased comprehension of brain processes permits enhancing behaviour prediction. The eye tracking methodology, by objectively quantifying and measuring the visual attention, permits clarifying this ambiguous issue. The authors prepare a task where subjects first see two assets and secondly the investment returns, which are presented as return percentage (R), change in value (C), and final value in Euro (V). The different scenarios combine the condition of gain vs loss and the dimension of high vs low amounts. The hypothesis that participants dedicate more time to positive information, in line with prospect theory, is confirmed especially when investment returns are expressed as C, since probably this value is perceived as more valuable information (Fehr and Tyran 2001). When returns are expressed as V or R, no substantial differences are found. These results confirm loss averse behaviour; the desire to avoid negative exposure override the general strong attraction to negative stimuli.

According to Kahneman and Tversky (1979), individuals give more weight to information that expresses the change relative to an initial value (generally called the reference point) than the absolute value. On this premise, the authors also test if investors spend more time looking at assets C or V.

The time spent looking at C is greater than V, confirming the hypothesis that subjects consider more the interesting relative values than the absolute ones. Change in value is the type of information that grabs more attention confirming that relative changes are more relevant than absolute values, in line with prospect theory.

Comparing the low gain- low loss and low gain- high loss conditions, it emerges that the time spent looking at C is lower in the second case, probably because investors try to reduce the exposition to losses as they become larger.

Finally, according to *mental accounting* principles (Thaler 1980, 1985), individuals tend to separate their money in different accounts, influencing consumption decisions. This behaviour is also displayed in the financial market with respect to investment behaviour (Odean 1998; Rockenbach 2004) and it is not consistent with standard financial theory according to which the value driving behaviour is the expected utility of the overall portfolio (Von Neumann and Morgenstern 1947; Savage 1954). By observing investors' ocular behaviour, it is possible to detect if they allocate more attention to the overall portfolio value or to the singular assets that compose it. Results confirm the mental accounting hypothesis and reveal that participants focus more on the units of the portfolio (V-gaining asset or V-losing asset) rather than on its global final value (V-portfolio).

Figures

Figure 1.
Proportion of rounds in which participants invested

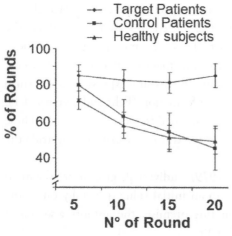

Source: adapted from Shiv et al. 2005.

Figure 2.
Activity in the ventral striatum

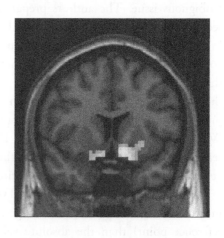

Source: Authors' elaboration.

Figure 3.
Time course of activity in ventral striatum

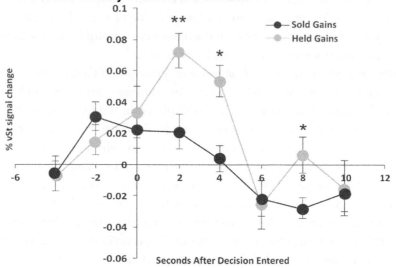

Source: adapted from Frydman et al. 2014.

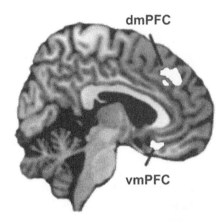

dmPFC

vmPFC

Figure 4.
Brain scan with ventromedial prefrontal cortex and dorsomedial prefrontal cortex highlighted

Source: Authors' elaboration.

Figure 5.
Eye gaze task

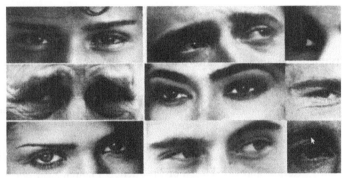

Source: Authors' elaboration.

Figure 6.
Neurofinance Lab at the Polytechnic University of Marche

Source: Authors' elaboration.

References

Barberis, N. and Xiong, W., (2012), «Realization utility», *Journal of Financial Economics*, 104, pp. 251-271.

Baron-Cohen, S., Wheelwright, S., Hill, J., Raste, Y. and Plumb, I., (2001), «The "Reading the Mind in the Eyes" Test Revised Version: A Study With Normal Adults, and Adults with Asperger Syndrome or High-Functioning Autism», *Journal of Child Psychology and Psychiatry*, 42, pp. 241-251.

Baumeister, R.F., Bratslavsky, E., Finkenauer, C. and Vohs K.D., (2001), «Bad Is Stronger Than Good», *Review of General Psychology*, 5, pp. 323-370.

Bechara A., Damasio H., Tranel D., Damasio A.R., (1997), «Deciding Advantageously Before Knowing the Advantageous Strategy», *Science*, 275, pp. 1293-1295.

Brunnermeier M.K., (2008), «Bubbles», in Durlauf S.N. and Blume, L.E. (eds.), *The New Palgrave Dictionary of Economics*, Palgrave Macmillan.

Camerer C., (2005), «How Neuroscience Can Inform Economics», *Journal of Economic Literature*, 43, pp. 9-64.

Camerer C. and Hogarth R., (1999), «The Effects of Financial Incentives in Experiments: A Review and Capital-Labor-Production Framework», *Journal of Risk and Uncertainty*, 19, pp. 7-42.

Damasio A.R., (1994), *Descartes' Error: Emotion, Reason, and The Human Brain*, New York, Grosset/Putnam.

De Martino B., O'Doherty J., Ray D., Bossaerts P. and Camerer C., (2013), «In the Mind of the Market: Theory of Mind Biases Value Computation During Financial Bubbles», *Neuron*, 79, pp. 1222-1231.

Fehr E. and Tyran J.R., (2001), «Does Money Illusion Matter?», *The American Economic Review*, 91(5), pp. 1239-1262.

Fiske, S.T., (1980), «Attention and Weight in Person Perception: the Impact of Negative and Extreme Behavior», *Journal of Personality and Social Psychology*, 38, pp. 889-906.

Frith C.D. and Frith U., (1999), «Interacting Minds—a Biological Basis», *Science*, 286, pp. 1692-1695.

Frydman C., Barberis N., Camerer C., Bossaerts P. and Rangel A., (2014), «Using Neural Data to Test a Theory of Investor Behavior: An Application to Realization Utility», *Journal of Finance,* 69, pp. 907-946.

Hensher D.A., (2010), «Hypothetical Bias, Choice Experiments and Willingness to Pay», *Transportation Research Part B: Methodological,* 44, pp. 735-752.

Ingersoll J. and Jin L., (2013), «Realization Utility with Reference-Dependent Preferences», *Review of Financial Studies,* 26, pp. 723-767.

Kable J.W. and Glimcher P.W., (2007), «The Neural Correlates of Subjective Value During Intertemporal Choice», *Nature Neuroscience,* 10, pp. 1625-1633.

Kahneman D. and Tversky A., (1979), «Prospect theory: An Analysis of Decision Under Risk», *Econometrica,* 47, pp. 263–91.

Knutson B. and Greer S.M., (2008), «Anticipatory Affect: Neural Correlates and Consequences for Choice», *Philosophical Transactions of the Royal Society B: Biological Sciences,* 363, pp. 3771-3786.

Loewenstein G.F., Weber E.U., Hsee C.K. and Welch N., (2001), «Risk as Feelings», *Psychological Bulletin,* 2, pp. 267-286.

Mehra R. and Prescott E.C., (1985), «The Equity Premium: A Puzzle», *Journal Monetary Economics,* 15, pp. 145-161.

Mitchell J.P., Banaji M.R. and Macrae C.N., (2005), «The Link Between Social Cognition and Self-Referential Thought in the Medial Prefrontal Cortex», *Journal of Cognitive Neuroscience,* 17(8), pp. 1306-1315.

Montague P.R. and Berns G.S., (2002), «Neural Economics and the Biological Substrates of Valuation», *Neuron,* 36, pp. 265-284.

Odean T., (1998), «Are Investors Reluctant to Realize their Losses?», *Journal of Finance,* 53(5), pp. 1775-1798.

Raggetti, G.M., Ceravolo M.G., Fattobene L. and Di Dio C., (2017), «Neural Correlates of Direct Access Trading in a Real Stock Market: An fMRI Investigation», *Frontiers in Neuroscience,* 11, pp. 1-14.

Rockenbach B., (2004), «The Behavioral Relevance of Mental Accounting for the Pricing of Financial Options», *Journal of Economic Behavior and Organization,* 53, pp. 513–527.

Savage L. J., (1954), *The Foundation of Statistics*, New York, Wiley.

Shavit T., Giorgetta C., Shani Y. and Ferlazzo F., (2010), «Using an Eye Tracker to Examine Behavioral Biases in Investment Tasks: An Experimental Study», *Journal of Behavioral Finance*, 11(4), pp. 185-194.

Shefrin H. and Statman M., (1985), «The Disposition to Sell Winners Too Early and Ride Losers Too Long: Theory and Evidence», *Journal of Finance*, 40 (3), pp. 777-790.

Shiv B., Loewenstein G., Bechara A., Damasio H. and Damasio A.R., (2005), «Investment Behavior and the Negative Side of Emotion», *Psychological Science*, 16(6), pp. 435-439.

Thaler R.H., (1980), «Toward a Positive Theory of Consumer Choice», *Journal of Economic Behavior and Organization*, 1, pp. 39-60.

Thaler R.H., (1985), «Mental Accounting and Consumer Choice», *Marketing Science*, 4, pp. 199-214.

Vlaev I., (2012), «How Different Are Real and Hypothetical Decisions? Overestimation, Contrast and Assimilation in Social Interaction», *Journal of Economic Psychology*, 33, pp. 963-972.

Von Neumann J. and Morgenstern O., (1947), *Theory of Games and Economic Behavior*, Princeton, Princeton University Press.

Weber M. and Camerer C., (1998), «The Disposition Effect in Securities Trading: An Experimental Analysis», *Journal of Economic Behavior and Organization*, 33, pp. 167-184.

Winecoff A., Clithero J.A., Carter R.M. et al. (2013), «Ventromedial Prefrontal Cortex Encodes Emotional Value», *The Journal of Neuroscience*, 33(27), pp. 11032-11039.

11. *Homo Oeconomicus*: Personality Neuroscience and Psychopathy
by Luca Passamonti

The concept of '*homo oeconomicus*' has dominated classic economic theories for decades. It posits that human beings act like 'rational' agents, especially when performing economical decision-making tasks that aim at maximising the utility function (defined as an indirect index of satisfaction and happiness). However, since its original development, several authors have challenged the validity of the concept of '*homo oeconomicus*', initially via theoretical counter-arguments and successively throughout empirical evidence showing that human beings often behave in 'irrational' ways that violate the utility function. These apparently 'illogic' or emotional behaviours are driven by ancient evolutionary forces that are mediated by brain 'hard-wired' mechanisms aimed at preserving the species. The new field of neuroeconomics originates from the intersection between behavioural economics and neuroscience and aims at understanding the brain basis of emotionally-driven biases in economical decision making. Research in neuroeconomics has provided robust data showing the existence of complex interactions between limbic emotional regions and phylogenetically more recent parts of the neocortex (especially different areas in the prefrontal cortex). The heuristic value of these studies has been enhanced by computational accounts that have formally modelled choice selection and decision making within specific mathematical frameworks. Yet, computational neuroscience of decision making needs to integrate individual variability in behaviour which is hypothesised to be driven by subject-specific attitudes towards different classes of stimuli (personality traits). Therefore, understanding how personality is mechanistically embedded in the brain has the potential to reveal an important source of variability in emotional bias during economic and non-economic decision making. Likewise, clinical studies of specific disorders of decision making, like psychopathy, carry out an added value in modernising the concept of '*homo oeconomicus*' and in providing new clues to understanding the origins of economic disasters.

In this chapter, I first examine how the concept of '*homo oeconomicus*' has been criticised by a series of studies in neuroeconomics, an emerging field of research that aims at exploring the brain basis of affective biases in economic choices. Next, I discuss the strong relationship between neuroeconomics and computational neuroscience of decision making and I describe also the importance of personality neuroscience to enhance our understanding of the inter-individual variability in decision making. Finally, I consider the special case of psychopathy as a key example of a neuropsychiatric disorder that may help to reveal the most intimate mechanisms of emotionally-driven mechanisms of choice selection.

11.1 The concept of '*homo oeconomicus*' and its critique

The concept of '*homo oeconomicus*' has been influential in several economic models and theoretic frameworks (Rittenberg and Tregarthen 2012). The classic portrait of the '*homo oeconomicus*' is that of a rational, selfish, ego-centric human being who continuously attempts to maximise the utility as a consumer and profit as a producer (Rittenberg and Tregarthen 2012). In the original definition by John Stuart Mill, the '*homo oeconomicus*' is described as "a human being who inevitably does that by which he may obtain the greatest amount of necessaries, conveniences, and luxuries, with the smallest quantity of labour and physical self-denial with which they can be obtained" (Persky 1995). The 'rationality' of the '*homo oeconomicus*' is, therefore, defined by his ability to maximise the utility function, which is, in economic terms, an indirect index of the satisfaction experienced by the consumer of goods. As assessing satisfaction may be very difficult, economists have introduced methods of representing it via more objective and measurable economic choices (Castagnoli and Calzi 1996). The utility function is, therefore, an indirect index of 'rationality' even though it does not necessarily indicate that the behaviour of an individual is 'rational' in ethical, moral or social terms. In contrast, 'rationality' within this context only denotes that the '*homo oeconomicus*' tries to achieve his objectives at the minimal cost possible. To compute the utility function, economists usually make assumptions about human preferences for different goods. For instance, if the preference for tea and coffee is considered to be equal, the corresponding utility function can be represented as: $u(c, t) = c + t$, where "u" is the utility function and "c" and "t" represent coffee and tea. A consumer who uses 1 gr of coffee and no tea has, therefore, a utility function of 1.

The notion of '*homo oeconomicus*' has been criticised not only at the theoretical level but, perhaps most importantly, on the basis of converging empirical findings that have repeatedly challenged its internal validity. For example, authors like Marshall, Polanyi, and Mauss have demonstrated that the social interactions across people significantly impact their decision making in economic terms and may significantly limit the utility function of single individuals, especially when this might negatively influence the society where these people live (Marshall 1972; Mauss 1924; Polanyi 1957). In other words, there are important ethical and societal constraints, particularly in more traditional societies, that influence the production and exchange of goods amongst people in a way that differs from what was predicted by the '*homo oeconomicus*' model. Such economic systems have been named 'gift' economy in contrast to the 'market' economy of the more classic economic theories (Mauss 1924).

Other empirical studies by Tversky and colleagues have criticised the hypothesis that investors are rational (Fox and Tversky 1995). In particular, Tversky has found that investors tend to display a risk-aversive behaviour when losing small amount of goods, while, curiously, they appear less affected by large losses, which obviously violates economic 'rationality (Fox and Tversky 1995)'. Further criticism of the model of '*homo oeconomicus*' has originated from the psychoanalytic tradition, which has emphasised the universal presence of 'internal' (and most of the time unconscious) conflicts in human beings, especially between short- and long-term objectives (e.g., eating a chocolate cake vs. losing weight) or between subject-specific goals and the overall societal values (Freud 1962). Such conflicts are thought to be the major determinants of apparently 'irrational' or contradictory behaviours which manifest themselves as inconsistent choices, functional 'paralysis', and neurotic behaviour. Another source of human irrational behaviour can be attributed to habits, laziness, behavioural 'mimicry' of peers or obedience to individuals with higher hierarchical status.

To conclude, since its initial introduction, the concept '*homo oeconomicus*' has been significantly debated and often considered as not realistic, over-simplistic, or even immoral. Who is the 'Homo Oeconomicus'?

- It is a key concept in classic economic theories.
- It is a model of human being who is characthesed by:

- Maximal 'rationality' (mainly intended as precision in calculation);
- High ability to *maximise* the *benefits* and *minimise* the *costs* (utility function) given the information available (e.g., during context evaluation).

11.2 Behavioural economics and neuroeconomics

The most substantial critique on the theory of the '*homo oeconomicus*' has been provided by behavioural economics, a field of research that examines real choices, including cognitive and emotional biases during economical decision making (de Tarde 1902). In sharp contrast to the concept of '*homo oeconomicus*', the behavioural economics has repeatedly emphasised that cooperation is a key element in economic transactions amongst human beings and, therefore, social and emotional biases in decision making should be included in naturalistic models of economical exchanges (Graham, Camerer and Loewenstein 2005). The growing field of neuroeconomics, which originates from the inter-disciplinary intersection between behavioural economics and neurosciences, has further corroborated the notion that there are important limitations in the conventional theories of economic 'rationality', as those represented by the concept of '*homo oeconomicus*' (Glimcher and Fehr 2013). More specifically, the field of neuroeconomics has provided converging evidence that even apparently 'rational' economic choices can be, in reality, guided by core emotional responses that in turn originate from human evolution and can be eventually studied in animal models. Decision making under risky and uncertain situations, loss aversion, inter-temporal choice, and choice selection within social contexts are the current major themes in neuroeconomics that attempt to address emotional biases in decision making.

For example, there is robust evidence that when decisions are made under risky or uncertain conditions, they become apparently less 'rational' as they violate the utility function (Tversky and Kahneman 1992). More specifically, during risky decision making, people tend to over-weight the probabilities of rare events while simultaneously under-weight the importance of other events that are more likely to happen (Levin, Schneider and Gaeth 1998). The activity in different parts of the prefrontal cortex (PFC), including the fronto-medial PFC has been found to be related to situations of uncertainty (Volz, Schubotz and von Cramon 2003). This is consistent with the idea that the PFC would be implicated in action and goal-planning even in the absence of any environmental information that may help guide choice selection (Paulus et al. 2001). The *insula* cortex is another critical region that has been found to be activated in uncertain situations; for example, when people play a 'double or nothing' gambling game (Paulus et al. 2003).

Another interesting aspect of human decision making is represented by the fact that individuals typically display strong aversion to losses, a form of 'irrational' behaviour that has been consistently found to bias potentially more efficient or 'rational' choices. In other words, the perceived cost of losing specific goods (e.g., amount of money) tends to be overall higher than the value of gaining the same goods. There are also inter-individual differences in aversion loss across people and this may be a key source of the high level of variability in the behavioural patterns during economical decision making, with some individuals showing more 'rational' behaviours than others under conditions in which it is more likely to lose rather than gain goods. Although with some controversies, it has been shown that patients with damage in the amygdala might display a lack of loss aversion and, consequently, have a potentially more 'rational' behaviour (De Martino, Camerer and Adolphs 2010). Finally, studies that have used peripheral markers of affective responses, like skin conductance, pupil dilatation, and heart rate, have showed that these physiological indices of emotional arousal tend to be increased during losses of goods than during gains of the equivalent amounts of goods (Hochman and Yechiam 2011; Sokol-Hessner et al. 2009).

Another central concept in behavioural economics and neuroeconomics is the notion that inter-temporal choice is an important source of bias in decision making. Briefly, inter-temporal choice represents how the relationship between costs and benefits is accounted over different time-scales. Although a 'rational' agent is expected to assign a different utility function to events occurring at different time-scales, it is evident that there are people who are particularly intolerant to delayed rewards, even when these are much larger than rewards that can be obtained over shorter periods of time (these people are often referred as displaying a form of impulsivity called "waiting impulsivity") (Dalley, Everitt and Robbins 2011). Regarding the neural systems governing inter-temporal choice, animal and human studies have converged in showing a critical involvement of limbic fronto-striatal loops as well as the important modulation of the dopaminergic, serotoninergic, and noradrenergic neurochemical systems (Winstanley et al. 2004).

The final major theme in neuroeconomics is represented by the study of social decision making, which includes the understanding of complex and reciprocal interactions amongst humans, like altruism, cooperation or social punishment. Key paradigms to understanding how people behave during social situations are represented by tasks, like the prisoner's dilemma and the ultimatum game, which I will describe in more detail in the following sections. In any case, the brain correlates of these social behaviours are still uncertain even if some neuroimaging studies have indicated that a series of brain regions, such as the *insula*, anterior cingulate cortex (ACC), dorsolateral PFC (DLPFC), and *ventral striatum*, may be particularly important in the orchestration and organisation of inter-personal interactions (Gabay et al. 2014).

11.3 Decision-making neuroscience and its relationship with neuroeconomics

From Plato's charioteer holding the 'horses of passion' (Ferrari 1985), to Freud's conscious *'ego'* that controls subconscious *'es'* (Freud 1962), there has been a long philosophical tradition that has considered 'reason' or 'logical thinking' and emotions as being opposed each other. This conceptualisation of the interaction between emotion and 'rationality' has also been popular in neuroscience where successful decision making has been traditionally viewed as depending on the intact pre-frontal cortex, which would, in turn, inhibit the affective responses generated within limbic and phylogenetically more ancient areas, like the amygdala, *ventral striatum*, hypothalamus, etc. Nevertheless, more recent models of the brain systems governing decision making have highlighted that, conversely to what was originally thought, decision making is not efficient without the necessary motivational and arousing component provided by the emotional inputs. This idea has originated from the work of Antonio Damasio on neurological patients with damage in the orbito-frontal cortex (OFC), which has been consistently shown to be a critical 'hub' in connecting limbic and emotional regions with other parts of the PFC involved in decision making (Damasio 1994). This working model has been successively formalised in the somatic marker hypothesis, which describes how visceral or internally generated emotions support decision making (Damasio 1994). More specifically, Damasio's group has provided evidence that during decision making, for example choice selection during a card game, the skin conductance (a peripheral measure of autonomic arousal) shows changes before critical choices are made, or even earlier than when people realise at a conscious level that they have made the wrong or correct choice (Tranel and Damasio 1994). Therefore, emotions are thought to be central in human decision making — which would explain why patients with damage in the OFC struggle to make the most important choices in their everyday life (Bechara, Damasio and Damasio 2000). All in all, emotions are considered to continuously shape and bias decision making and this is in sharp contrast to what was originally predicted by traditional economic theories.

Although the importance of emotion in decision making is increasingly recognised and studied, its role still needs to be formalised and incorporated into cutting-edge neuroscientific frameworks, especially those that study decision making from a computational prospective. I now move on to describe a popular computational model of decision making in neuroscience (the two-alternative forced choice) and its potential utility in neuroeconomics. It is implicit in the following discussion that there is a compelling necessity to include and formalise emotional inputs in models of decision making and choice selection.

The two-alternative forced choice (2AFC) and 'race' model are popular and relatively objective approaches to study and formalise the response times and 'internal' experience of individuals who are making choices (Fechner 1987). As displayed in Figure 1, in the race model (schematically represented as a horse race) evidence for each alternative is accumulated separately, and a decision made either when one of the accumulators reaches a predetermined threshold, or when a decision is forced and then the decision associated with the accumulator with the highest evidence is chosen. In a typical 2AFC task, the person is presented with two alternative and often contrasting choices, and only one of them is correct and associated with the target outcome (e.g., a reward). Usually, both options are showed simultaneously, although in some cases they can be presented sequentially (two-interval forced choice). A common variant of the 2AFC task used in cognitive neuroscience experiments is represented by the Posner cueing task, which employs a 2AFC design with two stimuli associated with two separate locations. During this paradigm, an arrow is used to cue which stimulus location the subject has to attend before an actual response between two separate locations is prompted and made. Participants' choices can also be rewarded according to the reinforcement probability learning theory, which is a theoretical framework that is used to study how reward interacts with decision making to enhance learning and guide efficient decision making. Another example of stimuli that can be employed in different versions of the 2AFC task is represented by the random dot kinetogram (Britten et al. 1993; Gold and Shadlen 2000). In this case, animals or humans have to pay attention to the centre of a computer screen in which a cloud of dots moving coherently towards one side of the screen is subsequently presented. In this task, a degree of randomness in the dot moving is introduced, with a remaining percentage of net coherent motion distributed across the random dots. The introduction of dot movement randomness permits the researchers to degrade the ability of participants to make clear decisions regarding the direction of the dots movement and, therefore, enables the manipulation of decision making. This method allows also to study decision making from a computational prospective, for example via using the drift-diffusion model.

Another way to bias decision making in the 2AFC task is to manipulate the stimulus' frequency. For example, if one stimulus is presented more often than another one, then participants tend to think that the likelihood of the appearance of the two alternative choices is different, whilst in reality it is not. It is also important to bear in mind that the computational models of the 2AFC are typically constructed under different assumptions, including that: i) the evidence which favours one alternative over the other one is accumulated and integrated over time; ii) there are random fluctuations that might increase the noise of decision making; and iii) the final choice is only made after sufficient evidence favouring one alternative choice over the other one has been progressively accumulated. Nevertheless, in different implementations of the computational models of 2AFC, it is also possible to track the evidence for the two alternative choices in a separate manner.

The drift-diffusion model (DDM) is an established mathematical framework that has been designed to model optimal decision making during 2AFC tasks (Ratcliff and McKoon 2008). The DDM assumes that a subject is accumulating evidence for one or the other alternative choice at each time step and that he-she is integrating that evidence until a decision threshold is reached. If the sensory stimulus necessary to accumulate evidence in favour of one decision over another is noisy, the accumulation to the threshold becomes stochastic rather than deterministic – this gives rise to the directed random walk-like behaviour of the model. The DDM has several advances and it has been found to describe accuracy and reaction times in human data during 2AFC and other tasks. The neurobiological validity of the DDM has also been supported by animal neurophysiological studies in which activity in the parietal and PFC has been recorded as well as in human research using fMRI (Krajbich and Rangel 2011; Mulder et al. 2012; Wiecki, Sofer and Frank 2013).

A limitation of current DDMs is the lack of inclusion of emotional input that in real life situations are known to significantly bias decision making. It would be important, therefore, that future implementation of the DDM, especially those which aim at modelling more naturalistic decision making will incorporate a formalisation of the emotional inputs that can alter the key parameters described in the computational model with the ultimate aim to better understand how emotions bias decision making.

11.4 The need to integrate emotions in decision-making models and the contribution of personality neuroscience

From what has been described so far, there is a clear necessity to augment the current theoretical and computational models of decision making to include the impact of the emotional inputs and their biasing effects on decision making. However, a major obstacle and challenge to reach this end is represented by the variability in how people experience emotions and how these can influence decision making. In other words, we need to better understand the brain basis of individual differences in emotional behaviour before we can reliably use this information to model how emotions shape and influence choice selection.

Recently, an emerging field of research named 'Personality Neuroscience' has been introduced with the aim of increasing our knowledge of the neurological roots underlying the high inter-individual differences in cognitive and emotional functions, as well as the variability in the enduring behavioural dispositions amongst human beings (DeYoung and Gray 2009; DeYoung et al. 2010). When referring to personality, I mean those groups of values, attitudes, personal memories, social relationships, habits, and skills that make the individuals the persons they are. The concept of personality is ancient and can be probably dated back to Hippocrates or even earlier (Figure 2). In Hippocrates' original description, people's temperaments were thought to be dependent on different typologies of humours. This is, with several obvious caveats, relatively similar to current neurobiological models of personality, which posit the importance of neurotransmitters in modulating individual differences in behaviour. More recently, it has led to several theories of 'personality traits' that have tried to explain and describe a series of relatively persisting personal features that are revealed when individuals face particular situations and environmental challenges (Allport 1937).

For instance, in threatening conditions (e.g., encountering a person with a knife), most of the people tend to react with anxiety (e.g., highly anxious individuals) while others may react aggressively (aggressive or antagonistic individuals). This does not necessarily imply that aggressive or anxious individuals will be aggressive or anxious in every single situation; in contrast, each specific personality trait mainly describes the likelihood that a certain individual will react in a characteristic manner given a determinate situation. In this context, it is also important to distinguish between 'trait' emotions and 'state' emotions (Spielberger 2010). This is because personality models have to take into account that all individuals can potentially experience and manifest any type of emotional state, although some states are more common than others in any specific person (e.g., anxiety will be often experienced by anxious people). Therefore, for 'trait' (e.g. anxiety traits), I mean a personality 'trait' that describes the behaviour of an individual in several circumstances, while for 'state' emotion, I refer to a short-term condition which can be present in any individual under certain conditions (e.g., acute anxiety as a result of a stimulus that is subjectively seen and perceived as potentially dangerous) (Spielberger 2010). In the context of decision making, it is hypothesised that both trait and state emotions can significantly bias choice selection and the associated economical decision-making processes. In the model of decision making that I propose (Figure 3), state and trait (personality) emotions are thought to impact and modulate different stages of the mechanisms underlying choice selection, from early stimulus processing and selection, to intermediate steps of context evaluation and, finally, to the codification of the internal value of any specific choice before an actual decision can be made. There is also some neuroanatomical and neurophysiological evidence that core brain emotional and limbic regions can influence ever later stages of the decision-making process including action selection and execution (Grezes et al. 2014; Toschi, Duggento and Passamonti 2017). This latter mechanism would represent a further way for emotions to bias choice selection and decision making. In any case, for the sake of simplicity, I describe the decision-making process as sequential, even if in no way I do imply that the neural underpinnings underlying each of these steps are sequential. In contrast, there is some evidence that the brain is able to implement each of these steps in a parallel rather than serial 'fashion', so it is likely that most of the decision-making steps that I describe in the next section are simultaneously implemented at the neural level. As displayed in Figure 3, in this modified version of the race model of decision making trait (i.e., personality) and state, emotions are able to significantly influence each step of the choice selection process. For instance, even in early sensorial processes, emotions can bias the intrinsic motivational value of each stimulus by altering an internal 'exchange rate'. In metaphorical terms, pre-existing personality factors can make people 'seeing' stimuli in a different way that can significantly bias their decision making regarding that given stimulus. The neural mechanisms underlying this hypothetical model are still relatively unknown and unexplored but see the text for a few examples of the brain regions which are thought to be implicated during this process. Likewise, the model assumes that later stages of the decision-making process, like context evaluation and assessment of benefits and risks in choice selection, can be significantly influenced by state and trait emotions.

The first step during which it is believed that individual differences in personality traits can significantly bias the downstream decision-mechanism processes is a relatively early and sensorial stage during which specific objects or inputs are processed and assessed. This could explain, in mechanistic terms, why some people are more prone than others in evaluating in a positive manner a rewarding stimulus (e.g., food) or, alternatively, to be more 'resistant' and resilient to the negative impact of certain situations or stimuli. This emotionally 'altered' early sensorial evaluation process can be formalised as a specific and subject-specific 'exchange' rate, when speaking in economic terms. In other words, trait and state emotions might significantly influence a sort of internal 'currency system', upon which subsequent choices are based. Although the brain mechanisms of the emotional bias on these initial sensory evaluation steps are poorly investigated and understood, there is emerging evidence from our research showing that the amygdala and other sub-cortical structures like the *ventral striatum* are implicated. More specifically, we found that individual traits linked to positive emotionality (e.g., behavioural activation system) predicted increased activation in the amygdala, *ventral striatum*, and OFC, while individuals were viewing pictures of appetising, relative to bland, food (Beaver et al. 2006). Furthermore, people with increased sensitivity to external stimuli (high external food sensitivity) were found to display enhanced connectivity between the amygdala, *ventral striatum*, and pre-motor cortex, as well as reduced connectivity between some PFC regions and the above-mentioned sub-cortical structures (i.e., amygdala and *ventral striatum*) (Passamonti et al. 2009). Together, these data neatly demonstrated that pre-existing personal attitudes towards certain classes of stimuli (in this case enhanced sensitivity to rewarding stimuli like food) may drive variability in the neural responses in cortical and sub-cortical brain networks that have been consistently implicated in emotional behaviour, its control, and more generally, in decision making and action selection processes. In other words, our findings can help explain, in mechanistic terms, the source of the heterogeneous responses that are often seen at the behavioural level during the selection of different choices, including economical ones (Passamonti et al. 2009).

Figure 4 summarises a series of findings that are described in more detail in Passamonti et al. 2009. In summary, it is hypothesised that pre-existing personality traits, which will be, in turn, 'hard-wired' within specific neural circuits, are able to significantly influence the early sensory processes that precede choice-selection and decision making regarding a particular set of stimuli. In this example, people with a high level of external food sensitivity are found to show enhanced connectivity patterns between limbic regions like the ventral striatum, the amygdala and, ultimately, the premotor cortex. At the same time, the same people were found to display reduced connectivity between the dorsal and ventral anterior cingulate cortex and sub-cortical areas including the amygdala and ventral striatum. This could help explain, in mechanistic terms, why these people tend to over-eat at the sight of food even if they are not hungry.

Similar brain mechanisms may underlie the processing of negative stimuli and may be, therefore, responsible for the bias towards some 'negatively charged' behavioural responses in certain individuals (e.g., the fact that anxious people tend to respond with anxiety and with decision making that can be significantly influenced by their current or 'trait' anxiety level). In this context, we found that individuals with high level of antagonistic traits tend to display increased amygdala response to social signals of threat (e.g., angry faces) and reduced activation in the PFC (the ventral anterior cingulate cortex - vACC) (Beaver et al. 2008). Consistently with the strong anatomical links between these regions, reduced connectivity between the amygdala and the vACC was also found in antagonistic individuals. Once again, these data could be important in explaining the high inter-individual variability when processing stimuli with an intrinsic emotional component and may reflect one of the earliest sources of the heterogeneity in decision making and choice selection. All in all, I believe that some hard-wired neural components reflecting inter-individual differences in personality can make different persons 'seeing' the same stimulus in different ways, which inherently biases their consequent choices regarding that stimuli. However, it is important to highlight, once again, that even if I describe these processes as sequential, by no means do I want to imply that these are also sequential processes at the neural level. This is because the methods that we employed (fMRI) have poor temporal resolution and we were not able to resolve the specific temporal dynamics of the underlying neuronal processes. In addition, it is quite surprising to see that many of the regions (e.g. those in the PFC), which have been traditionally implicated in late stages of decision making, showed in reality a strong modulation by personality traits, even in fMRI tasks that were mainly designed to assess relatively early sensorial processes rather than choice selection *per se* (i.e., processing emotional stimuli with minimal task or cognitive demand). This is corroborated by the evidence that even the passive viewing of emotionally 'charged' objects is, in principle, capable of recruiting key brain regions like the PFC, which has been traditionally implicated in high-level cognitive functions as decision making. Perhaps more importantly, this early 'engagement' of PFC regions by sensorial processes is thought to significantly vary from person to person which, in turn, would depend on the underlying 'natural' and subject-specific attitude (personality traits) towards specific sets of emotional stimuli (whichever positive or negative).

It is also important to mention that together with specific brain circuits, variability in the function of a series of key neurochemical systems can represent another fundamental source of individual differences in decision making and emotional processing. For example, heterogeneity in the functioning and anatomy of the serotoninergic system can mediate differences in how people process emotional stimuli or take decisions about them, both at the behavioural and neural levels. More specifically, tryptophan depletion (a dietary procedure that permits lowering the blood and brain levels of serotonin) has been found to mediate differences in decision making including moral decision making (Crockett *et al.* 2008). Interestingly, we also found that there was an interaction between individual differences in personality traits and the way in which tryptophan depletion could modulate the neural mechanisms underlying the processing of negative stimuli (angry faces) (Passamonti et al. 2012). In particular, we demonstrated that antagonistic people, relatively to their less antagonistic counterparts, displayed a greater effect of the tryptophan depletion procedure in terms of reducing the connectivity between the amygdala and vACC while processing angry faces (Passamonti et al. 2012). These data may help to explain why some pre-existing personality factors have an impact in determining the behavioural responses to psycho-active drugs and might also offer new insights to understand the way in which pharmacological agents can differently bias decision-making processes in different individuals. Figure 5 summarises the results of our studies described in detail in Passamonti et al. (2012). Briefly, tryptophan depletion --- a dietary procedure that is known to reduce the plasma and brain levels of serotonin --- changed the connectivity patterns between the ventral anterior cingulate cortex (in blue) and the amygdala (in red), especially in more antagonistic individuals, relative to their less antagonistic counterparts.

However, please note that although I discussed the serotoninergic system as an important element in biasing and guiding emotional processing and decision making, several other lines of research have demonstrated that this is not the only brain chemical that is able to influence choice selection and, more generally, brain functioning. Hormones or other neurotransmitters, like acetylcholine, noradrenaline, dopamine, and many other neurochemicals, have been found to impact large-scale neural networks with profound consequences in terms of behavioural choices and decision making. Nevertheless, a detailed description of the pharmacology of decision making is beyond the scope of this chapter and will not be further discussed.

I now move on to describe the final step in which personality traits are hypothesised to bias decision making. This is represented by the stage of context evaluation. As shown in Figure 3, after initial stimulus' assessment (during which a subject-specific exchange rate is set-up), the individual has now to determine which is the likelihood that the item or stimulus will be gained or lost, depending on external or environmental information available. As for earlier steps, some contingencies (losing or gaining) might be weighted in different ways according to individual differences in personality and subject-specific preferences. For example, some people are more risk-avoidant than others, which means that for certain people the risk of losing an item can be 'weighted' more than the estimation of the likelihood of obtaining the same object with same motivational value. It is also important to note that preventing the loss of an item can be equally rewarding as obtaining the same object, while blocking the gain of an object can be perceived as punishing as losing the same item. All these 'pros' and 'cons' are somehow rated (conscientiously or sub-conscientiously) by the individuals and are subject to important modulation of different personality traits. A paradigm, that in neuroeconomic studies has been emblematic to measure these context-dependant biases in decision making, is represented by the ultimatum game (Sanfey *et al.* 2003). In this task, there are two players. The first one (the proposer) is the person who is responsible for proposing how to divide a sum of money between him/herself and the other player (the responder). The latter, in turn, has to choose to either accept or reject the proposal from the first player. If the responder accepts the money offer, the money is split according to the proposal of the first player. If the second player rejects the proposal, neither player receives any money at all. As shown in Figure 6, the proposer (blue jacket) makes an offer to the responder (red jacket) on how to split up a certain sum of money. The responder has then to decide whether to accept or reject the offer bearing in mind that any time he/she rejects an offer, no player earns any money. In typical settings, the offers that are perceived as unfair (e.g., >70:30 split) are rarely accepted.

According to classic economic theories (e.g. '*homo oeconomicus*' model), the responder should always accept all offers as it is not rational to reject any offer considering that this leads to a loss of money. In reality, however, people do not behave as the '*homo oeconomicus*' theory predicts but, in contrast, they tend to accept only those offers that are perceived and evaluated as fair. In other words, most of the responders in the ultimatum game will only accept splits that do not evidently favour the proposer (in practice, a split less than 70:30 is rarely accepted).

Interestingly, two key brain regions have been found to be particularly important in mediating the decision-making processes of the responder: the *insula* and the dorso-lateral PFC (Sanfey *et al.* 2003). While it is likely that the activity in this latter region reflects the indispensable cognitive machinery to perform complex decision making-tasks (e.g. attention, working-memory, response inhibition, etc.), the *insula* activation has been thought to mediate those emotional components that are responsible of biasing choice selections. In other terms, it is believed that the *insula* activity is associated with the arousal or emotional aspects that accompany the receipt of an unfair offer (Sanfey *et al.* 2003). Given the prominent and reciprocal anatomical connections between the *insula* and DLPFC, it is also likely that their interplay or 'communication' represents another important mechanism of the bias in decision making during unfair offers, although this aspect has still been scarcely investigated.

However, even the likelihood of rejections of very unfair offers can be altered by strong social contexts and modulators. In a recent experiment lead by O'Callaghan, it has been indeed found that when the responder is presented with a specific social background regarding the proposer, the decision of rejecting an unfair offer might be significantly mitigated (O'Callaghan *et al.* 2015). As displayed in Figure 7, if the social situation of the proposer is framed in a prosocial or punishing fashion, it is possible to bias the rate of rejection or acceptance of unfair offers. This has been shown to be dependent on the integrity of the ventromedial prefrontal cortex and orbitofrontal cortex, as patients with the behavioural variant of frontotemporal dementia (bvFTD), a devastating neurodegenerative disorder that leads to significant damage in these regions, do not show a social framing effect when playing the ultimatum game (they tend to have more rejections even during the prosocial framing). For example, if the responder is told that the proposer has recently lost his/her job, it becomes more likely that the responder accepts an unfair offer from the proposer (and this perhaps may be true, especially for more empathic people) (O'Callaghan *et al.* 2015). In contrast, if the responder is told that the proposer has won money at the lottery, it becomes more likely for the responder to reject offers that in other circumstances would have been rated as fair and consequently accepted (O'Callaghan *et al.* 2015). All in all, the social framing of the offer can significantly bias the decision-making process in the responder and this is, once again, likely to be dependent on underlying differences in personality traits (e.g., more or less empathic people). Interestingly, patients with early stages of the behavioural variant of frontotemporal dementia, a devastating neurodegenerative disorder that is associated with significant damage in the OFC and medial PFC, have been found to be profoundly impaired in the evaluation of the social context during the ultimatum game; although they show normal acceptance and refusal rates during the ultimatum game trials in which there was no social framing (O'Callaghan *et al.* 2015). This highlights that some parts of the PFC are important in evaluating complex socio-affective stimuli (e.g., presence of discomfort in another person), which plays a major role in biasing decision making. This may also help explaining why, under some specific circumstances, patients with brain damage (e.g., OFC deficits) behave in a manner that appears even more 'rational' in economic terms.

We now move on to discuss another neuro-psychiatric condition which is, at the theoretical level, in keeping with the concept of the '*homo oeconomicus*': the psychopathic brain.

11.5 Neuroscience of psychopathy as a modern model of the '*homo oeconomicus*'

Traditionally, psychopathy has been defined by the presence of severe and persistent antisocial behaviour, lack of empathy and remorse and, more generally, blunted emotions (Hare 1970). Some forms of psychopathy have also been associated with highly disinhibited and impulsive behaviour and can also be characterised by strongly egocentric features at the inter-personal level (Lapierre, Braun, and Hodgins 1995). Adult individuals with high levels of psychopathic traits are also often considered to present an antisocial personality disorder, which is commonly associated with repeated delinquency, crime, and violence (De Brito and Hodgins 2009). In some circumstances, psychopathic traits manifest themselves with more 'covert' antisocial behaviours, like stealing, fire-setting or other forms of indirect violation of the rights of other people (Loeber and Schmaling 1985). From a developmental prospective, the psychopathic personality traits can be detected early during adolescence or even in childhood, especially in those children with conduct disorder, oppositional defiant disorder or attention deficit hyperactivity disorder, a group of relatively common paediatric conditions (Moffitt 1993). This epidemiological evidence has, thus, suggested a potentially strong neurodevelopmental origin of psychopathy and related antisocial behaviours (Moffitt 1993).

More recently, Raine and colleagues have proposed the working hypothesis that two major typologies of psychopathy would exist: the 'unsuccessful' and 'successful' psychopathy (Gao and Raine 2010; Ishikawa *et al.* 2001). The first form would be more characteristic of violent and incarcerated offenders, while the second group of psychopaths would be able to achieve their antisocial and psychopathic goals using covert and non-violent behaviours ('white collar' psychopaths) (Gao and Raine 2010). It has also been proposed that the group of unsuccessful psychopaths would have more neurological dysfunctions than the second group, especially in terms of cognitive functioning and intelligence quotient (Gao and Raine 2010). In contrast, the successful psychopaths would have intact or even enhanced cognitive skills, which would help them to achieve their psychopathic objectives without being caught or even noted by other people (Gao and Raine 2010). A central neurobiological deficit in both conditions would be, nonetheless, represented by the lack of empathy and by the general tendency to display 'flattened' affectivity (bluntness or emotional 'callousness'), which can be evaluated via a series of measures including personality questionnaires and peripheral measures of arousal, like the skin conductance response (Blair 2010). Psychopathy and blunted emotionality have also been associated to reduced function of the amygdala and *insula*, as well as to decreased response of the same regions during fear conditioning or while psychopathic people process socio-affective stimuli, like fearful, angry or sad faces (Blair 2007). Other regions that have been hypothesised to play a key role in psychopathy and antisocial behaviour are the OFC and the vACC, two highly interconnected limbic areas (Blair 2007). Interestingly, our group has found that many of these neurological deficits can already be detectable in adolescents and young adults with conduct disorder; a paediatric condition that anticipates the emergence of severe and pervasive antisocial behaviours in adulthood (Fairchild *et al.* 2011; Passamonti *et al.* 2010). More specifically, we found that youths with conduct disorders, relative to their peers with no antisocial behaviours, showed reduced response in the amygdala, *insula*, OFC, and vACC while processing angry or sad faces, relative to neutral faces (Passamonti *et al.* 2010) (Figure 8).

These deficits are probably dependent on an underlying neuroanatomical dysfunction in the form of reduced grey-matter density in the same regions (Fairchild *et al.* 2011) (Figure 9). Youths with conduct disorder, relative to their peers without antisocial behaviour, showed a reduced grey-matter density in the amygdala which may explain the functional alterations described in Figure 8, as well as the deficits in recognising the facial expression and the disturbances in the decision-making process.

The profound abnormalities in the limbic and para-limbic brain areas in adults with psychopathy and young people with conduct disorder are also reflected in a series of neuropsychological deficits, which include difficulty in recognising facial expressions (particularly fear, anger, and disgust), lack of empathy, and disturbances in decision making (Fairchild, Van Goozen, Calder, Stollery, and Goodyer, 2009; Fairchild *et al.* 2009). Interestingly, a neuropsychological study using the ultimatum game has found that incarcerated people with psychopathy and low levels of anxiety showed a behavioural pattern resembling that of neurological patients with ventromedial prefrontal cortex (vmPFC) or OFC lesions (Koenigs, Kruepke, and Newman 2010). More specifically, incarcerated psychopaths and vmPFC patients were less likely to reject unfair offers than patients with damage to other parts of the brain or incarcerated people without psychopathic traits (Koenigs, Kruepke, and Newman 2010).

If we interpret this set of results in the context of the decision-making model that I have discussed so far, it is possible to hypothesise that different types of psychopathy (successful vs. unsuccessful psychopathy) are related to distinct typologies of decision-making abnormalities, which will ultimately depend on whether the PFC or 'executive functions' are conserved (successful psychopathy) or not (unsuccessful psychopathy). In other words, I speculate that unsuccessful psychopaths are characterised by profound deficits in the exchange rate (or sensorial) steps of decision-making processes as well as by abnormalities in 'later' stages (context evaluation and attribution of internal value). This combined, or 'two-hits', deficit in the choice selection mechanisms, which is likely to have neurodevelopmental origins, would lead to highly abnormal behaviours, like aggression and violence. All in all, the 'unsuccessful' psychopaths would be highly insensitive to several socio-affective signals from other individuals that would originate from their deficits in processing these stimuli at the neural level. This, alongside the inability of these people to plan ahead and make sensible decisions on a long-term basis, is likely to lead to a highly chaotic life-style, which ultimately leads to incarceration or even death by assassination. On the opposite hand, people with more successful forms of psychopathy may have preserved or even enhanced cognitive skills, although their lack of the basic 'emotional machinery' to process key affective stimuli make them struggle to deal with emotions, especially those experienced by others (Gao and Raine 2010). This 'disconnection' between the 'emotional' and 'cognitive' brain may result in forms of decision-making that in some circumstances appear logical or even more rational than those typically made by normal individuals. In other words, some forms of psychopathy (i.e., successful psychopathy) may be in keeping with the classic 'portrait' of the '*homo oeconomicus*', which is that of a 'rational', 'selfish', and 'ego-centric' individual who maximises the utility function as a consumer and the profit as a producer (Rittenberg and Tregarthen 2012).

In this context, it is of interest to note that some forms of relatively 'mild' psychopathy or the presence of some psychopathic personality traits may have created an advance for some individuals from an evolutionary prospective. In other words, people with psychopathic elements in their personality may be able to escalate the social strata given their more 'rational' and 'emotionally-detached' cognitive skills. Essentially, if we imagine that psychopathy lies within a continuum spectrum with 'normal' behaviours and that there are no clear 'borders' or limits between 'healthy' people and 'psychopaths', we may then argue that the reason why psychopathic traits have been conserved or even selected throughout evolution is that they may have conferred a benefit in terms of survival chances. Consistently with this fascinating hypothesis, a recent population study in 3388 'healthy' individuals from the community has demonstrated that some psychopathic traits (e.g., those linked with blunted emotionality), were significantly linked to higher social and occupational status and leadership (Lilienfeld *et al.* 2014). In contrast, other forms of psychopathic characteristics (e.g., those associated with the 'unsuccessful' type of psychopathy) were negatively linked to the educational level and income (Lilienfeld *et al.* 2014). The potential dissociation between different aspects of psychopathy are, therefore, interesting and warrant further investigation at the behavioural, neuropsychological, and neural levels. All in all, elucidating the brain basis of psychopathy might have important implications for improving our knowledge of decision making and for revealing the most intimate mechanisms of those evolutionary processes that have shaped human beings throughout the centuries and millennia.

11.6 Conclusions

To summarise, I hope that this chapter has clarified some of the key concepts in the neuroscience of decision making and personality, and their links with neuroeconomics. Another important take-home message from this chapter is that the concept of '*homo oeconomicus*', although highly debated, could be still potentially useful within specific experimental settings, especially those that aim to improve our understanding of complex and not yet fully understood neuro-psychiatric conditions, like psychopathy and some forms of brain damage affecting the prefrontal cortex. More studies using computational approaches and formal models of behaviour are also needed to reveal the core neurobiological processes that govern decision making during economical and non-economical choice selection. A better understanding of these mechanisms has the potential to inform economic models with the ultimate aim to tackle, predict, and contextualise the apparently 'irrational' human behaviours. On a large or macro-economic scale, this will also have obvious implications to improve the management and rationalisation of our economic resources, and to reduce or even prevent economic disasters.

Figures

Figure 1.
Model of decision making

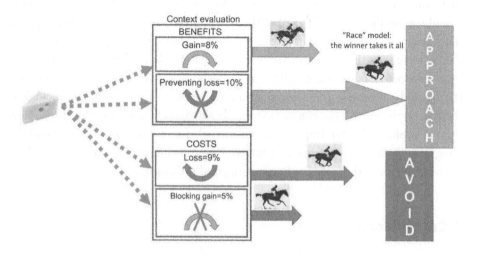

Source: Authors' elaboration.

Figure 2.
Four temperaments: Hippocrates (460-370 BC)

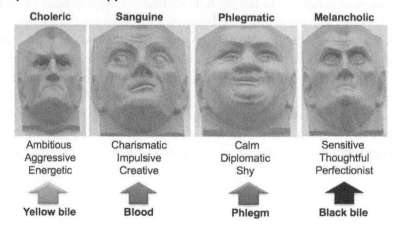

Source: Authors' elaboration.

Figure 3.
Decision making model

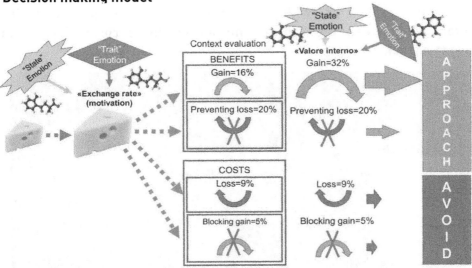

Source: Authors' elaboration.

Figure 4.
Neurobiological model of the exchange-rate step of decision making

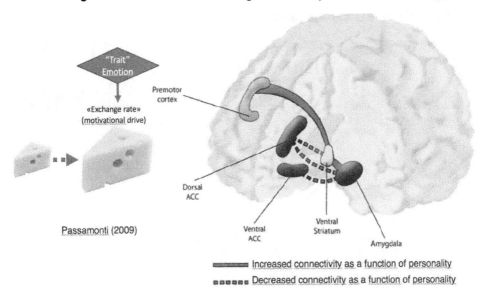

Figure 5.

Lowered levels of tryptophan (and consequently serotonin) in antagonistic people are associated with decreased connectivity (dotted yellow line/arrow) between the ventral anterior cingulate cortex (cyan) and amygdala (red).

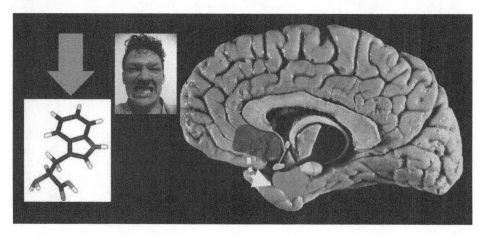

Source: Authors' elaboration.

Figure 6.

Schematic of the ultimatum game.

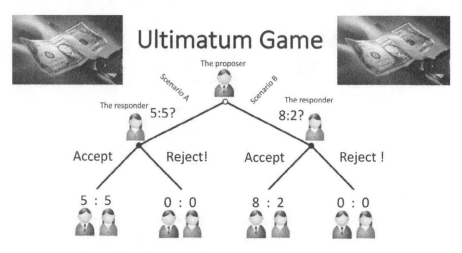

Source: Authors' elaboration.

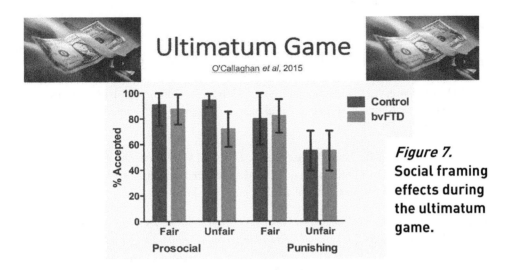

Figure 7.
Social framing effects during the ultimatum game.

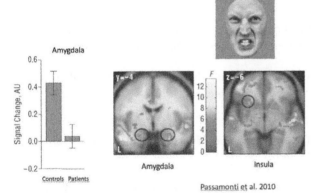

Figure 8.
Enconding of angry faces in conduct disorderressions.

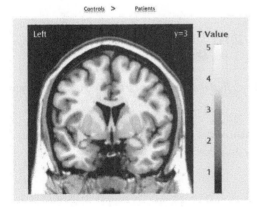

Figure 9.
Voxel Based Morphometry (VBM).

Fairchild et al. 2011

References

Allport, G.W., (1937), *Personality: A psychological interpretation*, Henry Holt.

Beaver, J.D., Lawrence, A.D., Passamonti, L. and Calder, A.J., (2008), «Appetitive Motivation Predicts the Neural Response to Facial Signals of Aggression», *Journal of Neuroscience*, 28(11), pp. 2719-2725.

Beaver, J.D., Lawrence, A.D., van Ditzhuijzen, J., Davis, M.H., Woods, A. and Calder, A.J., (2006), «Individual Differences in Reward Drive Predict Neural Responses to Images of Food», *Journal of Neuroscience*, 26(19), pp. 5160-5166.

Bechara, A., Damasio, H. and Damasio, A.R., (2000), «Emotion, Decision Making and the Orbitofrontal Cortex», *Cerebral Cortex*, 10(3), pp. 295-307.

Blair, R.J.R., (2007), «The Amygdala and Ventromedial Prefrontal Cortex in Morality and Psychopathy», *Trends in Cognitive Sciences*, 11(9), pp. 387-392.

Blair, R.J.R., (2010), «Psychopathy, Frustration, and Reactive Aggression: The Role of Ventromedial Prefrontal Cortex», *British Journal of Psychology*, 101(3), pp. 383-399.

Britten, K.H., Shadlen, M.N., Newsome, W.T. and Movshon, J.A., (1993), «Responses of Neurons in Macaque MT to Stochastic Motion Signals», *Visual Neuroscience*, 10(6), pp. 1157-1169.

Castagnoli, E. and Calzi, M.L., (1996), «Expected Utility without Utility», *Theory and Decision*, 41(3), pp. 281-301.

Crockett, M.J., Clark, L., Tabibnia, G., Lieberman, M.D. and Robbins, T.W., (2008), «Serotonin Modulates Behavioral Reactions to Unfairness», *Science*, 320(5884), pp. 1739-1739.

Dalley, J.W., Everitt, B.J. and Robbins, T.W., (2011), «Impulsivity, Compulsivity, and Top-Down Cognitive Control», *Neuron*, 69(4), pp. 680-694.

Damasio, A.R., (1994), *Descartes' Error: Emotion, Rationality and the Human Brain*, Putnam Publishing.

De Brito, S.A. and Hodgins, S., (2009), «Antisocial Personality Disorder. Personality, Personality Disorder and Violence», 42, pp. 133-153.

De Martino, B., Camerer, C.F. and Adolphs, R., (2010), «Amygdala Damage Eliminates Monetary Loss Aversion», *Proceedings of the National Academy of Sciences*, 107(8), pp. 3788-3792.

de Tarde, G., (1902), *Psychologie économique,* (Vol. 2), Félix Alcan, Éd., Ancienne Libr. Germer Baillière et Cie.

DeYoung, C.G. and Gray, J.R. (2009), «Personality Neuroscience: Explaining Individual Differences in Affect, Behaviour and Cognition», *The Cambridge handbook of personality psychology*, pp. 323-346.

DeYoung, C.G., Hirsh, J.B., Shane, M.S., Papademetris, X., Rajeevan, N. and Gray, J.R., (2010), «Testing Predictions from Personality Neuroscience: Brain Structure and the Big Five», *Psychological Science*, 21(6), pp. 820-828.

Fairchild, G., Passamonti, L., Hurford, G., Hagan, C.C., von dem Hagen, E.A.H., van Goozen, S.H.M. et al., (2011), «Brain Structure Abnormalities in Early-Onset and Adolescent-Onset Conduct Disorder» *American Journal of Psychiatry*, 168(6), pp. 624-633.

Fairchild, G., Van Goozen, S.H.M., Calder, A.J., Stollery, S.J. and Goodyer, I.M., (2009), «Deficits in Facial Expression Recognition in Male Adolescents with Early-onset or Adolescence-onset Conduct Disorder», *Journal of Child Psychology and Psychiatry*, 50(5), pp. 627-636.

Fairchild, G., van Goozen, S.H.M., Stollery, S.J., Aitken, M.R.F., Savage, J., Moore, S.C. et al., (2009), «Decision Making And Executive Function In Male Adolescents With Early-onset or Adolescence-onset Conduct Disorder and Control Subjects», *Biological Psychiatry*, 66(2), pp. 162-168.

Fechner, G.T., (1860), *Elemente der Psychophysik*, 2 Bd. Leipzig: Breit-kopf and Härtel [2. und 3. unveränderte Auflage, hrsg. von W. Wundt, 1889 und 1907].

Fechner, G.T., (1987), «My Own Viewpoint on Mental Measurement (1887)», *Psychological Research*, 49(4), pp. 213-219.

Ferrari, G.R.F., (1985), «The Struggle in the Soul: Plato, Phaedrus 253c7-255a1», *Ancient Philosophy*, 5(1), pp. 1-10.

Fox, C.R. and Tversky, A., (1995), «Ambiguity Aversion and Comparative Ignorance», *The Quarterly Journal of Economics*, 110(3), pp. 585-603.

Freud, S., (1962), *The ego and the id*, WW Norton and Company.

Gabay, A.S., Radua, J., Kempton, M.J. and Mehta, M.A., (2014), «The Ultimatum Game and the Brain: A Meta-Analysis of Neuroimaging Studies», *Neuroscience & Biobehavioral Reviews*, 47, pp. 549-558.

Gao, Y. and Raine, A., (2010), «Successful and Unsuccessful Psychopaths: A Neurobiological Model». *Behavioral Sciences & the Law*, 28(2), pp. 194-210.

Glimcher, P.W. and Fehr, E., (2013), *Neuroeconomics: Decision making and the brain*, Academic Press.

Gold, J.I. and Shadlen, M.N., (2000), «Representation of a perceptual Decision In Developing Oculomotor Commands», *Nature*, 404(6776), pp. 390-394.

Graham, J., Camerer, C.F. and Loewenstein, G., (2005), «Adam Smith, Behavioral Economist», *The Journal of Economic Perspectives*, 19(3), pp. 131-145.

Grezes, J., Valabregue, R., Gholipour, B. and Chevallier, C., (2014), «A Direct Amygdala-Motor Pathway for Emotional Displays to Influence Action: A Diffusion Tensor Imaging Study», *Human Brain Mapping*, 35(12), pp. 5974-5983.

Hare, R.D., (1970), *Psychopathy: Theory and research*, Brendan Maher.

Hochman, G. and Yechiam, E., (2011), «Loss Aversion in the Eye and in the Heart: The Autonomic Nervous System's Responses To Losses», *Journal of Behavioral Decision Making*, 24(2), pp. 140-156.

Ishikawa, S.S., Raine, A., Lencz, T., Bihrle, S. and Lacasse, L., (2001), «Autonomic Stress Reactivity and Executive Functions in Successful and Unsuccessful Criminal Psychopaths From The Community», *Journal of Abnormal Psychology*, 110(3), p. 423.

Koenigs, M., Kruepke, M. and Newman, J.P., (2010), «Economic Decision-Making in Psychopathy: A Comparison with Ventromedial Prefrontal Lesion Patients» *Neuropsychologia*, 48(7), pp. 2198-2204.

Krajbich, I. and Rangel, A., (2011), «Multialternative Drift-Diffusion Model Predicts the Relationship Between Visual Fixations and Choice In Value-Based Decisions», *Proceedings of the National Academy of Sciences*, 108(33), pp. 13852-13857.

Lapierre, D., Braun, C.M.J. and Hodgins, S., (1995), «Ventral frontal Deficits in Psychopathy: Neuropsychological Test Findings», *Neuropsychologia*, 33(2), pp. 139-151.

Levin, I. P., Schneider, S. L. and Gaeth, G.J., (1998), «All Frames Are Not Created Equal: A Typology and Critical Analysis Of Framing Effects», *Organizational Behavior and Human Decision Processes*, 76(2), pp. 149-188.

Lilienfeld, S.O., Latzman, R.D., Watts, A.L., Smith, S.F. and Dutton, K., (2014), «Correlates of Psychopathic Personality Traits in Everyday Life: Results from a Large Community Survey», *Frontiers in Psychology*, p. 5.

Loeber, R. and Schmaling, K.B., (1985), «Empirical Evidence for Overt And Covert Patterns of Antisocial Conduct Problems: A Metaanalysis», *Journal of Abnormal Child Psychology*, 13(2), 337-353.

Marshall, S., (1972), «The Original Affluent Society», *Stone Age Economics*, Marshall Sahlins, pp. 1-27.

Mauss, M., (1924), *The Gift: The Form and Reason for Exchange in Archaic Community*, WW Norton.

Moffitt, T.E., (1993), «Adolescence-Limited and Life-Course-Persistent Antisocial Behavior: A Developmental Taxonomy», *Psychological Review*, 100(4), p. 674.

Mulder, M. J., Wagenmakers, E.-J., Ratcliff, R., Boekel, W. and Forstmann, B. U. (2012), «Bias in the Brain: A Diffusion Model Analysis of Prior Probability and Potential Payoff», *Journal of Neuroscience*, 32(7), pp. 2335-2343.

O'Callaghan, C., Bertoux, M., Irish, M., Shine, J. M., Wong, S., Spiliopoulos, L. et al. (2015), «Fair Play: Social Norm Compliance Failures in Behavioural Variant Frontotemporal Dementia», *Brain*, 139(1), pp. 204-216.

Passamonti, L., Crockett, M.J., Apergis-Schoute, A.M., Clark, L., Rowe, J.B., Calder, A.J. et al., (2012), «Effects of Acute Tryptophan Depletion on Prefrontal-Amygdala Connectivity While Viewing Facial Signals of aggression», *Biological Psychiatry*, 71(1), pp. 36-43.

Passamonti, L., Fairchild, G., Goodyer, I.M., Hurford, G., Hagan, C.C., Rowe, J.B. et al., (2010), «Neural Abnormalities in Early-Onset and Adolescence-onset Conduct Disorder», *Archives of General Psychiatry*, 67(7), pp. 729-738.

Passamonti, L., Rowe, J.B., Ewbank, M., Hampshire, A., Keane, J. and Calder, A.J. (2008), «Connectivity from the Ventral Anterior Cingulate to the Amygdala Is Modulated By Appetitive Motivation in Response to Facial Signals Of Aggression», *Neuroimage*, 43(3), pp. 562-570.

Passamonti, L., Rowe, J. B., Schwarzbauer, C., Ewbank, M. P., Von Dem Hagen, E. and Calder, A. J., (2009), «Personality Predicts the Brain's Response to Viewing Appetizing Foods: The Neural Basis of a Risk Factor for Overeating», *Journal of Neuroscience*, 29(1), pp. 43-51.

Paulus, M. P., Hozack, N., Zauscher, B., McDowell, J. E., Frank, L., Brown, G. G. et al., (2001), «Prefrontal, Parietal, and Temporal Cortex Networks Underlie Decision-Making in the Presence Of Uncertainty», *Neuroimage*, 13(1), pp. 91-100.

Paulus, M.P., Rogalsky, C., Simmons, A., Feinstein, J.S. and Stein, M.B., (2003), «Increased Activation in the Right Insula During Risk-Taking Decision Making Is Related to Harm Avoidance and Neuroticism», *Neuroimage*, 19(4), pp. 1439-1448.

Persky, J., (1995), «Retrospectives: The Ethology of Homo Economicus», *The Journal of Economic Perspectives*, 9(2), pp. 221-231.

Polanyi, K., (1957), *The Great Transformation*, Beacon Hill (Beacon Press).

Ratcliff, R. and McKoon, G., (2008), «The Diffusion Decision Model: Theory and Data for Two-Choice Decision Tasks», *Neural Computation*, 20(4), pp. 873-922.

Rittenberg, L. and Tregarthen, T., (2012), *Principles of Microeconomics* (Version 2.0). Washington, DC, Flat World Knowledge, Inc.

Sanfey, A.G., Rilling, J.K., Aronson, J.A., Nystrom, L.E. and Cohen, J.D., (2003), «The Neural Basis of Economic Decision-Making in the Ultimatum Game», *Science*, 300(5626), pp. 1755-1758.

Sokol-Hessner, P., Hsu, M., Curley, N.G., Delgado, M.R., Camerer, C.F. and Phelps, E.A., (2009), «Thinking Like a Trader Selectively Reduces Individuals' Loss Aversion», *Proceedings of the National Academy of Sciences*, 106(13), pp. 5035-5040.

Spielberger, C.D., (2010), *State-Trait Anxiety Inventory*. Wiley Online Library.

Toschi, N., Duggento, A. and Passamonti, L., (2017), «Functional Connectivity In Amygdalar-Sensory/(Pre) Motor Networks at Rest: New Evidence from the Human Connectome Project», *European Journal of Neuroscience*, 45(9), pp. 1224-1229.

Tranel, D, and Damasio, H., (1994), «Neuroanatomical Correlates Of Electrodermal Skin Conductance Responses», *Psychophysiology*, 31(5), pp. 427-438.

Tversky, A. and Kahneman, D., (1992), «Advances in Prospect Theory: Cumulative Representation of Uncertainty», *Journal of Risk and Uncertainty*, 5(4), 2pp. 97-323.

Volz, K.G., Schubotz, R.I. and von Cramon, D.Y., (2003), «Predicting Events of Varying Probability: Uncertainty Investigated by fMRI», *Neuroimage*, 19(2), pp. 271-280.

Wiecki, T.V., Sofer, I. and Frank, M.J., (2013), «HDDM: Hierarchical Bayesian Estimation of the Drift-Diffusion Model in Python», *Frontiers in Neuroinformatics*, p. 7.

Winstanley, C.A., Dalley, J.W., Theobald, D.E.H. and Robbins, T.W., (2004), «Fractionating Impulsivity: Contrasting Effects of Central 5-HT Depletion on Different Measures Of Impulsive Behavior», *Neuropsychopharmacology*, 29(7), p. 1331.

Part IV
New Curiosites about the Brain

12. A Viable Systems Approach (VSA) to Social Neurosciences

by Sergio Barile, Francesca Iandolo, Stefano Armenia

The decision-making process is part of everyday life of organisations and it continuously depends, and has an influence, on the contexts in which organisations themselves live and operate.

Traditionally, studies on decision processes have referred to articulated procedures, mainly based on calculus, thus giving the process a rational characterisation (von Neumann and Morgenstern 1947).

However, recent studies on bounded rationality (March and Simon 1958), as well as on the decision intended as a social construction (Cohen, March and Olsen 1972) put emphasis on the influence that non-rational elements have on decision processes. An essential contribution to addressing the current complexity and the unpredictability of the markets, as well as the behaviour of business operators comes from two fields of study: behavioural economics and neuroscience, as well as from the link between these two disciplines: the so-called "neuroeconomics".

To face these issues related to decision making in complex contexts, in this work we will refer to the conceptualisation of the Viable Systems Approach (VSA) that distinguishes between two kinds of decisions; the ones related to problem solving and the ones related to decision making (Barile 2009; Barile *et al.* 2016). According to VSA, we can define problem solving as the adoption of theories, models, techniques and tools that are already known; in this sense, we can define it as the ability to use existing knowledge, as the problems the decision-maker faces are not related to the availability of information but to the knowledge gap experienced that results from the lack of interpretation capabilities.

Decision making, instead, is related to the need to identify or develop new theories, models, techniques, and tools that are not already known to the decision maker. According to these concepts, which are the factors that culminate in a right or wrong choice, and the elements of knowledge that can contribute to define a solution to a given problem? The Viable Systems Approach (VSA), with the notions of consonance and resonance, measures the appropriateness of a specific decision. Such a model bases its dynamics on the following concepts: information variety, interpretation schemes, and value categories that will be described in what follows.

Representing a viable system through decision making and problem solving activities characterising the dynamics and the evolution of knowledge acquisition (Barile 2008), makes it possible to identify significant properties associated with the decision process. The possible paths of resolution of a specific decision making problem starts from a perception deriving from the external context and from the knowledge owned by each subject. This process, developed through abduction, induction and deduction, can be repeated infinite times before it gives a solution to the problem, which becomes a new interpretation scheme. However, in some cases, this sequence may not bring a solution; the possible paths are explained in Figure 1.

To better explain this process, it can be useful to clarify the concept of deduction, which consists of the appropriate application of established models or simple interpretation schemes to analogous situations. According to the perspective adopted herein, a decision maker's strong beliefs, convictions, and interpretation schemes are crucial in defining a problem and the dynamics which converge towards a certain choice. A decision consists of prospecting a solution to a problem but, as we have seen before, is not true in all cases. In order to investigate how the decision maker develops the (decision making) process, according to the various levels of knowledge of the elements that take part in the process, it is fundamental to understand how knowledge is stored within viable systems.

Starting from the considerations above, the aim of this work is to propose a theoretical model based on the concepts developed within the Viable Systems Approach (VSA) and translate it at an applicative level through the system dynamics methodology.

Starting from a review of the main conceptualisations proposed by VSA, we will translate them within a VSA-based System Dynamics (SD) model.

12.1 The Viable Systems Approach: the viable system as an information variety

VSA is a theoretical approach that starts from Beer's viable system model (Beer 1972) that defines viable a system if it "survives, remains united and is integral, is homeostatically balanced both internally and externally and possesses mechanisms and opportunities for growth and learning, development and adaptation, which allow it to become increasingly effective within its environment" (Beer 1985).

Starting from these conceptualisations, VSA suggests some developments that refer to the simultaneous observation of phenomena, both from a structural perspective (static) and from a systemic perspective (dynamic), and defines viable as the system that is also able to survive in its context of reference (Barile 2009; Barile and Saviano 2011). Accordingly, the ultimate purpose of each viable system is survival, which depends on the ability of the system itself to create relationships and interactions of harmony with the relevant entities present in its context of reference (Golinelli 2002, 2005; Barile 2008, 2009).

Moreover, VSA proposes a substantial isomorphism between a viable system and an Information Variety; the latter is the 'knowledge patrimony' that each system owns and is articulated in three dimensions: information units, interpretation schemes, value categories (Barile 2009).

Information units are the most external level of the variety and express the "structural composition of knowledge" (Barile 2009), as they are what a system can *perceive* with its senses, or elaborate from the outside. These external data, through an elaborating process, become information.

Interpretation schemes can be defined as the "forms" of knowledge (Barile 2009) that enable each viable system to *organise information* rationally, as they are the way information units are 'filtered' and transformed into information.

Finally, value categories can be defined as the strong beliefs of a system that is the set of values that deeply orientate each system in the decision-making processes. In this sense, they can be seen as the "resistance" that knowledge possesses oppose to change (Barile 2009) and are related to the acceptance or refusal of messages, elaborations, etc., as they represent the most subjective and the deepest level of information variety.

Information variety can be represented as follows:

$$V_{inf}(k) = (U_{inf}(k), S_{int}(k), C_{val}(k))$$

where:

V_{inf} *(k)* = Information Variety of viable system K;
U_{inf} *(k)* = Information Units of the information variety of viable system K;
S_{int}*(k)* = Interpretation Schemes of the information variety of viable system K;
C_{val}*(k)* = Value Categories of the information variety of viable system K.

According to VSA, each information variety, when interacting with other information varieties, has an evolutionary path that is influenced by *Consonance* and *Resonance* (Barile 2009). Consonance is the potential condition of compatibility and/or complementarity between interacting systems or varieties; resonance represents the consequent effect of these harmonic interactions between two or more systemic entities and is influenced by the pre-existent conditions of consonance (Barile 2009). Consonance and resonance are the drivers that orient a viable system's behaviour and, consequently, its knowledge.

As *Consonance* between two (or more) different information varieties has been defined as the major or minor potential that the two (or more) information varieties have in aligning their knowledge due to the information units used, it can be represented as follows:

$$C_{ons} = \lim_{u1 \to u2} V_{inf1} - V_{inf2} / u_1 - u_2 = \delta V_{inf} / \delta u$$

Resonance, instead, represents the change in the levels of Consonance and expresses the intensity with which it can grow or decrease over time. It can be represented as follows:

$$R_{es} = \lim_{u1 \to u2} C_{ons1} - C_{ons2} / u_1 - u_2 = \delta C_{ons} / \delta u$$

From the above, consonance can be defined as a line of action for the viable system, and involves the implementation/preservation of the conditions of harmony, correspondence, alignment and dialogue with the context of reference; it expresses the fundamental need of the system to match the values, cultures and needs of the surrounding society and to find recognition and consideration among the different entities that populate it (Golinelli 2005).

Resonance, on the other hand, occurs in the modification of the levels of consonance; in essence, it represents the way in which an information variety moves dynamically into the context in which it expresses its viability, and represents the level of sensitivity that it manifests towards the other systems with which it interacts with the perception of new information (Barile 2009). Therefore, resonance, unlike consonance that may exist or not, also has a direction that qualifies the evolution of consonance over time; it can be positive, when the change in consonance increases over time, or negative, when consonance undergoes a reduction (Carrubbo *et al.* 2017). Starting from these considerations, in the following, we will develop a theoretical System Dynamics model that, based on VSA conceptualisations, simulates the knowledge process.

12.2 Can System Dynamics constitute a viable quantitative manifestation for a VSA?

Starting from the considerations laid out in the previous paragraph, in this section we will argue and try to demonstrate that System Dynamics can be a viable quantitative method to translate VSA concepts into a simulation model; thus, we will now start shaping the foundations of a system dynamics model based on VSA concepts by analysing the process of knowledge creation (Barile 2009; Iandolo *et al.* 2017).

System Dynamics has its roots in Systems Thinking; it was developed in the late 1950s by J. W. Forrester at MIT and was first described at length in Forrester's book, *Industrial Dynamics* (Forrester 1961) with some additional principles presented in later works (Forrester 1969; Forrester 1971). It is a modelling and simulation methodology particularly fit at describing complex, non-linear, counter-intuitive feedback-driven behaviours, also characterised by feedback relationships and delays acting in the system. A central tenet of system dynamics is that the complex behaviours of organisational and social systems are the result of ongoing accumulations—of people, material or financial assets, information, or even biological or psychological states—and both balancing and reinforcing feedback mechanisms. The concepts of accumulation and feedback have been discussed in various forms for centuries (Richardson 1991). System Dynamics (Sterman 2001) is also a computer-based modelling method that makes use of formal models in order to understand the elements of complex systems over time. The main goal of System Dynamics is to understand how a system's behaviour emerges and uses this understanding to gain insights on how policy changes in that system might alter its behaviour. System Dynamics uniquely offers the practical application of all these concepts in the form of computerised models in which alternative policies and scenarios can be tested in a systematic way that answers both "what if" and "why" (Tank-Nielsen 1980; Morecroft 1985). Its main elements are *feedback loops* and *delays* that give rise to dynamic complexity, inherent in socio-economic systems and processes, through quantitative simulations (Sterman 2001).

In other words, SD is a methodology for understanding, discussing and simulating complex systems over time (Sterman 2001) and it has been widely used in many management, engineering, social and environmental application areas.

Some of the most important systems dynamics' concepts are the following (Zock 2004):

- **Stocks and Flows**: stocks (or levels) consist of accumulation within the systems while flows (or rates) are the transport of some content of one level to another.
- **Time delays**: as levels are changed only by the rates, the rates' change is measured in a determined time interval.
- **Feedback loops**: a decision alters the state of the world but, at the same time, indirectly influences itself defining the situation we will face in the future and triggering side effects and delayed reactions. Feedback loops can be positive or negative. Positive loops consist of reinforcing or amplifying what is happening in the system. Negative loops, instead, counteract and create balance and equilibrium.
- **Accumulation**: the levels, or stocks, are integrations. These are variables that cannot change instantaneously; they accumulate or integrate over time according to the results of actions in the system.
- **Endogenous point of view**: it refers to the existence of a closed boundary, which means the dynamic behaviour arises within the internal feedback loop structure of the system (Richardson 1991).

In the system dynamics methodology, the structure of a system can be conceptualised through a Causal Loop Diagram (CLD), which is a map of the feedback present in the system. It is worth mentioning that such a structure can be classified according to the way feedback loops interact with each other, producing sometimes a few clearly recognisable structures, called system archetypes, that display a typical behaviour, which, thus, can be inferred (at least qualitatively) from the evidenced systemic structure of a system.

A system dynamics model consists of an interlocking set of differential and algebraic equations developed from a broad spectrum of relevant measured and experiential data. A completed model may contain scores or hundreds of such equations along with the appropriate numerical inputs. Modelling is an iterative process of scope selection, hypothesis generation, causal diagramming, quantification, reliability testing, and policy analysis. The refinement process continues until the model is able to satisfy requirements concerning its realism, robustness, flexibility, clarity, ability to reproduce historical patterns, and ability to generate useful insights. These numerous requirements help to ensure that a model is reliable and useful not only for studying the past but also for exploring possible futures (Forrester and Senge 1980; Homer 1996)

The calibration of a System Dynamics' model's numerical inputs—its initial values, constants, and functional relationships—merits special mention. In System Dynamics modelling, variables are not automatically excluded from consideration if recorded measurements on them are lacking. Most things in the world are not measured, including many that experience tells us are important. When subject matter experts agree that a factor may be important, it is included in the model, and then the best effort is made to quantify it; whether through (in approximately this order of preference) the use of recorded measurements, inference from related data, logic, educated guesswork, or adjustments needed to provide a better simulated fit to history (Homer 1996; Graham 1980). Uncertainties abound in model calibration, which is one of the reasons that sensitivity testing is critical. Sensitivity testing of a well-built System Dynamics model typically reveals that its policy implications are unaffected by changes to most calibration uncertainties (Forrester 1969; Forrester 1971). However, even when some uncertainties are found to affect policy findings, modelling contributes by identifying the few key areas—out of the overwhelming number of possibilities—in which policy makers should focus their limited resources for metrics' creation and measurement (Figure 2).

In SD, the system can also be analysed through a simulation, which is possible after the construction of a Stock and Flows Diagram (SFD). A SFD is a quantitative assessment of the system. The dynamics are pictured in the SFD and the model formulation is done by the elaboration of equations that expresses how the variables are interconnected with others and how the accumulation process is determined by the change in the flows altering the state of the system levels (Figure 3).

To quantify the system, Stocks and Flows are used and the subsequent model is simulated with the use of computer software. A general representation of stocks and flows is illustrated in Figure 4.

The structure above corresponds to the following differential equation:

$$\text{Stock}(t) = \int (\text{inflow}(t) - \text{outflow}(t))dt + \text{Stock}(t_0)$$

Building a SD model generally goes through a sequence of specific phases that can be summarised by the Figure 5.

It is interesting to note that the process of building a SD model is inherently circular, both in its qualitative phase (the Systems Thinking one, where we essentially build causal loop diagrams to understand the basic structure of the system under analysis) and in its quantitative one as, in fact, from each phase one may want to go back to review the hypotheses that were built in previous phases.

As shown in the next figure, the learning curve goes through a well-known process of "trial-error-refinement" (Figure 6), where the refinement happens at the end of each cognitive cycle and after having learned how to modify the model in order to make it more similar to the reality (hence, to better shape the problem we are attempting to solve).

System Dynamics models are normally constructed for further understanding of a complex system but they are often misunderstood for predictive models. However, the purpose of the method (and its main strength) is that it can capture underlying connections among system elements that cannot be easily perceived, it can identify and represent delays that affect the effectiveness of a policy and, finally, it can remove the personal ideology and bias from the actual computations (Sterman 2001).

In other words, System Dynamics is a valuable quantitative approach to delve into understanding how a system works, what are its key/high-leverage points and how it can react to certain badly-designed policies by resisting change (just because the change effort was directed towards the points with the lowest capability to change) and, thus, present some counter-intuitive behaviours (which is a way to demonstrate how humans are characterised by bounded rationality, unable to manage too many "interdependencies", and correctly and coherently forecast the overall system behaviour).

Armenia *et al.* (2013) describe how issues, such as those just depicted, are key challenges for policy makers, which need effective tools to reduce uncertainty and understand the possible impacts of their policies, ensure long-term thinking, effectively manage crisis and the "unknown unknown", efficiently communicate the reasons for certain decisions as well as their impacts (thus generate involvement), ultimately encouraging behavioural change and uptake through cooperation and systems thinking, and eventually creating not only a shared better knowledge but also providing the basis for a sort of social wisdom.

Given the above and as also reported in Armenia, Barile and Iandolo (2015), the authors believe that the SD methodology can constitute an effective way to support building quantitative models that are described according to the VSA approach; also given the intrinsic systemic nature of the VSA approach itself and the inherent capability of SD to be able to model even the most complex and abstract concepts, it is, nonetheless, a framework which is born by the considerations that revolve around the concept of knowledge creation.

The model depicted in Figure 7, similarly to the one already commented and depicted in Figure 6, describes the way in which an individual takes decisions (acts), observes the results of his actions so to be able to control, in the short-term, the outcomes by adapting decisions, and from a longer perspective, to adapt his mental models, hence even radically changing his basic assumptions and, thus, implementing radical changes in his strategies.

12.3 Evidencing the Systemic Structure of the Learning Process

Understanding how a system works is a key task in order to be able to act on those high leverage points that are capable of bringing consistent and permanent change. A generalisation of Sterman's learning structure (depicted in Figure 7) can be found in the model formulation of Peirce's System of Inquiry, depicted in Figure 8, where events are observed, hypotheses are formed and then developed to be tested and, once tested, their outcomes are evaluated and matched to the originally observed events. In this main feedback process, there are two lower dominance control loops (one to support hypotheses' formation and one to monitor tests' implementation).

In other words, Peirce states that by gathering information while observing events outcomes (i.e., the system's behaviour), we usually generate new hypotheses with reference to what might have given rise to them. Once these hypotheses are generated, they need to be tested in order to determine their validity. Testing such hypotheses, thus, generates new information (which is related to the tests' outcomes). This information is matched with the initial information that generated the hypotheses and the information gap is used to eventually drop any hypotheses that have been ascertained as non-applicable (because they do not produce valuable results), thus supporting the process of new hypotheses generation. On the other hand, this generates a certain understanding about the system structure and the world around itself. Such an understanding brings new learning and, hence, new knowledge through which it is possible to perform a better Events Selection (Events' refinement).

The CLD of Peirce's qualitative model reported in Figure 8 has been depicted through the use of the Vensim* software and is reported in the Figure 9.

The above causal-loop diagram of Pierce's System of Inquiry can, of course, be transformed into a SFD, which has been developed again through the use of the Vensim˙ software as shown in Figure 10.

The VSA theory shows us, however, a different reading of Peirce's model of Inquiry, which can be summarised by the diagram in Figure 11.

In fact, new hypotheses are formed through an **Abduction** process (trial and error type) up to a tipping point where **Induction** helps to develop testable hypothesis, which, if successful, lead to a **Deduction** process through outcomes' observation that will lead to new knowledge. This process is inherently dynamic and circular (converging in spirals to an ultimate situation in which we are satisfied with the generated understanding, learning and new knowledge); so deduction could lead also to dropping previous hypotheses (which, however, constitute new information, understanding and knowledge) and starting again developing new ones by observing once more events and systems' behaviours through a new approach filtered by the newly obtained knowledge.

If we define a graphical 2-dimensional behaviour curve for such a process, we could use the one depicted in Figure 12, which is basically the product of two functions; one representing the trial and error dynamics ($y=a^x$) and the other the process of induction/deduction following the progressive understanding of a problem through the development and testing of hypotheses ($y=e^{-x}$).

If we match Peirce's System of Inquiry with the VSA process of knowledge creation, knowledge alignment, capability to create new hypotheses on the problem to be solved and, hence, new information which, in turn, produces a new understanding and, hence again, new knowledge, we can easily redesign previously derived CLDs and SFDs into the VSA SFD (Figure 13).

Where:

- Actual Information = Knowledge patrimony = V_{inf}
- Current Knowledge = Knowledge alignment = $(dV_{inf} / du) = C_{ons}$
- Knowledge Change = Change in Knowledge patrimony = $(dC_{ons} / du) = R_{es}$

This is a typical SD structure formed by one main, high-dominance feedback loop with two lower dominance feedback loops (Figure 14).

This is a well-known second-order feedback structure, displaying two stocks, each feeding the other one's flow.

The state-space representation of this system structure is the following:

$$\dot{x}_1(t) = a_{11} * x_1(t) + a_{12} * x_2(t)$$

$$\dot{x}_2(t) = a_{21} * x_1(t) + a_{22} * x_2(t)$$

with the following matrix notation:

$$\dot{X}(t) = AX(t)$$

where the gain matrix A is:

$$A = \begin{bmatrix} a_{11} & a_{12} \\ a_{21} & a_{22} \end{bmatrix}.$$

This can be further generalised by the Figure 15.

Where:

$$\dot{x} = ay - bx$$
$$\dot{y} = -cx + dy$$

By simplifying the model (2 loops, d = 0 – in the case for which there is no confrontation with previously available knowledge; rather the new knowledge is just integrated into the old one in a process of continuous growth of knowledge – which is a reasonable assumption), we have the following:

$$\dot{x} = ay - bx$$
$$\dot{y} = -cx$$

$$\ddot{x} = a\dot{y} - b\dot{x} = \left(a\frac{\dot{y}}{\dot{x}} - b \right) \dot{x} = \left(-\frac{acx}{ay - bx} - b \right) \dot{x}$$

$$\ddot{x} = -acx - b\dot{x}$$

$$\ddot{x} + b\dot{x} + acx = 0$$

That is:

$$a(d2y/dx)(x) + b(dy/dx)(x) + c(x) = 0$$

If we use the typical VSA concept to substitute for the constant a, b and c, we have the following:

- $a = C_{val}$
- $b = - S_{int}$
- $c = - K$

12.4 Conclusions

The aim of this work was a first attempt to propose a quantifiable SD-model for the VSA and for the VSA-based definition of decision making process that, according to this perspective, is based on the use of a fundamental application that characterises the decision making approach through learning and problem solving.

Given the inherent capability of System Dynamics to grasp the intrinsic complexity of systems and the presence of articulated feedback loops, we decided to adopt such a methodology, given also its circular nature in the process of learning and understanding, as well as of knowledge acquisition when dealing with complex issues.

System Dynamics, in fact, allows defining models that can be populated with data and can be simulated in order to obtain insights on behaviour over time of the variables of interest, as well as of the decision makers that operate within organisations.

However, the model is still at a theoretical stage and will have to be further developed and conceptualised by clarifying how the three-loop structure determines the typical behaviour in knowledge-creation, as well as how interactions work, for example, by considering at least two different subjects, with different perspectives, interacting in the same environment.

Figures

Figure 1.
Possible resolving paths for a decision-making process

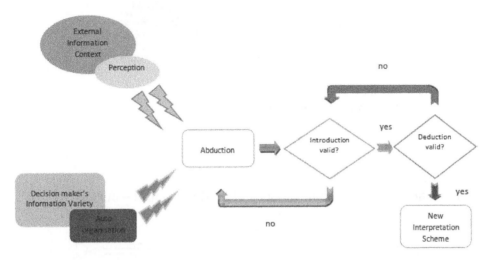

Source: Barile, 2009.

Figure 2.
A causal-loop diagram (CLD) depicting a negative feedback-loop

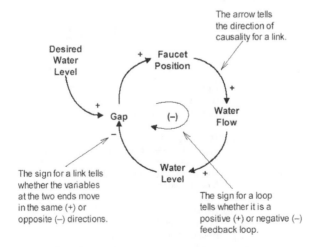

Source: Authors' own elaboration of The Fifth Discipline, P. Senge (1990).

Figure 3.
A diagram that translates (into stocks & flows notation - SFD) the CLD in Figure 1

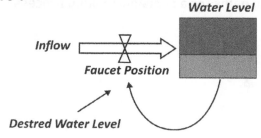

Water Level
Inflow
Faucet Position
Destred Water Level

Source: Authors' own.

Figure 4.
A stock accumulates the difference of its flows (input – output)

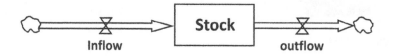

Stock
Inflow
outflow

Figure 5.
Phases in SD modelling

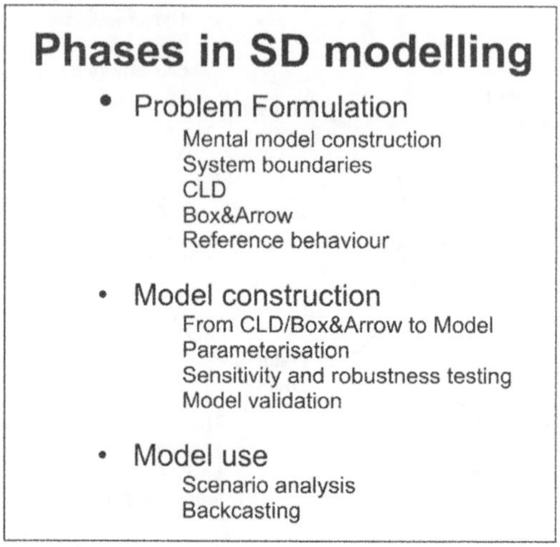

Phases in SD modelling
• Problem Formulation
Mental model construction
System boundaries
CLD
Box&Arrow
Reference behaviour
• Model construction
From CLD/Box&Arrow to Model
Parameterisation
Sensitivity and robustness testing
Model validation
• Model use
Scenario analysis
Backcasting

Source: Authors' own.

Figure 6.
A CLD describing the learning process

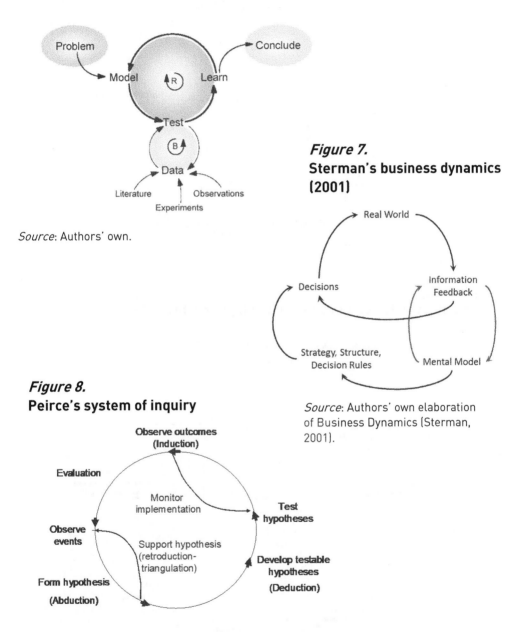

Source: Authors' own.

Figure 7.
Sterman's business dynamics (2001)

Source: Authors' own elaboration of Business Dynamics (Sterman, 2001).

Figure 8.
Peirce's system of inquiry

Source: Authors' elaboration.

Figure 9.
CLD of the model in Fig. 7

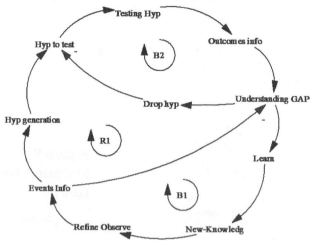

Source: Authors' elaboration.

Figure 10.
Translation of Peirce's system of inquiry into a first SFD

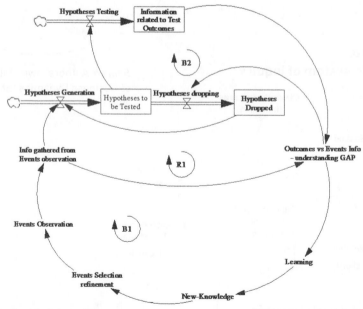

Source: Authors' elaboration.

Figure 11.
VSA reading of Peirce's approach to inquiry

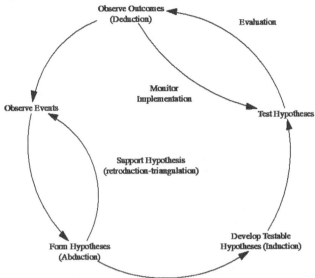

Source: Authors' elaboration.

Figure 12.
VSA 4CS curve

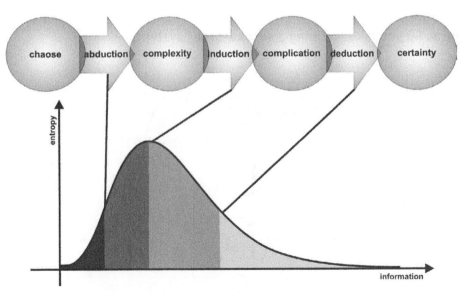

Source: Adaptation from Barile, 2009, www.asvsa.org

Figure 13.
A SD-description of the VSA-based model on knowledge

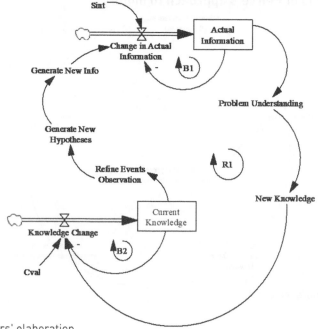

Source: Authors' elaboration.

Figure 14.
Generic SD-model describing a second-order system

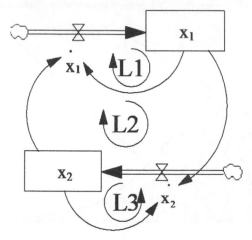

Source: Authors' own elaboration on Guneralp.

Figure 15.
Further generalisation of model in Fig. 14

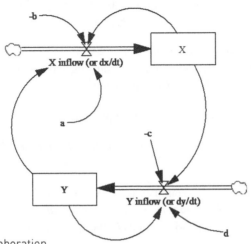

Source: Authors' elaboration.

References

Armenia S., Barile, S. and Iandolo, F., (2015), «Merging Viable Systems Approach (vSa) and System Dynamics to Evaluate Sustainable Value Creation», *Advances in Business Management. Towards Systemic Approach*, p. 50-52.

Armenia S, Carlini C., Onori R. and Saullo A.P., (2013), «Policy Modelling As A New Area For Research: Perspectives for a Systems Thinking and System Dynamics Approach?», in *Proceedings of the EURAM 2013 Conference*.

Barile S., (2009), *Management sistemico vitale*, Giappichelli.

Barile S., (2008), *L'impresa come sistema. Contributi sull'Approccio Sistemico Vitale* (ASV), Giappichelli.

Barile S. and Saviano M., (2011), «Foundations of Systems Thinking: The Structure-Systems Paradigm», *Contributions to Theoretical and Practical Evidences in Management. A Viable Systems Approach (VSA)*, Various Authors, International Printing, Avellino, pp. 1-25.

Barile S., Di Nauta P. and Iandolo F., (2016), *La decostruzione della complessità*, Collana Studi di Management e Organizzazione Aziendale, Minerva Bancaria.

Beer S., (1972), *Brain of the Firm*, The Penguin Press.

Beer S., (1985), *Diagnosing the System for Organizations*, John Wiley.

Carrubbo L., Iandolo, F., Pitardi, V. and Calabrese M., (2017), «The Viable Decision Maker for CAS Survival: How to Change and Adapt Through Fitting Process», *Journal of Service Theory and Practice*, 27(5).

Cohen, M., March, J. and Olsen, J., (1972), «A Garbage Can Model of Organizational choice», *Administrative Science Quarterly*, vol. 17, n 1, pp. 1-25.

Forrester J.W., (1961), *Industrial Dynamics*, M.I.T. Press, Cambridge, Massachussetts.

Forrester J.W., (1969), *Urban Dynamics*, MIT Press.

Forrester J.W., (1971), «Counterintuitive Behavior of Social Systems», *Technology Review*, 73, pp. 53-68.

Forrester J.W. and Senge P.M., (1980), «Tests for Building Confidence in System Dynamics Models», *TIMS Studies in the Management Sciences,* 14, North-Holland Publishing Company pp. 209-228.

Golinelli G.M., (2002), *L'approccio sistemico al governo dell'impresa. L'impresa sistema vitale*, vol. 1, Cedam.

Golinelli G.M., (2005), *L'approccio sistemico al governo dell'impresa. L'impresa sistema vitale*, Cedam.

Graham A.K., (1980), «Parameter Estimation in System Dynamics Modeling», in Randers, J, ed., *Elements of the System Dynamics Method,* MIT Press, pp. 143-161.

Güneralp B., (2004), «A Principle on Structure-Behavior Relations in System Dynamics Models», *Proceedings of the 2004 International System Dynamics Conference*, Oxford, Albany, New York, System Dynamics Society.

Homer J.B., (1996), «Why we Iterate: Scientific Modeling in Theory and Practice», *System Dynamics Review*, 12, pp. 1-19.

Iandolo, F., Armenia, S. and Carrubbo, L., (2017), «A System Dynamics Simulation Model For Sustainable Value Through the Viable Systems Approach», in Gummesson, E., Mele, C. and Polese, F., (Eds.), *Service Dominant Logic, Network and Systems Theory and Service Science: Integrating three Perspectives for a New Service Agenda*, Giannin,.

March, J. G., and Simon, H. A., (1958), *Organizations*, John Wiley and Sons.

Morecroft, J.D.W., (1985), «Rationality in the Analysis of Behavioral Simulation Models», *Manage Science,* 31, pp. 900-916.

Peirce C.S., (1967), «Collected Papers of Charles Sanders Peirce», in Volume III *Exact logic* (Published papers) and Volume IV *The Simplest Mathematics*, edited by Hartshorne C. and Weiss P., two volumes in one, Wiess, Belknap Press, pp. xiv + 602.

Richardson, G.P., (1991), *Feedback Thought in Social Science and Systems Theory*, University of Pennsylvania Press.

Senge P., (1990), *The Fifth Discipline: The Art and Practice of the Learning Organization*, Doubleday/Currency.

Sterman J., (2001), «System Dynamics Modeling: Tools for Learning in a Complex World», *California Management Review*, 43, pp. 8-25.

Tank-Nielsen C., (1980), «Sensitivity Analysis in System Dynamics», in Randers, J, ed., *Elements of the System Dynamics Method*, MIT Press, pp. 185-202.

Von Neumann J. and Morgenstern O., (1947), *Theory of Games and Economic Behavior*, 2nd ed., Princeton University Press.

Zock, Alexander, (2004), «A Critical Review of the Use of System Dynamics for Organizational Consulting Projects», *at CD-ROM of Proceedings*, Oxford System Dynamics Conference, System Dynamics Society.

13. Eye Movements and Investment Behaviour

by Maria Gabriella Ceravolo, Vincenzo Farina, Lucrezia Fattobene, Lucia Leonelli[1]

In 1986, the psychologist, Weiskrantz, reported the bizarre condition of a patient who, regardless of his claim of total blindness, had intact visual functions. The oxymoron 'blindsight' was, therefore, coined and used to indicate the ability of some people to accurately *sense* some visual stimulus even though they were unable to see it *consciously*; in other words, it is when the brain sees what the subject does not. This is only one example indicating that brain activity is not strictly continuous with awareness and conscious experience. Neuroscience has clarified the existence of two different types of processes in the brain: controlled and automatic (Schneider and Shiffrin 1977). The former are serial, effortful and evoked deliberately; oppositely, the latter occurring in parallel are effortless and reflexive (Camerer 2005). Moreover, while for controlled processes, people have good introspective access, this does not occur for automatic ones. There is now extensive evidence that a great part of the brain's activity occurs automatically and below the threshold of consciousness.

Behavioural economics and finance have absorbed knowledge from the discipline of psychology and sociology to improve the description and the prediction of individual decision making and – at an aggregated level – of market outcome. Experimental economics and finance offer the advantages of all experimental methods,

[1] We are immensely grateful to Prof. GM. Raggetti for his precious help in conceiving the design and fostering interdisciplinary collaborations. We would like to thank all the researchers of the NEUROFIN research group: Prof. A. Carretta, Prof. N. Mercuri, Prof. R. Floris, Prof. F. Garaci, Dr. M. Pierantozzi and Dr. Rocco Cerroni. We would also like to thank Dr. Lucia Pepa for her technical assistance and practical support with the eye tracking technology.

i.e. the possibility of measuring observable choices, of reproducing the setting to verify findings and of manipulating conditions. Besides these incommensurable advantages offered by these disciplines, they both suffer from the limitation of focusing on choice outcomes and not on the underlying processes of the decision making. Neuroeconomics, instead, grasping all the positive aspects of these research fields, adds the revolutionary advantages related to opening the black box. This recent discipline, bridging neuroscience, psychology and economics, challenges the consolidated assumptions in economics and finance that the decision-making process consists of a unitary system and behaviour is the result of rational choice, underpinning the relevance of automatic and affective systems during the interaction with cognitive and controlled systems. Moreover, enriching the research methodologies with new techniques (brain imaging, brain stimulation, lesion studies, eye tracking, etc.), neuroeconomics aims at objectively detecting, quantifying and measuring some variables related to both the systems and to the processes of perception, learning, information processing, computation, elaboration, integration, and so on.

13.1 Eye tracking and economic and financial decision making

The eye tracking studies conducted in economics and finance have, up to now, focused on two types of decision making: individual and strategic. The former considers single subjects who have to choose between different options; in the latter, subjects interact with other people and their decisions are related to other people's possible reactions. The basic assumption, on which the eye-tracking methodology relies, is the "eye-mind hypothesis", according to which there is "no appreciable [time] lag between what is fixated and what is processed" (Just and Carpenter 1976). The eye-mind relationship assumes a close relationship between what the eyes are gazing at and the mind is engaged with.[2]

Different researchers used eye tracking to study whether decision making is systematic and rational,[3] complying with neoclassical models, or based on intuitive

---

[2] Generally, the main phases of an experiment consist of i) preparation, during which material, questionnaires, stimuli, etc. are set up, ii) validation, asking experts to comment, revise and provide critical suggestions, iii) pilot study that is a small scale preliminary study to evaluate feasibility, iv) fine tuning, to incorporate all the suggestions emerging from the previous phase, v) experiment, to collect data, and finally, vi) data analysis.

[3] It is important to underline that when using the words *rational* and *irrational,* we usually refer to a comparison with standard and classical models. In this sense, it is considered rational for a

and heuristic approaches; the majority of these studies support the last view, underlying the relevance of the eye tracking methodology in exploring new theoretical frameworks. The studies that exploit eye tracking in marketing research are so numerous and sophisticated that reviewing them fall outside the aim of this work. In accounting, the number of studies is significantly lower; researchers have concentrated on financial reports (Grigg and Griffin 2014), key audit matters (KAMs) in auditors' reports (Sirois, Bédard and Brera 2015), measures' communication and performance evaluation of the Balanced Score Card (Chen, Jermias, and Panggabean 2016), and so on. Also, in the financial research field, the number of studies is negligible but not at all the findings that have emerged. Husser and Wirth (2014) examine the effectiveness of disclaimers in mutual fund disclosure, testing if extrapolation bias (the belief in performance persistence, also called the hot-hand effect) is able to explain the return-chasing behaviours of investors. To observe and to measure investors' attention, the unobtrusive methodology of eye tracking represented the best approach, providing measures such as *gaze duration*. The analysis revealed that investors display an attentional bias toward performance data and that the disclaimer is not effective in reducing extrapolation bias. Moreover, the findings reveal that subjects are more attracted by graphical information to performance data than to graphical information about mutual fund philosophy. Another interesting study is that of Shavit *et al.* (2010) who exploit eye tracking to test investors' biases, such as mental accounting, loss aversion, prospect theory and confirm that underlying decision-making models are not in line with neoclassical ones (for a review of this study, please see Chapter 10). Duclos (2015) investigates how investors process graphical financial information, reporting that the last trading days of a stock strongly affect both decision making and investor behaviour, through an end-anchoring effect. Rubaltelli, Agnoli and Franchin (2016) study investors' behaviour and graphical presentation of past performance, focusing on individual differences. The authors classify participants according to their Emotional Intelligence trait, which expresses individual differences in the management of emotions related to decisions, and use eye tracking to measure *pupil dilation* and capture individuals' affective arousal. They test if subjects more sensitive to affective reactions (high emotional intelligence trait) show higher arousal (larger pupil dilation)

---

behaviour that mirrors what is predicted by classical models, and vice-versa. These two adjectives represent simple labels that economists use to categorise behaviour relative to their own models. Psychology and neuroscience, on the other hand, inform us that all brain evaluations and subjects' behaviours are the result of evolutionary needs and respond to the two main goals planned in the genetic heritage: reproduction and avoidance of death. Therefore, what is considered *irrational* from an economic point of view is usually perfectly *rational* from a neuroscientific perspective.

when observing the graph of past performance. They also test whether high arousal is associated to a greater (lower) probability of investment in the case of positive (negative) past performance or if it is associated with the tendency to invest additional money independently from past performances. Results reveal that participants with high emotional intelligence are more sensitive to a negative affective cue, i.e. negative trend of past performance. Moreover, eye movements have been found to be predictive of investment strategy; investors with larger pupil dilation were less prone to sell their stocks than participants with smaller pupil dilation, independently from past performances (the interaction between variables of pupil dilation and type of chart was not significant). This study is relevant also in showing that an eye-tracking variable (pupil dilation) mediates the effect of the psychological factor (emotional intelligence trait) on investment strategy. Overall, the research suggests the need to consider individual differences, such as sensitivity to affective information in financial decision making and risk taking behaviour.

In this brief review, we presented all the published papers, to the best of our knowledge, that deal with financial issues and employed the technology of tracking eye movements. On the whole, these studies highlight the value added by the application of neuroscientific assumptions and techniques to advance the financial theoretical framework.

13.2 Investor behaviour and the Key Investor Information Document (KIID)

We performed an experimental study[4], exploiting an eye-tracking device to investigate the process of attention allocation during the visual exploration of financial products'.

Recently, the European Commission replaced the Simplified Prospectus (SP) for UCITS introduced in 2001 with the shorter and more concise KIID that should provide investors with all the information they need to take their investment decisions. After having assessed that *the more information the better* is true only when information is actually processed and understood, the European Commission has suggested promoting a short, plainly-worded, consumer-friendly and comparable across Europe document that aims at both improving investors' protection and the single market in UCITS. In a few words, regulators suggested, "keep it short and simple" (KISS), but

---

[4] Preliminary version of the research has been presented at the 2017 FINEST Conference (Trani), and at the 2017 International Rome Conference of Money, Banking and Finance (Palermo).

tell all (Burn 2010). The underlying idea of a simpler disclosure document is the reduction of investors' information overload to facilitate their cognitive process of paying attention, reading and understanding the main characteristics of the investment product they are going to buy.

After several tests were conducted on investors and intermediaries, using both quantitative (survey) and qualitative (telephone interviews, focus group) research techniques, a final standardised template, KIID, has been achieved. When drafting it, management companies have to follow a specific content and layout[5] that include the title, objectives and investment policy, risk - reward profile, charges, past performance and some practical information.

Some studies have investigated the efficacy of this new financial disclosure document. Walther (2015) compares the perceived quality - broken down into 10 dimensions - of KIID and SP finding that the first is better evaluated than the second in all the different categories. He also reports that participants suffer less information overload in the case of KIID, affecting the probability of naïve diversification. Oehler, Hofer and Wendt (2014) reveal that subjects find the document moderately appropriate in reporting the key characteristics, suggesting the need to produce even easier and more comprehensible documents. The presence of visual distractors in the frame of the disclosure documents has been investigated by Hillenbrand and Schmelzer (2015) who found that they lead to gather less correct information, invest more and expect smaller return variance.

Previous empirical evidence on the new information disclosure document relies on data collected through self-reported measures that suffer from a number of methodological problems and biases.[6] A more objective way to collect data is offered by the eye tracking tool, which allows detecting where and what subjects look at (and do not look at), and for how long, regarding the scan path[7] and changes in subjects' pupils dilatations during exposition to stimuli. The research objective of our research was to detect, in an objective way, the process of investors' attention allocation during the reading of financial product disclosure documents. Moreover, we tried to investigate if the format of the documents' presentation influenced attention patterns. To this aim, we measured the ocular behaviour of students while reading the KIID in

---

[5] The template is provided in the CESR/10-794 consultation paper.

[6] Eye tracking measures are more accurate and reliable than self-reported ones; also, in the case of observational behaviour, actual view differs from claimed view (O'Connell *et al.* 2011).

[7] A scan path is defined as the sum of fixations and saccades where the former are a period of time when the eye is stationary and gathers visual information and the latter are fast ballistic movements that redirect gaze.

his standard version (Figure 2) and in a manipulated version where the position of the main sources of information has been changed (Figure 3 displays an example of one of the manipulated format)

Overall, our results underpin the existence of an influence of the presentational format on the physiological mechanisms underlying the reading of financial documents.

13.3 Conclusions

Summing up, we show that i) attention allocation differs across the different sections of the KIID, ii) presentational format modulates the attention allocated to the main sections of the KIID, and iii) although it does not impact on subjects' scan path, it also modulates the overall attention dedicated to the document. Moreover, iv) the way information is communicated influences the attention dedicated to the different visual stimuli, and v) the evaluation of products' financial attractiveness.

A future development of our work should compare samples of subjects with different characteristics so to measure the impact of single psycho-social features on attention distribution and judgement. Also the relationship between emotions, physiological reactions, and financial decision making could be explored more in depth; since the rapid adjustment of pupil diameter - a correlate of autonomic nervous system activation - has been associated to both cognitive and affective information processing, we suggest to exploit the eye tracking research tool in order to study pupil dilation during financial decisions, as a new research frontier in the so-called field of neuro-finance. Moreover, an integration of the eye tracking with the EEG and the fMRI investigation tools would provide better insight into temporal dynamics of brain networks involved in financial decisions.

Our study supports the need to investigate the neurobiological processes related to the visual exploration of disclosure documents. In this sense, the eye tracking can be regarded as a new methodology in the regulators' toolkit to study the influence of specific features of financial disclosure documents on attention distribution patterns and individuals' behavior.

Figures

Figure 1. The eye tracking technology

Source:
Authors'
elaboration.

Figure 2. Example of standard KIID

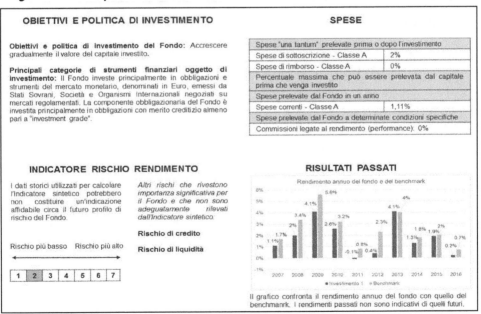

Source: Authors' elaboration.

Figure 3.
Example of KIID with blocks of information rotated

Source: Authors' elaboration.

References

Burn, L., (2010), «KISS, But Tell All: Short-Form Disclosure for Retail Investors», *Capital Markets Law Journal*, 5(2), pp. 141-168.

Camerer, C., (2005), «How Neuroscience Can Inform Economics», *Journal of Economic Literature*, 43, pp. 9-64.

Chen, Y., Jermias, J. and Panggabean, T., (2016), «The Role of Visual Attention in the Managerial Judgment of Balanced-Scorecard Performance Evaluation: Insights from Using an Eye-Tracking Device», *Journal of Accounting Research*, 54(1), pp. 113-145.

Duclos, R., (2015), «The Psychology of Investment Behavior: (De)biasing Financial Decision making One Graph at a Time», *Journal of Consumer Psychology*, 25 (2), pp. 317-325.

Grigg, L. and Griffin, A. L., (2014), «A Role of Eye-Tracking Research in Accounting and Financial Reporting?», in: Horsley, M. et al., (eds.), *Current Trends in Eye-Tracking Research, Cham, Switzerland: Springer International Publishing*, pp. 225-230.

Hillenbrand A. and Schmelzer A., (2015), *Beyond Information: Disclosure, Distracted Attention, and Investor Behavior*, MPI Collective Goods Preprint, No. 2015/20.

Hüsser A. and Wirth W., (2014), «Do Investors Show an Attentional Bias toward Past Performance? An Eye-Tracking Experiment on Visual Attention to Mutual Fund Disclosures in Simplified Fund Prospectuses», *Journal of Financial Services Marketing*, 19(3), pp. 169-185.

Just M.A. and Carpenter P.A., (1976), «Eye Fixations and Cognitive Processes», *Cognitive Psychology*, 8(4), pp. 441-480,

Oehler A, Höfer A. and Wendt S., (2014), «Do Key Investor Information Documents Enhance Retail Investors' Understanding of Financial Products? Empirical Evidence», *Journal of Financial Regulation and Compliance*, 22, pp. 115-127.

Rubaltelli E., Agnoli S. and Franchin L., (2016), «Sensitivity to Affective Information and Investors' Evaluation of Past Performance: An Eye-tracking Study», *Journal of Behavioral Decision Making*, 29, pp. 295-306.

Schneider W. and Shiffrin R.M., (1977), «Controlled and Automatic Human Information Processing: I. Detection, Search and Attention», *Psychological Review*, 84(1), pp. 1-66.

Shavit T., Giorgetta C., Shani Y. and Ferlazzo F., (2010), «Using an Eye Tracker to Examine Behavioral Biases in Investment Tasks: An Experimental Study», *Journal of Behavioral Finance*, 11(4), pp. 185-194.

Sirois L. P., Bédard J. and Bera P., (2015), *The Informational Value of Key Audit Matters in the Auditor's Report: Evidence from an Eye-Tracking Study*, Mimeo (conference paper).

Walther T., (2015), «Key Investor Documents and Their Consequences on Investor Behaviour», *Journal of Business Economics*, 85, pp. 129-156.

14. Neuroeconomics and Insurance: a Look Forward

by Riccardo Guerrini [1]

> *Lightness*
> *Quickness*
> *Exactitude*
> *Visibility*
> *Multiplicity*
> *Consistency*
> (Italo Calvino: "Six memos for the next millennium")

The insurance industry is facing a delicate transition period: the forthcoming introduction of the new Insurance Distribution Directive (IDD) in February 2018, which brings new rules of professionalism and transparency in the distribution of insurance products; the persistence of low interest rates on government bonds; the entrance of new risk scenarios (cyber-risk, terrorism, climate changes, etc.) that are deeply changing the traditional figure of the insurer, pushing him towards achieving an advanced level of competences. The insurer of the future will not be limited to act as a matching figure between a client and an insurance company (a so-called "intermediary") but will be requested to develop a skilled professional profile with multiple abilities, in order to handle an increasing number of requests, work on multiple software platforms (computer programs, e-mails, apps, social networks) - sometimes even at the same time - and try to find a solution to the multiple needs of

---

[1] The views expressed in this work are those of the author and do not in any way bind the responsibility of the group.

the customers. For these reasons, an insurer will have to be a person with ever-growing competencies and with a wide range of uncommon talents.

Recent findings in the field of Neurosciences and, more specifically Neuroeconomics, can make significant progress also in the field of insurance. We are already talking about the change from the "Internet of Things" (domotics, as an example) to the "Internet of Emotions" ("We are what we feel" - David Shing). Neuroeconomics and neuromarketing can make substantial changes in the relationship with customers regarding the purchase and management of insurance policies; there will be a stronger awareness in the insurers generated by a new type of approach, not just based on the expectation of a personal gain but influenced by a "win-win" perspective (where both the customer and the insurer can benefit from mutual exchanges of knowledge and will). Neuromarketing can assist insurance companies in improving the construction of clear and comprehensible policy booklets, optimising the way to present a product to the customer (graphic design, spot advertising, and brochures); a better understanding of the emotions generated by the customer-insurer relationship will improve both the demand and the offer of insurances of any kind.

Such evolution is also expected to provide social benefits, in a not-so-far future. One of the most problematic aspects in Italy, for an expansion of insurance culture, lies in the "fatalistic" thinking of a large part of mass customers. Perhaps the time has come to move from a type of sales based on negative emotions to an approach that can instill confidence in the future, in each customer (if a seller gives a customer sitting in front of him any reason to get up and leave, the customer himself will be disappointed and prejudiced each time he sits not only in front of the same seller but also in front of anyone who will try to talk about insurance with him). Moreover, an insurance policy is sometimes (maybe too often!) requested by the client when a negative event has already occurred (as in cases when a company asks for insurance against fire just after having suffered a fire incident); a change from an *ex-post* mentality (to intervene after something has happened) to a mindset aimed at prevention could significantly lower insurance premiums within a few years.

The study of socio-economic behaviours, as described in the Ultimatum Game, is useful to understand the choice of many potential customers who interrupt, sometimes abruptly, a negotiation presuming they have to pay too high a price for what an insurance policy would offer (think of a type of insurance policy that provides a guarantee against theft of a portable asset - machine or jewellery - to which a franchise is considered too high by the buyer). The knowledge of the mechanisms that exist in the Dictator Game helps to predict the consumer's behaviour and, therefore, his decisions when he considers buying insurance products. Certainly, an insurance company that offers market products, which leave low margins of choice, will be disliked by the customer who is under the impression of unilateral imposition; conversely, he could prefer a company that will offer him the freedom to choose the guarantees to insure. In the future, there will be more need for "tailor-made" policies that adapt as much as possible to the individual needs, rather than simple-stipulated, pre-packaged policies.

In the humble opinion of the writer, a viable choice might be the exploitation of the "Reward mechanism" in personal insurance products (so-called "Retail" segment) in the absence of claims in the previous year. For example, there might be relevant benefits to the clientele, when introducing an annual discount percentage (namely about 3-4%) on the premium of healthcare policies, which is often considerable. The use of the "Reward mechanism" can prove helpful in a wide variety of conditions; for example, a Third Party Insurance could include a commercial reward for the head of the family (a free family cinema entry, or something similar), since the premium for such insurance is not overly expensive. Again, Home or Injury insurance policies could include discounts on the next annual premium or benefits, like an increase of the insured sums by a predetermined percentage (namely 3%).

Even in the field of loss management, the introduction of new technologies can contribute to a general lowering of insurance premiums; for example, the awareness of having a "black box" installed on their car seems to increase drivers' prudence. A loss is, by definition, a "future and uncertain event", so the probability of "uncertainty" can be narrowed by trying to prevent the causes of loss as much as possible. This can be done both at the macro level and at the micro level, by raising customers' awareness about a negative "risk-event" ratio and stimulating the adoption of precautionary measures or lifestyle changes.

In conclusion, the coming year will be crucial for moving to a new and more complete insurer profile. Neurosciences can be of great help to those who want to be part of a new era. Maybe, there will be a new discipline that we will call Neuroinsurance.

To Alberto

Some Reflections and Perspectives

The contributions collected in this book concern the results of scientific researches carried out by neuroeconomists affiliated to different disciplines. The interdisciplinary vision of Neuroeconomics and the new and different methods used for neurobiological investigations are no longer an insurmountable complexity even for micro-economics scholars. The collection and the measurement of neural correlates of decision-making processes are an important source of new information and data about the brain's role in the behavior of the economic operator. The variability of his preferences, choices and individual decisions is better clarified considering also the mechanisms and processes, chemical-physical, activated in the neural substrate of every brain function. They are initiated, automatically and unconsciously, by the exogenous sensory stimuli received and processed by the brain. It is time to consider the role of the phenomena mentioned also in micro-economic studies. The scientific results offered by the neuroeconomists are the new food for conservative micro-economist's thought: they hint to them some theoretical integrations, changes, updates and innovations in experimental protocols and methods. The researches presented show how the behavior of an economic agent is influenced by the impulses deriving from neural circuits activated by each sensory input received and processed. These proceedings explore how those impulses are conditioned by emotions, arousal and mental states caused by themselves. The results obtained in Neuroeconomics underline the complexity of brain functions and the difficulty to understand (and to forecast) the human behavior. Only with an interdisciplinary vision and new methods one can attempt the scientific challenge mentioned. All this should increase the curiosity of young researchers, in micro-economics, and should reinforce their motivation to innovate the traditional conceptual schemes, recovering the ancient suggestions of Adam Smith. A long time ago, Smith proposed to consider the role of mental factors in individual behavior to clarify economic phenomena. With Neuroeconomics, that suggestion becomes even more relevant. But resorting to Neuroeconomics means, as it is cleared in this book, conducting research together with neuroscientists, physiologists, biologists, neuroradiologists, neuropsychologists, psychologists, geneticists, molecular medicine researchers, nanotechnologists, computer scientists, scientists of Artificial Intelligence, and others. This, in reality, is the substantial change that Neuroeconomics imposes, taking up the fundamental invitation of Adam Smith. This "1ª Officina di Neuroeconomia" is the most innovative way to accept that suggestion. The curiosity and interest among the participants were surprising: we can foresee a remarkable development for this new scientific discipline also in our academic context.

GianMario Raggetti
UNIVPM, Ancona

List of Contributors

Maria **Albanese** is a consultant neurologist at the Neurology Unit of "Tor Vergata" University Hospital in Rome. She studied medicine at the University of Rome "Tor Vergata", qualifying in 2008. Earlier in her career, she was a Research Fellow at the Department of Neurology of Jagiellonian University, Krakow (Poland). In 2013 she performed her PhD in Neuroscience, exploring the role of CSF biomarkers in the field of neuroinflammatory diseases, with particular focus on Multiple Sclerosis. Currently, she is involved in several scientific projects and clinical trials for the diagnosis and pharmacotherapy of neurodegenerative pathologies.

Stefano **Armenia** is a Research Fellow in the Analysis of Dynamical Systems at the "Research Department" of the Link Campus University of Rome and President of SYDIC, the Italian Chapter of the System Dynamics Society. He has a degree in Computer Engineering, Industrial Automation & Control Systems, a Ph.D. in Business Engineering and a Master in Management and Business Administration. His research interests deal with the analysis of complex systems dynamics in many fields: logistics and transportation, finance, technological innovation, policy modeling and assessment of impacts of innovation and new technologies on organizational processes.

Sergio **Barile** is Full Professor of Business Management at Sapienza University of Rome, where he is Head of the Management Department. His research includes business management, systems theory, decision theory and complexity. He founded the Association for Research on Viable Systems (ASVSA) and is one of the main references for the studies on Viable Systems Approach (ASV). He sits many editorial boards of journals dealing with business management, and is author of numerous books and articles (European Management Journal, Journal of Service Theory and Practice, Journal of Service Management, Systems Research and Behavioral Science, Service Science). In 2015 he received the Evert Gummesson Outstanding Research Award.

Maria Gabriella **Ceravolo,** MD, PhD in Neurosciences, Neurologist, is Full Professor of Physical and Rehabilitation Medicine at Università Politecnica delle Marche. Her scientific research mainly focuses on the assessment, prognosis and rehabilitation of motor and cognitive impairment in subjects with brain diseases. Her recent studies concern the neural correlates of financial decisions in healthy subjects. She co-authored the book "Neuroeconomia…Neurofinanza: I correlati neurali del Direct Access Trading", published by McGraw-Hill in 2017, and contributed to organize the *1ˢᵗ Officina di Neuroeconomia*.

Rocco **Cerroni** is a Medical Doctor resident in Neurology at Clinical Neurological Unit, University of Rome "Tor Vergata". He graduated in Medicine and Surgery and qualified for medical practice at Univerity of Rome "Cattolica del Sacro Cuore", where he performed clinical research activities at Alzheimer Centre and received a particular training in Neuropsychology. He is particularly interested in movement disorders and Neuropsychology and currently performs clinical research activities at Movement Disorders Centre at University of Rome "Tor Vergata".

Girolamo **Crisi,** MD, is a specialist in Diagnostic Radiology and Neurology with added qualification in Neuroradiology. He is Director of the Neuroradiology Unit and Chief of the Department of Diagnostic of the Hospital and University of Parma, Italy.

Giuseppe **di Pellegrino,** MD, PhD, is Professor of Cognitive Neuroscience at the Department of Psychology, University of Bologna. He was trained as neurologist and has carried out research in psychology and cognitive neuroscience in many laboratories, both in Italy and abroad. He has investigated the neural and cognitive mechanisms of selective attention and space representation, using a variety of methodological approaches, ranging from single-cell recordings in animals, to behavioral, eye-movement, electroencephalographic and psycho-physiological measurements in humans. His current research focuses on the functional mechanisms of cognitive control and decision-making. He has authored many research articles published in peer-reviewed, international journals.

Mara **Fabri** is Associate Professor of Physiology at Department of Clinical and Experimental Medicine at Università Politecnica delle Marche, Ancona. She is Member of the Italian Society of Physiology (SIF), the Italian Society of Neurosciences (SINS), the European Society for Neurosciences (ESN), the Society for Neurosciences (SFN), the International Brain research Organization (IBRO), and the Italian Society of Psychophysiology (SIPF). Her research interests concern anatomo-functional organization of central sensory systems, in particular somatic sensory areas, studied with neuroanatomic techniques and electrophysiological recordings; neurotransmitters of mammals somatosensory areas by immunocytochemical and neural tracing techniques; and interhemispheric connectivity of human brain with functional MRI.

Vincenzo **Farina** is Associate Professor of Financial Markets and Institutions in the Department of Management and law at the University of Rome "Tor Vergata" and Adjunct Professor of Financial Management and Financial Markets in the Department of Finance at Bocconi University. He is member of scientific board of PhD in "Economia Aziendale",

University of Rome "Tor Vergata". His research has been published in *Journal of Banking & Finance, European Financial Management, European Management Review, Applied Financial Economics*, and *Corporate Governance*, among others.

Lucrezia **Fattobene** is a Research Fellow at Università Politecnica delle Marche, Ancona, and University of Rome "Tor Vergata". Before earning a Ph.D. in Management from the University of Rome "Tor Vergata" in 2016, she was a visiting research scholar at the Rotterdam School of Management, Erasmus University. Her main fields of research are Neuroeconomics, Behavioural Finance, and Corporate Governance. She is interested in the neurobiology of financial decision making, particularly in the neural correlates and in the process of attention allocation in financial decisions, which she investigates via fMRI and eye-tracking. She contributed to organize the *1ˢᵗ Officina di Neuroeconomia*. Her research has been published in international journals such as Frontiers in Neuroscience and Journal of Management and Governance, among others.

Riccardo **Guerrini** is a head office in an insurance agency in Rome. He has specialist knowledge of Motor, Retail and Life insurance products, and of management of claims.

Frank **Hartmann** is Full Professor of Management Accounting and Management Control at the Rotterdam School of Management, Erasmus University. He is also Dean of Executive Education and member of the Executive Board of the school. His main academic activities involve research and teaching on managerial decision making. His research is published nationally and internationally, and his teaching, development and consulting experiences are aimed at audiences that range from undergraduate level students to certified controllers, and executives. Frank's current work is in the neurobiology of financial decision making and the role that theories play in improving daily management practice.

Francesca **Iandolo** is Research Fellow and Adjunct Professor in Management at Sapienza University of Rome. She holds a PhD in Management with a dissertation thesis on Viable Systems Approach (vSa), value creation and sustainability. Her research interests are Viable Systems Approach (vSa), Value Theory, Corporate Sustainability, Business Ethics. She participated to several national and international conferences as discussant and published on national and international journals. She is chartered accountant and junior consultant for private companies.

Lucia **Leonelli**, PhD, is Associate Professor of at the School of Economics, Department of Management and Law, University of Rome "Tor Vergata". She is Coordinator of the undergraduate program in Economics and Finance, University of Rome "Tor Vergata". Her main field of interest are Payment Systems and Neurofinance.

Gianpiero **Lugli** main academic role was Full Professor at the Economics Department of Parma University. Professor Lugli has served as Dean as well as Executive President of the Italian

Marketing Society (SIM). Since November 2016, Professor Lugli has retired from the University. The main area of scientific interest are Retail Economics, Consumer Behaviour, Neuromarketing and Neuroshopping.

Simona **Luzzi** is Associate Professor of Neurology at Università Politecnica delle Marche, and Director of the Centre of Cognitive Impairment and Dementias, at the Neurology Clinic, Ancona. She qualified in Medicine at the University of Perugia and trained in Neurology at University of Ancona. Her research area is cognitive neurology. Special interests include the progressive aphasias, temporo-frontal lobe degeneration and neuropsychology of neurodegenerative brain diseases.

Nicola Biagio **Mercuri** is Full Professor of Neurology at the Department of System Medicine University of Rome "Tor Vergata", Italy. He is Director of the preclinical research of the IRCCS Fondazione Santa Lucia. Specialised in neurology in 1982. He has interest in neuronal electrophysiology, actions of psychoactive drugs/neurohormones. Its clinical activity is mainly devoted to movement, mood and sleep disorders. In the 1982 he worked in the Max Planck Institute for psychiatry of Munich Germany and in the 1985/1986 MIT Cambridge USA. He has published more than 300 papers having a h-index of 52 on Scopus and 59 on Google Scholar.

Luca **Passamonti** is a Senior Clinical Research Fellow and NHS Honorary Consultant Neurology at the University of Cambridge and Cambridge University Hospital. Dr Passamonti studies the brain mechanisms underlying behavioural variability, and their role in neuropsychiatric disorders ("Personality Neuroscience"). For instance, he considers the neural underpinnings of individual differences in personality traits as neuroticism, impulsivity, and aggression. Improving our knowledge of the neurological roots of personality is not only of interest theoretically but also has the potential to lead to new and brain-based approaches to manage complex neuropsychiatric disorders.

Gabriele **Polonara** is Associate Professor of Neuroradiology at Department of Odontostomatologic and Specialized Clinical Sciences at Università Politecnica delle Marche, Ancona and Head of the Neuroradiology Unit of the "Ospedali Riuniti di Ancona". He is Member of the Italian Society of Neuroradiology (AINR), Italian Society of Radiology (SIRM), European Society of Neuroradiology (ESNR), European Society of Radiology (ESR). He is also a Member of the Board of the Neuroradiology Section of the Italian Society of Radiology. His research interests concern anatomo-functional organization of central sensory systems, interhemispheric connectivity of human brain with functional MRI, brain tumours, neurodegenerative diseases.

GianMario **Raggetti** is Full Professor of Behavioral Finance at the School of Economics and Scientific Director of the Center for Health care Management (CMS) at the School of Medicine, Università Politecnica delle Marche, Ancona. At the CMS, he stimulates and coordinates several interdisciplinary researches in Neuroeconomics. The results of his neuro-biological investigations, carried out together with neurologists, physiologists, neuropsychologists, neuroradiologists, on the role of the brain in economic and financial decision-making, are published in scientific journals and presented at national and international seminars. His commitment to spread the innovative views and methods of Neuroscience research in Economics and Finance is continuous: this to stimulate the scientific curiosity of students and researchers in the domestic academic context towards Neuroconomics. His idea of an annual rendez-vous with "*Officina di Neuroeconomia*" his consistent with his, personal and professional, responsibility.

Manuela **Sellitto** is a senior postdoc and a lecturer in Neuroscience of Intertemporal Choice at the Department of Comparative Psychology, Heinrich-Heine University of Düsseldorf. She obtained a BSc in Psychology and a MSc in Neuropsychology, and an international PhD in Cognitive Neuroscience both at the University of Bologna and at Bangor University. Her main interest is human decision-making, particularly the behavioral and neural bases of intertemporal choice and temporal discounting, as well as social discounting, which she investigates via behavioral paradigms and fMRI. She has published in international scientific journals and she has collaborations with both Italian and foreign labs.